Aboriginal
Stories

Aboriginal Stories

Illustrated by Roger Hart

A.W. Reed

With Word List
English—Aboriginal
Aboriginal—English

REED

Reed Books
a part of Reed Books Australia
Level 9, North Tower
1-5 Railway St.
Chatswood, NSW 2067

This edition first published 1994
Reprinted 1994, 1995

National Library of Australia
Cataloguing-in-Publication Data
Reed, A.W. (Alexander Wyclif), 1908-1979

Aboriginal Stories and Word List

ISBN 0 7301 0481 8

[1]. Aborigines, Australian—Legends.
2. Australian languages. I. Reed, A.W. (Alexander
Wyclif), 1908-1979. Aboriginal stories of
Australia. II. Reed, A.W.(Alexander Wyclif),
1908-1979. Aboriginal Words Of Australia. III.
Title. IV. Title: Aboriginal stories of Australia.
V. Title: Aboriginal words of Australia.

398.2049915

Typeset in Australia
Printed by Australian Print Group
Maryborough Victoria.

CONTENTS

INTRODUCTION

IN recent years there has been increased interest in the Australian Aboriginals, who at one time were regarded as so primitive in their outlook and culture that little purpose was to be served by investigating and preserving their anthropological records. It is only when we are in danger of losing something that we begin to value it, and the large number of books describing the life, customs, arts, and skills of the Aboriginals is ample proof of this renewal of interest.

It is important that white Australians should appreciate the wealth of imagination displayed in Aboriginal legend. It is part of the literature of Australia. We shall not put our roots down into the soil until we have incorporated their folklore into the indigenous literature of the southern continent, and can see the land through the eyes of the primitive, clever, imaginative people who had to fight to gain their nourishment from Mother Earth. It is remarkable that in an environment of desert wastes and infertile soil, as well as in well-watered country, the imagination of the Aboriginals should produce tales that are both beautiful and amusing, and that they should find human characteristics and poetry in bird and beast, in the sky above them, in sun, moon, and stars, and even in reptiles and insects.

They lived close to the soil, these children of nature. They were dependent on her for sustenance, and in the teeming animal life and in the barren places alike they found evidence of the work of a Creator Spirit, and promise of Bullima, the after-life, where game abounded, there was soft grass to lie on, refreshing streams, and soft breezes. From their physical needs a majestic conception of nature was evolved, with beneficent spirit ancestors—and the corresponding spirits of evil that are inimical to mankind.

The legends contained in this book have been gathered from many different sources. It is a comprehensive collection which originated among different tribes and can be regarded as a typical sampling of the beliefs of Aboriginals in every part of Australia.

Coming from widely divergent sources, it is natural that there should be inconsistencies and contradictory elements. This is particularly the case in the Creation myths and the folklore concerning animals when the land was still in the Dreamtime. From some legends we learn that animals and insects were brought to life at the touch of Yhi, the Sun Goddess, and that Man, the final creation, was made in the bodily and mental form of Baiame, the Great Spirit.

Other widespread legends say that all living things first took the form of men, and gradually achieved individual characteristics as animals. This is a reasonable explanation of the origin of totemism, which exercised a considerable influence on Aboriginal life. It is a vast subject, especially as totemism took different forms in various parts of the country. The presentation of myths and legends in a form which is acceptable to the present day must necessarily depart from the spirit of the Eternal Dreamtime in many respects. To the Aboriginal the stories were not simply pleasant tales to beguile the evening hours. As Professor A. P. Elkin remarked, "Mythology is not just a matter of words and records, but of action and life, for the cult societies, the totemic lodges, do not spend their time at meetings reciting and chanting only; they also re-enact myths, and do so because the heroes and ancestors were, in their belief, actual persons and totemic beings; what they did in the course of their labours must now be done in ritual and the places associated with them must be visited and cared for. For the most part, the details of any myth are only important because they enable the present-day men to walk the path with fidelity, which leads into the sacred dreamtime, the source of life."*

So far as possible, continuity of theme runs through the collection, but because of the widespread origin of the tales, the reader should consider each legend as a self-contained narrative, without attempting to put it in the context of other stories in the same chapter. For this reason animals sometimes appear as

*The Australian Aborigines, A. P. Elkin, Angus & Robertson, 4th edn. 1964, p. 244.

men, and at other times in their natural form. Similarly there are several conceptions of the Father-God, the Great Spirit, Baiame. In some he is Culture hero, father and creator of his people, towards whom created man aspires; in others he is a great wirinun, plagued by faithless and foolish wives.

The value of this compilation may well lie in its representative nature. With hundreds of tribes and hundreds of languages, there was no homogeneity of nomenclature, but there was a common ethos which can be readily found by sampling the variant legends of different tribes.

An arbitrary selection of Aboriginal names for living creatures has been made and adhered to throughout in order to avoid confusion, but it will be appreciated that such names varied according to tribe and locality. A glossary of names and Aboriginal terms is given in an appendix.

Many books have been used freely as source material, but variant accounts have been compared and the tales rewritten in a form that it is hoped will appeal to readers of the present time. The modern version of Mrs Langloh Parker's books of Eulalie tradition, edited by H. Drake-Brockman and published by Angus and Robertson in 1953 are particularly valuable. *Myths and Legends of the Australian Aboriginals* by Dr W. Ramsay Smith and published by George G. Harrap & Co. in 1930 is the largest collection previously published.

A. W. Reed

Creation Myths

YHI BRINGS LIFE TO THE WORLD

IN the beginning the world lay quiet, in utter darkness. There was no vegetation, no living or moving thing on the bare bones of the mountains. No wind blew across the peaks. There was no sound to break the silence.

The world was not dead. It was asleep, waiting for the soft touch of life and light. Undead things lay asleep in icy caverns in the mountains. Somewhere in the immensity of space Yhi stirred in her sleep, waiting for the whisper of Baiame, the Great Spirit, to come to her.

Then the whisper came, the whisper that woke the world. Sleep fell away from the goddess like a garment falling to her feet. Her eyes opened and the darkness was dispelled by their shining. There were coruscations of light in her body. The endless night fled. The Nullarbor Plain was bathed in a radiance that revealed its sterile wastes.

Yhi floated down to earth and began a pilgrimage that took her far to the west, to the east, to north, and south. Where her feet rested on the ground, there the earth leaped in ecstasy. Grass, shrubs, trees, and flowers sprang from it, lifting themselves towards the radiant source of light. Yhi's tracks crossed and re-crossed until the whole earth was clothed with vegetation.

Her first joyous task completed, Yhi, the sun goddess, rested on the Nullarbor Plain, looked around her, and knew that the Great Spirit was pleased with the result of her labour.

"The work of creation is well begun," Baiame said, "but it has only begun. The world is full of beauty, but it needs dancing life to fulfil its destiny. Take your light into the caverns of earth and see what will happen."

Yhi rose and made her way into the gloomy spaces beneath the surface. There were no seeds there to spring to life at her touch. Harsh shadows lurked behind the light. Evil spirits shouted, "No, no, no," until the caverns vibrated with voices that boomed and echoed in the darkness. The shadows softened. Twinkling points of light sparkled in an opal mist. Dim forms stirred restlessly.

"Sleep, sleep, sleep," the evil spirits wailed, but the shapes had been waiting for the caressing warmth of the sun goddess. Filmy wings opened, bodies raised themselves on long legs, metallic colours began to glow. Soon Yhi was surrounded by myriads of insects, creeping, flying, swarming from every dark corner. She retreated slowly. They followed her out into the world, into the sunshine, into the embrace of the waiting grass and leaves and flowers. The evil chanting died away and was lost in a confusion of vain echoes. There was work for the insects to do in the world, and time for play, and time to adore the goddess.

"Caves in the mountains, the eternal ice," whispered Baiame. Yhi sped up the hill slopes, gilding their tops, shining on the snow. She disappeared into the caverns, chilled by the black ice that hung from the roofs and walls, ice that lay hard and un-yielding, frozen lakes in ice-bound darkness.

Light is a hard thing, and a gentle thing. It can be fierce and relentless, it can be penetrating, it can be warm and soothing. Icicles dripped clear water. Death came to life in the water. There came a moving film over the ice. It grew deeper. Blocks of ice floated to the surface, diminished, lost their identity in the rejoicing of unimprisoned water. Vague shapes wavered and swam to the top – shapes which resolved themselves into fish, snakes, reptiles. The lake overflowed, leaped through the doorways of caves, rushed down the mountain sides, gave water to the thirsty plants, and sought the distant sea. From the river the reptiles scrambled ashore to find a new home in grass and rocks, while fish played in the leaping waters and were glad.

"There are yet more caves in the mountains," whispered Baiame.

There was a feeling of expectancy. Yhi entered the caves again, but found no stubborn blocks of ice to test her strength. She went into cave after cave and was met by a torrent of life, of feather and fur and naked skin. Birds and animals gathered round her, singing in their own voices, racing down the slopes, choosing homes for themselves, drinking in a new world of light, colour, sound, and movement.

"It is good. My world is alive," Baiame said.

Yhi took his hand and called in a golden voice to all the things she had brought to life.

"This is the land of Baiame. It is yours for ever, to enjoy. Baiame is the Great Spirit. He will guard you and listen to your requests. I have nearly finished my work, so you must listen to my words.

The flowers lifted themselves toward the radiant sun goddess.

"I shall send you the seasons of summer and winter – summer with warmth which ripens fruit ready for eating, winter for sleeping while the cold winds sweep through the world and blow away the refuse of summer. These are changes that I shall send you. There are other changes that will happen to you, the creatures of my love.

"Soon I shall leave you and live far above in the sky. When you die your bodies will remain here, but your spirits will come to live with me."

She rose from the earth and dwindled to a ball of light in the sky, and sank slowly behind the western hills. All living things sorrowed, and their hearts were filled with fear, for with the departure of Yhi darkness rushed back into the world.

Long hours passed, and sorrow was soothed by sleep. Suddenly there was a twittering of birds, for the wakeful ones had seen a glimmer of light in the east. It grew stronger and more birds joined in until there came a full-throated chorus as Yhi appeared in splendour and flooded the plains with her morning light.

One by one the birds and animals woke up, as they have done every morning since that first dawn. After the first shock of darkness they knew that day would succeed night, that there would always be a new sunrise and sunset, giving hours of daylight for work and play, and night for sleeping.

The river spirit and the lake spirit grieve most of all when Yhi sinks to rest. They long for her warmth and light. They mount up into the sky, striving with all their might to reach the sun goddess. Yhi smiles on them and they dissolve into drops of water which fall back upon the earth as rain and dew, freshening the grass and the flowers and bringing new life.

One last deed remained to be done, because the dark hours of night were frightening for some of the creatures. Yhi sent the Morning Star to herald her coming each day. Then, feeling sorry for the star in her loneliness, she gave her Bahloo, the Moon, for her husband. A sigh of satisfaction arose from the earth when the white moon sailed majestically across the sky, giving birth to myriads of stars, making a new glory in the heavens.

THE STRANGE SHAPE OF ANIMALS

WHEN animals were brought to life from the frozen depths of earth by the sun goddess, who shall tell what they were like? There are some who say that they had the form of men and women, and others that they had many different shapes. We can be certain of only one thing . . . that after a time they grew tired of the forms that Baiame had given them, and were seized by vague longings.

Those who lived in the water wanted to be on dry land. Those who walked on the earth wished to feel the freedom of the sky. There was not a single animal that was not possessed by this strange discontent. They grew sad and hid themselves away from Yhi. The cheerful sound of their voices was no longer heard, and the green plants wilted in sympathy with their friends the creatures.

Looking down in her slow crossing of the sky, Yhi realised that sorrow lay heavily on the earth. For the last time she descended from the sky and stood on the Nullarbor Plain. From every direction a tide of animal life flowed in towards her.

"She has come back! The goddess will listen to our requests," they shouted.

"Come closer," she called to them. "Tell me what is troubling you."

A babble of voices answered her. Waves of sound surged around her. She held up her hands.

"Stop! Stop!" she called. "I cannot hear what you are saying when you all speak at once. One by one, please."

She beckoned to Wombat, who craved a body that could wriggle into shady places where he could hide from others.

He was followed by Kangaroo, who wanted strong legs for leaping and a tail with which to balance himself.

Bat said he wanted wings so that he could fly through the air like a bird.

Lizard was tired of wriggling on his belly and needed legs to support himself.

Poor Platypus could not make up his mind what he wanted, and ended up with the parts of many animals.

15

Yhi smiled as they came and made their wants known to her. She smiled because their forms were so bizarre; she smiled tenderly because she realised that with the transfiguration of their bodies, life would change for her little creatures.

Mopoke, who had asked for large, shining eyes, would have to hide in dim places by day and hunt only at night.

Stick Insect would need to remain unmoving for hours on the branches of trees till he almost turned into a twig.

Pelican would have to learn to stand motionless with his long legs in the water before he could snap up an unwary fish.

She smiled wistfully because she knew that the granting of their wishes would not bring contentment to her little ones. The restless surge of life that seeks and demands would take them away from her. Other changes would come, suddenly or slowly, in mysterious ways, and by strange adventures. The world was to be full of change.

She dismissed them and watched them disperse to every quarter of the earth before she rose up for the last time into the sky.

The story of these changes has been told round campfires for a thousand years. When men and women came to live in the great continent, and saw the creeping, crawling, jumping, swift-running, flying, burrowing wild life on which they depended for their food, they invented strange tales to account for the habits of the creatures that Baiame had given to them. As we crouch round the embers with them, sheltered from the wind by the low fence of woven branches, let us also listen to tales that have come from the heart of a people who are closer than we are to the gods of nature.

THE FIRST MAN

Now the labours of Yhi, the sun goddess, were over. Her warmth and tenderness had brought living creatures to the earth and they basked in her love. Now that she had left them, they were under the care of the Great Spirit. In the spirit of Baiame was thought, intelligence, life; but it had no body.

"I cannot appear to my children and yours," Baiame told Yhi. "I will clothe the power of my thought in flesh. Then they will see me and know that I am indeed their Father."

"The gods are one creation and the animals another," Yhi replied. "To put your spirit into the form of an animal would debase it; they would not respect you."

"Then I will put a little part only into the animals," said Baiame. He gave a small portion of his power of thought to birds, and insects, and reptiles, and fish, and to animals. They were governed by that part of thought which is known to man as instinct.

But Baiame was not yet satisfied.

"My whole mind must be put into something that has life and is worthy of the gift," he said. "I will need to make a new creation."

From the processes of thought, the joining together of atoms and microscopic grains of dust, the forming of blood and sinews, cartilage and flesh, and the convolutions of the substance of the brain, he formed an animal that walked erect on two legs. It had hands that could fashion tools and weapons and the wit to use them; above all, it had a brain that could obey the impulses of the spirit; and so Man, who was greater than all other animals, was fashioned as a vessel for the mind-power of the Great Spirit.

This was done in secret. No other eye saw the making of Man, and the minutes of eternity went by in the last great act of creation. The world became dark and sorrowful at the absence of the Great Spirit. Floods ravaged the land. The animals took refuge in a cave high up in the mountains. From time to time one of them went to the entrance to see if the floods had subsided; but there was nothing to be seen except the emptiness of the land and the endless swirling of the waters under a sunless sky.

Baiame stood in the form of Man who rules over all creation.

Goanna, wise among the reptiles, went to look for himself, and returned hurriedly.

"I have seen a round, shining light like the moon. It is resting outside the cave," he announced.

"Nonsense!" said Eagle. "Bahloo is in the sky."

"I said it was *like* the moon. That is how it appears to me."

Eagle went out. On his return everyone looked at him expectantly.

"It is a kangaroo," Eagle said quickly. "It has two bright eyes, so it is silly to say that it is like the moon. The eyes shine so brightly that their light pierced my body."

"This is a strange thing," said the animals. "Goanna says it is like the moon, and Eagle says it is like a kangaroo. Which are we to believe? Crow, you are the cleverest of us all. You go out and look, and come back and tell us what this strange being is really like."

Crow preened his feathers, but made no move until they pushed him forward. Then he squawked loudly and fluttered up into a crevice in the rock where none could touch him.

"Leave me alone," he called fiercely. "I am not interested. This is a thing that birds and animals should have nothing to do with. If we keep quiet it will probably go away."

"If Crow is afraid, I'll go," Mouse said bravely. He crept out on silent paws, but when he came back he could not speak. One after the other the birds and animals tiptoed to the entrance and looked at the strange being that stood there in the half light. There were many arguments, because the little part of Baiame's mind that was in each of them recognised a little part of the whole mind that was clothed in flesh outside the cave.

The unchanging night lasted for a period which could not be measured in sunrises and sunsets, which were but a paling and a brightening of the grey mist. The animals grew hungry. Eagle killed Rat and ate his body. It was the signal for widespread slaughter. Larger animals tore smaller ones to pieces and devoured their flesh. Baiame heard their tumult and left the mountain, saddened that the animals had discovered the pleasure that comes with the death of others.

As he went Yhi flooded the world with light. The remaining animals came out of the cave and gathered together on the hilltop. There on the pinnacle of the roof of the world they saw the Great Spirit revealed to them at last. Baiame stood before

19

them in the form of Man, of Man who rules over all creation because he has the soul and intelligence of Baiame in a human body.

*   *   *   *

As he walked through the earth, the Man that was the thought-power of Baiame was lonely. Strange feelings surged through him, undiscovered desires. He needed a companion to share the wonder of the world, and he sought for one fruitlessly. He went to Kangaroo and Wombat, Snake and Lizard, Bird and Flying Fox, Fish and Eel, Insect and Earthworm, but in vain. He was kin to them because they loved the Great Spirit, but there was only a little part of Baiame's mind in each of them, and it was not enough to satisfy the hunger of Man's spirit.

He turned to trees, and to grasses, and to flowers. Their beauty intoxicated him, but they appealed only to his senses, for the eternal spirit of Baiame had not been conferred on them. The flaming flowers of the waratah, the golden glory of the wattle, the scented leaves and grey bark of the eucalypts were a delight to eyes and nose. He drew deep breaths of fresh perfume, but still his soul was not at rest.

In the evening he went to sleep near a grass yacca tree. All night he was troubled with strange dreams, in which his desires seemed to be on the point of fruition. When he woke again he found that Yhi had thrown her rays across the plain. They seemed to be concentrated on the tall flower stalk of the yacca tree. He gazed at it for a long while, until he was roused by the sound of heavy breathing. He looked round and was astonished to see that the whole animal creation had gathered together on the plain. In the air was a feeling of expectancy.

He looked back at the tree. It was changing. The flower stalk grew shorter and rounder. Limbs began to form, and with a shock Man realized that the tree was changing into a two-legged creature like himself.

But there was a difference. The limbs were smooth and soft, rounded breasts swelled before his eyes, there was a proud tilt to the shapely head. Man held out his hands to Woman. She clasped them and stepped gracefully across the grassy base of the tree. Man held her in his arms and together they surveyed the waiting world. The animals danced with delight and then ran off into the distance, satisfied that the loneliness of Man was ended.

The loneliness was ended; the duty and obligations of Man began. Woman came slowly to full life and communion with her husband. He hunted food for her. He sought shelter for her. He showed her love and tenderness, which are the fruits of the spirit. He taught her the names of birds and animals and their ways. She learned to love him, and to work for him, to be the other part of him that he needed for the satisfying of his longings and needs.

Baiame smiled. "When I show myself to the little things I have created," he mused, "I shall be well content to show myself in the form of a Man!"

THE GIFT OF FLOWERS

Baiame remained for a long while on earth as a man. He loved Tya, the world which, it is said, was once a piece of the sun itself. He made his home in a mountain, talking with the animals and the men and women whom he had created. There was communion of spirit between them, for the period of rest after the labours of creation were a refreshment to the Great Spirit. Day after day Yhi smiled at him as she moved across the vault of the sky, while round his earthly home the flowers bloomed in profusion.

One day he spoke to the men and women, and to the animals which crowded round him.

"The time has come for me to leave you, my children. While the earth was young you needed me, but now you are fully grown. It is better that you live by yourselves."

A low moan went up, but he smiled and said, "Do not be sad. Little children have no real minds of their own. When I am gone, and only then, you will learn to take your proper places in the world. If I were to remain here for ever you would come to me with all your troubles, and you would never learn to stand up for yourselves. But do not fear. Even though I shall return to my true home in the sky, in the bright patch of the Milky Way, I shall still be your Father Spirit. When you really need me, I shall be with you. Sometimes I shall return to earth, and then I shall take the form of a man so that you will recognise me."

The animals dispersed slowly, but the men and women lingered. They had delighted in the flowers which grew so profusely round the mountain of Baiame and were loth to leave the many-coloured carpet with the sweet perfume. They lay on the carpet during the long nights looking up at the Milky Way, imagining that they could still see the Great Spirit.

A vague unease disturbed their minds. They could not tell what it was until a woman cried out, "The flowers are gone!"

It was true. Men and women had understood Baiame's last message, and even animals, in whom Baiame had planted a little of his mind, knew that the Great Spirit had not left them for ever; but the flowers had no minds. All they knew was that the

Father-Spirit was no longer with them, and that Yhi, the sun goddess was far away.

"He has left us," they murmured. Their drooping leaves and petals fell to the ground, and one by one they died.

"Look!" the woman cried again. "There are no flowers left anywhere!"

As far as the eye could reach the earth was bare and brown. The circle of dead and dying plants was spreading through the whole world. Death of flowers raced ahead of the searching women, and all the raindrops sent by the spirits of the sky, and all the smiles of Yhi could not arrest it.

The air was filled with the black bodies of the bees as they flew frantically from one dead plant to another in search of honey.

"Now we shall have no honey," the women cried. "There is only the sweet gum of the trees that Baiame left, but they are his and we may not touch them."

Even while they were speaking, trees grew up round them, and down their trunks flowed a clear liquid that quickly hardened. One woman, more venturesome than the rest, scraped some off with her finger and put it in her mouth.

"It is sweet," she cried. "Baiame has seen our plight and sent this food to us. These are not his sacred trees, which we would never touch. Come and eat."

So their hunger was appeased, and they knew that Baiame still cared for them. Yet generation after generation was born and died, and still there were no flowers in the world. They were only a memory to the oldest people, a story that was told and scarcely believed by those who had been born long after the Death of Flowers. The stories grew with the telling, but no matter how fertile the imaginations of the tellers, the imagination could not equal the reality.

High in his starry home Baiame felt sorry for the descendants of his creation. He put into their minds a longing they could not resist. Gradually some of the men left their own camp grounds and gathered together at the foot of the mountain where Baiame had once lived as a man. They felt as though they were being drawn by invisible cords, up the endless slopes of the mountain and into the vast depression which had been made when Baiame lay down on the carpet of flowers. And there was Baiame himself, holding out his hands, gathering them to himself as a hen gathers her chickens, and lifting them up to the starry sky.

"Come and see my home, little children," he said in a deep voice that reverberated through the heavens and set the stars dancing in their courses.

He set them down on a cloud, and a great sigh echoed through the Milky Way, because as far as they could see there was a glowing carpet of colour, brighter than any rainbow, and with all the colours of the great bow they had seen after rain.

"The stories you have heard were true," Baiame said. "Once earth was covered with flowers like these, but never again. Yet my heart is sorrowful for you, and for your friends who will never see this sight. Gather armfuls of flowers now and take them back to earth with you. Take as many as you can. They will fruit and their seeds will take root, to gladden the hearts of you and your children and your children's children for ever."

The gentle hand set them down again on the solid ground. Dropping flowers as they went, they ran to their own tribes, and scattered the largesse that the Father Spirit had given them. It could not be expected that the flowers would bloom as they did in the days of Baiame, in the Dreamtime; but never again will Earth be without flowers while the Great Spirit continues to watch over his people.

THE PLAGUE OF INSECTS

WHILE he remained on Tya, the earth, Baiame let his imagination run riot. He fashioned mountains, covering them with trees and spreading a blue mist over them; he delighted in sending water spinning and laughing down their sides; he lined the banks with fragile plants that drank from the streams and bent over them in gratitude; at other times he swept his hand across the land and smoothed it into mallee-covered plains and sandy desert wastes. Tya grew and took form in his skilful fingers. Above it the pellucid wonder of the sky changed in colour from earliest dawn, when the stars winked out, to the brazen blue of midday, and the soft veils of evening.

As the sun rose in the mornings he looked at his handiwork, at the swaying trees and moving water, and he breathed soft winds across it, sending a million plants dancing with joy.

But like a wind on the embers of a camp fire, the jealousy of Marmoo, the Spirit of Evil, was also fanned to flame.

"Baiame's heart is too full of pride," said Marmoo to his wife. "Anyone could make a world out of Tya; but Baiame's vanity will be his downfall."

"What can you do?" she asked. "You have not tried to make a world for yourself."

"I can do something better than that. I will spoil his precious world for him."

"How?"

"You will see," he said knowingly, and strode off into the dark forest where none could see him. In secrecy he made the insect tribe – beetles, flies, bugs, snails, worms, and a thousand other tiny creatures that crawled, and burrowed, and flew. There are tribes who say that the sun goddess Yhi brought to life all the animals, and birds, and insects that Baiame had created, but this is a story of Marmoo and his wickedness that is told by other camp fires.

For an endless time Marmoo laboured, breathing life into them, and sending them out of the forest in swarms. The sky was dark with flying insects, the ground became a heaving, crawling mass, and still Marmoo went on with his work.

The insects became a devouring host spreading out from the dark forest. They ate the grass, they bit the leaves from the trees. No plant was safe from them. The earth grew bare and ugly, the scent of flowers was replaced by the noxious smell of the plagues that devoured the living things that Baiame had made. Even the music of streams and waterfalls was drowned by the whirr of wings and the clashing jaws of the insect tribe.

Looking down with pride from his mountain home, Baiame saw the brown tide rolling over the plains and swarming up the foothills. The fair land he had made was being eaten up by the ravening hosts of Marmoo.

The Great Spirit was furious that his fair land should be so wantonly destroyed, but he felt he could get rid of the plague. He knew that it had been sent by Marmoo. Calling up one of the stronger winds, he sat down again to watch the dispersal of the insect swarms.

The wind whistled shrilly over the plain, but the insects clung with clawed feet to the tree trunks, or burrowed into the soil. Before the day was done Baiame knew that he would need help from his fellow spirits. He travelled quickly to the home of Nungeena, who lived in a waterfall hidden in a fertile valley in the mountains.

"Come with me and see what has happened to the beautiful land I made," he said.

Nungeena was appalled at the sight.

"Your valley, too, will soon be like this," Baiame warned her. "The plague is coming closer. Unless you help me, your stream will be choked with creeping, crawling, slimy things, and there will be no place for you to live."

Nungeena acted swiftly. She called her attendant spirits to her and asked them, "What have you seen as you came to me?"

The spirits sighed. "We have seen insects everywhere. The whole earth is being eaten up by them, Mother. What can we do to stop them?"

The Mother Spirit smiled. "I have a plan," she said, "but you must help me."

Her fingers flashed quickly in the sunshine, lifting colour from the flowers, weaving an intricate pattern in the air. When it was finished they saw the graceful form of a lyre bird standing in front of her.

"What is this, Mother?" they asked.

The ground became a heaving, crawling mass of insects.

"It is a lyre bird. Look!"

She waved her hand again and the lyre bird moved, spreading its tail for all the spirits to admire. It flapped its wings and circled Nungeena.

"Wonderful!" cried the spirits. "But how can it help us to get rid of the plague?"

"See for yourselves," Nungeena replied. As they watched, the beautiful bird snapped at the advance guard of the insect tribe, which had already reached the Mother Spirit's resting place.

"We must work fast," Nungeena said to her attendants. "Birds are beautiful creatures, but it is more important that they should eat the insects quickly. We must set to work to make as many birds as we can. To work!"

Nungeena made other birds, and each one was different. The other spirits copied her as well as they could.

The younger spirits were clumsy. They made ugly-looking birds like the magpie and the butcher-bird but even these, as soon as they were made, began to snap up the insects.

The spirits who came from the watery regions of the world made birds that could swim and wade in the swamps and rivers. These began to eat the insects that were flying over the stream.

The spirits of the coastal lands made gulls, and though these graceful birds are more fond of fish, they too joined in the great insect feast.

The night spirits who put the flowers to sleep made the mopokes and the nightjars.

The swiftest of the spirits made the fantails, the swallows, and the fly-catchers, and the air was filled with the snapping of their beaks.

The little spirits that spent their lives among the flowers fashioned robins, wrens, and mistletoe birds.

When they were all made the air was full of the sound and movement of wings. Baiame was delighted.

"They are so beautiful that they must have voices to match," he said, and to each he gave the songs that have since rung through the bush and valleys, and across the plains of Tya. The harsh call of the crow and the raucous laughter of the kookaburra drowned the other sounds.

"Do you call that beautiful?" Nungeena asked incredulously.

"It is a pleasant sound in my ears," Baiame retorted. He

turned to the birds who by this time had eaten all the insects that had ventured into the valley of the Mother Spirit.

"Go forth and destroy the hordes of Marmoo," he ordered.

Still singing, they circled round him and then fanned out like the spokes of a wheel, flying ever further away until they met fresh insect swarms that were denuding the earth of its vegetation. What a feast day for the birds! Never since have they been so fully fed; but they are always hoping that Marmoo will send them another bounteous harvest.

THE FIRST INITIATION CEREMONY

THE first corroboree and initiation ceremony the world has ever known was held at Googoorewon, the place of trees, while Baiame was still living on earth, and animals were still men.

The Great Spirit, who at that time had appeared to the tribes of men as a wirinun or medicine man, called his people together from their distant hunting grounds. Many tribes were there as the representatives of the animal world. There were the Wahn, the Crows; Du-mer, the Brown Pigeons; Baiamul, the Black Swans; Madhi, the Dogs; and many others.

As tribe after tribe came to the place Baiame had chosen for them, the excitement increased. Old friends greeted each other and inquired anxiously if anyone knew the purpose of the meeting, but none could read the mind of Baiame. The expectation, mingled a little with fear, increased hourly.

Yet it was a joyous occasion. Gifts were exchanged, marriage contracts were arranged, and those who had brought valuable possessions bartered them for others. There was dancing and singing every night until the fires burned low, and men and women could scarcely keep awake.

After several days Baiame summoned the men and addressed them as he stood outside his wurley.

"It is good for you to enjoy yourselves," he told them, "but now the serious business must begin. The real purpose of our meeting together in this place is to prepare the young men for manhood. You are men. You know what must be done because I have implanted these thoughts in your mind. First you must make a bora ground. Then the bullroarers will sound, the boys will leave their mothers, and you who are older will accept the responsibility of training them."

The men spent several days clearing the ground, earthing up the protecting walls, and cutting a path through the scrub. Most of them worked quickly and silently, as tried warriors should do, but they were interrupted all the time by the senseless chatter and laughter of the Madhi tribe. Little notice was taken of them at first, for they were well known to be empty-headed. It was thought that when the bora ground began to take shape in the scrub the Madhi would be overawed by the solemnity of the coming rites. Occasionally a wirinun appealed to them to be quiet and help with the work; but they took no notice.

After a while threatening looks were cast at them, and the wirinuns warned them that if they would not be silent, the Great Spirit would be angry with them. The Madhis laughed contemptuously. They swaggered round the workmen making insulting remarks, criticising what was being done, and making rude gestures at the medicine men.

Baiame had been observing them closely. He had said nothing because he thought they stood in awe of the wirinuns. He believed that when the time of initiation drew near they would realise that as fully grown and tested men they must set an example to the boys. When it was evident that their bad manners and impudent behaviour were getting worse and worse, he decided that the time had come to punish them, for it was essential that the tribes should be protected and the initiates taken safely through their ordeal. He strode into their midst and spoke so loudly and sternly that they all stopped to listen.

"I am grieved at the behaviour of the Madhi," the great wirinun said. "My people live happily because they obey the laws I have made for them. Yet you, the Madhi, are proud and rebellious. You have not listened to the wise men; you are making a mockery of this solemn occasion. Very well: you may go on laughing and howling to your hearts' content. No longer will I dignify you with the name or appearance of men. Go your way, Madhi, and continue your howling."

One by one the Madhi dropped on all fours. Hair grew thickly over their bodies, their arms changed to legs, their hands and feet to paws. They tried to call out to Baiame and tell him they were sorry for what they had done. It was too late. No words but barking and howling noises came out of their mouths. They were scared by their own noise and fled yelping into the scrub. The noise died away in the distance.

Everyone was now afraid of Baiame. They had known him only as a friend. Now he had shown himself as a wirinun who would not be trifled with. In the shelter of the wurleys and around the camp fires that night the story of the day's events was told over and over again.

Next morning, when Baiame walked into the circle where a

31

One by one the Madhi dropped on all fours.

group of women was gathered, they fell silent and looked at him apprehensively.

"Why are you not grinding seeds for flour?" he asked.

No one replied.

"Come," said Baiame jestingly. "I am not going to eat you, but by tonight I will be hungry. If the cakes are not ready, anything may happen."

One of the older women plucked up courage to speak.

"Oh sir, do not think us idle. A strange thing has happened. Our grinding stones have left us."

Baiame roared with laughter.

"I have heard of women leaving grinding stones, but never of grinding stones leaving of their own accord. Can't you think of a better story to tell than that?"

"It is true, sir," she insisted. "There is not one left in the camp."

Baiame looked round about.

"Certainly they are not here," he admitted, "but that does not mean that they grew legs and walked away. I expect you lent them to the Du-mer?"

"No, no, no, we did not," came a chorus of voices.

"Yes, yes, yes, you did. Go and get them at once."

Frightened by the fate of the Madhis, the women did not argue. They knew they had not lent the stones to the Brown Pigeons; still, they went from one group to another asking, "Have you seen our grinding stones?" but the answer was always "No".

"Listen!" cried one of the girls. "What is that noise?"

They stopped and heard a peculiar drumming noise overhead.

"The Wunda! The spirits are here!" cried a voice.

They ran back as quickly as they could and told Baiame that they had heard the Wunda.

The wirinun stroked his beard and said thoughtfully, "Perhaps I have done you an injustice. Let us go and visit the Du-mer and see for ourselves."

He took up his magic weapons and went towards the camp of the Du-mer women, followed at a respectful distance by the other women. The Du-mer camp was deserted, but one woman, sharper-eyed than the others, saw a grinding stone gliding between the bushes. Baiame hurried after it, still followed by the women, while overhead the drumming of the Wunda went on monotonously.

33

"It is being carried by a Wunda whom we cannot see," Baiame said.

They broke through the scrub and an astonishing sight met their eyes. Hundreds of grinding stones were streaming across the bare plain, and running after them were the Du-mer women. As they looked the Du-mers were changed into Brown Pigeons which flapped their wings and flew towards the bush.

"Follow! Follow!" cried Baiame. Over streams and across country they ran. But the stones were carried faster than they could run and were lost to sight in the distance. Yet Baiame urged the women on.

"Look!" he said at last. "This is where the chase ends."

A stony mountain rose from the open plain. It was Mount Dirangibirra. When they reached it they found it was composed entirely of grinding stones. Ever since that day the tribes who want the best stones for grinding always go to Mount Dirangibirra to secure them.

*   *   *   *

While the weird noise of the bullroarers rose and fell, the women huddled together in camp, fearful of the mysteries that may be attended only by men. The boys had been taken away by their guardians and only the women and children were left.

On the bora ground the young men summoned to their defence the fortitude that had been gained through long years of privation, pain, and loneliness. There had been times when they were driven to the very edge of madness and hysteria, but they were as nothing to the tests they now had to endure. They remembered the freezing, fireless cold of night and the strange noises that had come out of the darkness when the elder brothers had driven them away from their camps; the long day's hunting, the first thrill of seeing a stone-tipped spear sink into their prey, the thirsty trek back to the camp, the pride with which they had thrown the kill on the ground for all to admire, the shattering realisation that others would eat it while they, the hunters, were forced to go hungry. These experiences had befallen them when they were young and in their innocence they had thought that the endurance of such tests would bring with them the privileges of manhood.

But Baiame had instructed his wirinuns wisely.

"My children must be strong," he told them. "Strong to father

34

sons, to care for their women, to overcome appetite and pain and fear. They must learn the wisdom of the tribes, the mystery of water and all the stars of heaven, of winds that blow, the flight of the bee to its honey store, the food that is hidden under the earth, the seeing eye that can follow the light-footed trail of the kangaroo rat over stony ground. Teach them!"

Through blackened, bleeding lips the young men tried to follow the chanting of the wirinuns. The initiates were stretched out on the hot sand while ants crawled on their bare skin, and investigated the clay patterns painted on their bodies. The blood trickled slowly across their thighs and was licked up by the thirsty soil. No food or water had been given to them for many days, and the blood roared in their ears like thunder. Memory was blotted out as the old lore was chanted by the wirinuns. The thunder changed to the sound of a waterfall as the churingas whirled on and on. If one of the young men succumbed to fatigue his head was jerked back and a fresh gash reminded him that he had slackened the grasp of his mind.

Through the nights of spring the singing, the telling, the whispering, the endless whirring of the churingas kept on – until early one morning, when the bushes looked like men crouching in the dim light, the last act was performed. The elder brothers sat on their bodies until their ribs cracked in the cave of their chests and the breath was pressed out of their lungs, while the wirinuns, with sharp flints and heavy pounding stones, knocked out their front teeth.

The sound of the churingas died away, and in the hush of dawn the young men stood up, their eyes shining, to face the world with the experience and all the pride of men.

*   *   *   *

Weeks had passed slowly by, and presently the mothers looked forward to seeing their sons again. They would admire them as they proudly took their place with the seasoned hunters and warriors. Privately, when no one was looking, they would weep over the smashed teeth and gashed bodies of the men who such a short while before had been little boys. They did not want to meet them at the bora ground, so they packed their few possessions and began the long march back to their own tribal lands.

One day a middle-aged woman walked into the camp and fell in front of them, beating her breast and crying, "You have

35

deserted me. Shame on you! May you all be mothers of twins!"

"What is the matter? What is wrong with you?" they asked, gathering round her.

"I could not keep up with you," she sobbed. "My children were many, and they were small. They grew tired. The quicker you walked, the more slowly they went. Not one of you looked back. Not one of you would help. We could not find the water holes, and one by one my children died and now not one is left to me."

She scrambled to her feet, her eyes glaring, and cursed them.

"You would not wait for us. You were in too much of a hurry to get here. You did not care that you had killed my children. You are here now, and here you will remain. Goo gool gai ya! Turn into trees – every one of you!"

She fell backwards, her tongue protruding from her mouth, with her sightless eyes turned upwards. The women tried to reach her, but their feet were rooted to the ground. As they bent over her their outstretched arms turned into branches, their fingers into twigs and leaves, their legs and bodies into tree trunks. The wind rustled through them and they wailed in agony.

Other tribes of women heard the unusual noise and rushed to them to see what was happening. As they came close they were changed into other shapes – the Baiamuls to Black Swans, the Ooboons to Blue-tongued Lizards sliding across the grass. The Du-mers flew overhead cooing with the sound that the Wundas had made when they stole the grinding stones. And from the dead body of Millin-nulu-nubba, the bereaved mother, came the little bird Millin-nulu-nubba who keeps on crying, "Goo gool gai ya! Turn into trees!"

*   *   *   *

Back at the bora ground Baiame welcomed the young men who had conquered appetite, pain, and fear.

"Welcome," said the wise old wirinun. "You are all men now. The women have started on their homeward way. We shall follow. They are burdened by their children, and we shall quickly catch them up."

The trail was easy to follow. Baiame's own dog raced ahead and reached the glade where the trees, that had so lately been women, bent their heads towards the ground. Animals scuttled out of her way. The dog lay down under a bush and gave birth to pups, which had the bodies of dogs and the heads of porcupines. They were so fierce that no one dare go near them. Men call them the Eer-moonans, the long-toothed monsters of the dark shades, who tear travellers limb from limb with their sharp teeth.

Baiame went sadly back to his home in the mountains. The greatest initiation ceremony ever known was ended; but women had been turned into trees, men to dogs, whole tribes to reptiles and birds, and even his own dog had left him and given birth to monsters.

But Baiame is old and wise. From evil comes good; and he knew that when the sharp memories of the initiation were over, the world would be richer because of the presence of the plants and animals that had come from his great bora.

THE WIVES OF BAIAME

BEFORE leaving the world to go to his home in the Milky Way, Baiame climbed the ladder of stone steps to the summit of Mount Oobi-oobi, whose peak is in Bullima. There, when he made his last departure, his wives were attached to a crystal rock, as a remembrance of the time when Baiame looked and spoke as a man and walked upon the earth.

Long before their petrification, Birra-nulu and Kunnan-beili, the women chosen to be his wives, were young and foolish. He could never trust them out of his sight for long.

"I want you to be careful and listen to what I am about to say," he told them one day. "I am going out to search for honey. While I am away, take your digging-sticks and get some yams, and as many frogs as you can find. Take them to the spring at Coorigil and wait for me there. But whatever you do, don't bathe in the spring. The water at that place is only for drinking."

He opened his hand and a bee flew out, trailing a tuft of white down. The Great Spirit ran after it and was soon lost to sight.

"He'll be gone a long time," said Birra-nulu. "He'll never give up till the bee has reached its home in a tree. Let's get to work, and then perhaps we can have some fun while he's away."

They worked so quickly that in a short time their bags were full of food, and this they carried to the spring.

"The water looks cool, and I am hot. What would you do if you were me?" Kunnan-beili asked.

"I would go for a swim. What would you do if you were me, Kunnan-beili?"

"I would go for a swim."

They looked at each other and burst out laughing.

"Old Baiame warned us not to go, but sometimes I think he's just a silly old man who doesn't understand what girls are like. Let's go!"

They took off their girdles and jumped into the spring, shouting with delight at the shock of the cold water. Deep down in the spring two menacing shapes began to stir. Silently they swam up through the clear water, unnoticed by the young women. Two huge mouths gaped wide and the jaws of the Kurrias, the crocodile guardians of the pool, closed over them. At one moment the laughter of the girls filled the glade, then silence fell as the birds stopped singing, and even the gentle breeze died away. Birds and animals looked in horror at the eddies on the surface of the pool, and the grim shapes that vanished in its depths.

The Kurrias did not sink to the bottom. They knew that the bodies of the women in their bellies were the wives of Baiame, and their only thought was to escape before the god discovered what had happened to them. Halfway down the bore of the spring was a channel which led to the Narran river. They crawled along the narrow passage, pushing the water in front of them. Down the Narran river they sped. The water heaped itself in front of their bodies in a wave that spread over the banks and surged against the tree trunks, leaving the bed of the river empty behind them.

Baiame had gathered his supply of honey. He went quickly to the Coorigil spring, wondering what mischief his women might have been getting up to during his absence. He called out to them, but there was no answer. He heard the croaking of frogs in the dilly bags which had been placed in the shade of the trees, and on the edge of the spring he saw their girdles, left where they had thrown them when they went to bathe.

He walked to the edge and saw that the surface of the pool was far below its usual level. The blood beat in his temples and his hands tightened over his weapons when he realised that the women had disobeyed him and had been swallowed by the Kurrias. He scrambled down the steep bank, and hope returned when he saw the black tunnel through the rock.

Crouching on hands and knees, he crawled along it and came out on the empty river bed. He knew that the crocodiles would move slowly, dragged down by the weight of Birra-nulu and Kunnan-beili. The dry river bed twisted and turned in front of him, but Baiame climbed on to the bank and strode across country to where he could see a distant gleam of silver, which indicated that the Kurrias were still travelling downstream. The pebbles slipped and slid down the river bank as he rushed onwards, forming the ridges that now lead towards the Narran River.

He came to a place where the river spread out into a shallow lake, and sat down to wait. Presently he saw a towering wave

39

The young women climbed shakily to their feet.

coming rapidly towards him. It spread over the lake and the Kurrias came ashore at the very spot where he was waiting. He sprang to his feet and before they had time to rush him, he had fitted a spear to his woomera and pierced one of them through the head, pinning it to the ground. The other he struck with his nullanulla, stunning it for a moment. Avoiding their lashing tails he cut off their heads and slit their bellies with his flint knife.

The bodies of his wives rolled out on the bank. They lay still, covered with thick slime. Now Baiame searched until he found a nest of red ants. He gathered a quantity of them and placed them on the girls' bodies, where they ran to and fro, licking up the coat of slime until their skins shone in the sunlight. Roused by the tickling of many tiny feet and the bites of many ants, the young women stirred, sat up, and climbed shakily to their feet.

They hung their heads in shame when they saw their husband looking at them.

"We are sorry. We were very foolish," they said.

Baiame smiled at them. He was always tolerant with his light-headed wives.

"Your adventure has ended happily," he said. "Maybe it will teach you to listen to your husband another time. There is always a reason for the orders I give you. If it had not been for me you would still be lying inside the Kurrias, and your bodies would have been eaten away by the juices of their bellies. Will you promise me never to go swimming in any pool or billabong or river without my permission?"

"We will! We will!" answered Birra-nulu and Kunnan-beili.

BAIAME AND THE LAND OF WOMEN

At the end of the world, beyond the mountain where Baiame the Great Spirit lived, there was once a land inhabited only by women. These women were famous for their skill in making weapons – spears, boomerangs, and nullanullas. They traded them with men for meat and possum skins which they needed for food and warmth, because there were no animals on the other side of Baiame's mountain. Hunters were equally glad to trade with them, for the weapons that the women made were the finest in the world.

It was difficult to reach the land of women. A vast waterless plain had to be traversed. Then the traveller could proceed no further because his way was barred by a deep lake. No one was allowed to cross it. The traveller would place his load of meat and skins on the bank and retire. When he was out of sight the women would paddle across the lake in their canoes and exchange the gifts for weapons. Yet in spite of the high cost and heavy labour, men were ready to go to such lengths for the sake of the beautiful weapons that conferred honour and dignity on those who owned them.

But there are always rebels who will not conform to the pattern set by others. Such a man was Wurrunah.

"It is ridiculous that men should be content to accept what women are prepared to give them," he complained to his brothers. "After all, they are only women, and men should be their masters. If no one else will do it, I will show them how they ought to be treated."

"How can you possibly do this?" they asked him. "No one is allowed to cross the lake. We shall not be able to approach them."

Wurrunah laughed scornfully.

"Men are always more clever than women," he replied. "Women make them weak by their wiles; but if a man is strong and determined he will always win. I'll tell you what we shall do.

"First, we must enlist the help of a number of trusty men. We will take no food, no rugs. Instead each man will bring with him a live animal. It doesn't matter what it is so long as it is alive."

"What will we do with the animals?"

"Never mind. You must trust me. I shall tell you what to do when we get there."

With some difficulty a band of men was gathered together and a curious procession set out across the sun-scorched plain. Wurrunah was in the lead, followed by his brothers. After them came a number of men, each carrying a live animal, well-roped and slung across his back.

When at length they reached the edge of the lake, Wurrunah gave his instructions.

"First of all I will turn my two brothers into white swans. They will swim across the lake. The women will notice them and, as they have never seen any birds except Wahn, and Mullian who is Baiame's messenger, they will launch their canoes and try to catch the birds. In the meantime I will go round the lake. When I reach the women's camp I will gather up their complete stock of weapons. This is sure to bring the women back in a hurry. As soon as I see them approaching, I will shout. When I have given the signal I want you to release your animals. The attention of the women will be distracted by them, and while they are going back and chasing the animals, I will make my escape. Then we shall meet and I shall distribute the weapons among you."

Wurrunah conjured up his most powerful magic. His brothers were changed into two beautiful white swans which glided across the calm lake waters. The women, amazed at the sight, launched their canoes and set off in pursuit.

Wurrunah crept up to the deserted camp and tied all the weapons he could find into a bundle, and placed them on his back. As he left the camp, doubled up under his load, the women saw him. They abandoned the chase of the white swans and paddled furiously towards the shore. Wurrunah gave a loud shout, and his men released the animals. Never had the women seen such a sight before. They leaped ashore and ran in all directions trying to capture them. In the confusion Wurrunah made his escape and passed the weapons over to his followers.

They felt no further allegiance towards him. Each man took his newly-gained, treasured possession and hurried away to the plain and the long journey back to his home. But Wurrunah was elated with his success. He had conquered the redoubtable women, and felt power flowing through his body. He lifted his eyes up to the summit of the lofty mountain where it was said that the Great Spirit lived, and in a mood of defiance began to climb the sacred slopes. He had not gone far before black thunderclouds rolled across the peak, and vivid shafts of lightning lit the gloom. One spear-point of light stabbed down the mountain side and struck his body. Wurrunah fell to earth, bruised and defenceless. The newly-won power ebbed away. The magic departed from him, and there was none left to turn his brothers back to their true form. Sobbing for breath, he turned his footsteps towards the plain.

As he plodded across it, Eagle-hawk soared far above him. Mullian had seen the clouds gathering and knew that his master had called him. His attention was caught by two white dots floating on the lake far beneath. He swooped down and was enraged to find that Baiame's preserves had been invaded by the swans. He attacked them fiercely, tearing out their feathers until they drifted across the water in a white cloud.

The swan brothers cried out to their brother for help. Wurrunah heard them from far away, but was powerless. He could only stand and wring his hands. Yet help was close at hand. The mischievous crows, the birds called Wahn, had made their nests in the sacred mountain, under the very beaks of their enemies the Eagle-hawks. They heard the despairing cries of the swans as they sank lower in the water, and took pity on them. They too were rebels against the might of Baiame. They plucked the black feathers from their plumage and scattered them over the swans until they were warm again, and able to swim ashore.

Baiame looked down and was amused at their temerity, and touched by their kindness to the swans; as a reward he allowed the swans to live and decreed that all the swans of Australia would have black feathers instead of white.

Legends of Sun, Moon and Stars

WHY KOOKABURRA LAUGHS AT DAWN

SOME time when the world was young, birds and animals had grown to an enormous size. They were as big as mountains and they lived in darkness that was lit only by the dim light of the stars. The animals were quarrelsome, for it was difficult to find food enough to support their enormous bodies. Baiame had begun his acts of creation, but had not yet determined what form his people would take. These animals he had made were his first experiments.

The world was not a comfortable place in which gods could live. Baiame preferred to remain in his home in the Milky Way which he shared with another powerful spirit, whose name was Punjel. In the frosty realms of the sky it was cold, and every day the gods collected firewood, which they piled in a heap in front of their celestial wurley.

"Why do we gather all this wood but never set it alight?" Punjel asked plaintively.

"We have no fire. Fire is found only in the world below."

"Then why don't we go down and get some for ourselves? I am cold."

"You must remain cold for a while longer," Baiame told him. "The time will come. You cannot hasten the processes of creation."

Punjel was prepared to argue, but his attention was attracted by an unusual sight. Both he and Baiame were able to see clearly in the half-light that enveloped the world. They saw that Eagle and Emu were fighting over the carcase of some animal. Emu managed to snatch it away from Eagle. He rushed towards his nest with the other bird hot in pursuit. Eagle's beak was stretched out and he was pulling the tail feathers from the fleeing bird. Emu did not dare to stay by the nest. He ran straight on into the dense undergrowth and was lost to sight. Eagle stopped, and began to walk back towards the Emu nest. He looked in and saw two white eggs glimmering in the darkness. He picked one of them out with his beak, transferred it to his claw, and with a wicked smile on his face, threw it up in the air with all his might.

45

Punjel had been watching closely. The egg soared upwards, higher and higher, and as it came closer to him it seemed to grow so large that it blotted out his view of the world. Instinctively Punjel put out his hand to catch it, but it slipped through his fingers and smashed against the wood pile outside the wurley. It broke into a thousand pieces, and the timber was splashed with white and gold. As the two great spirits watched, the shattered egg burst into flames, the wood was kindled, and as it had been stored for so long and was tinder-dry, it burned furiously. The gods drew near to warm their bodies.

Presently they looked down. The stars had paled before the intense glow of the fire, and the whole world was lit up by the flames. They drew their breath quickly at the sight. Never before had they seen such beauty. Mountain tops were touched with pure gold; trees were like a feathery green garment on the hillsides; silver streams and waterfalls adorned a land that shone in splendour. Even the arid plains were glowing with a thousand bright colours; while the clouds that drifted over the earth's face were gossamer veils that enhanced her loveliness.

"This is your doing, Baiame," said Punjel. "Under cover of darkness you have been making the world beautiful so that we may enjoy it forever."

Baiame smiled: "Not for us alone, Punjel. The huge animals of the darkness have had their day. Now it is time to people this world of mine with little animals, small birds and reptiles, even tiny insects that we can scarcely see, and to put silvery fish into the rivers and lakes."

As he was speaking the fire began to die down, and some of the beauty was concealed again.

"What is the use of making such a world if no one is able to see it?" Punjel asked.

"Now that we have the gift of fire in the heavens," Baiame replied, "we will never let it go out. At night it will die down till no one can see it, but in the morning I shall light it again. Men will call it the sun, but we know that it is a new woodpile burning brightly to waken all living things from sleep."

"What is sleep?" asked Punjel.

"Sleep is a gentle spirit that closes men's eyes and soothes the thoughts out of their heads. It is a time of resting. Living things need sleep."

"Do you mean that they are dead?"

"No, no. It is hard to tell you, because you do not know it, but sleep is a not-living that keeps men alive."

Punjel shook his head in a puzzled fashion. "I don't understand, Baiame," he said. "If you say it is good, it must be good. But if men are living yet not living, and their eyes are closed, they will not know when the fire is lit, and they will go on and on in this thing that you call sleep, which is like death."

"They will open their eyes to the fire each day," Baiame assured him. "I shall hang a bright star in the east, and by that they will know that the fire is to be lit again, and that light is coming back to the world."

"How can they know when the star is there, if their eyes are shut?"

"There will be a noise that will wake them when the star shines."

"What kind of noise? Who will make it?"

"That is for you to find out, Punjel. Since you are so concerned lest my little ones should not wake up each day, you must try to find a way of letting them know."

Punjel went back into his wurley, and tried to think. "I could carry stones up to the Milky Way and drop them on the earth," he thought, "but then they might hurt Baiame's people when they fell. Anyway, that would not be a happy sound to wake everyone. They might be afraid."

After thinking for a long time, he went down to earth and wandered through the bush. He listened to the branches of trees creaking together in the wind, to water trickling over stones, to the thudding of the paws of animals on the ground; but none of these things satisfied him.

Then he heard a sound of laughter, and went to see what it was. He found Kookaburra perched on the branch of a tree, laughing happily to himself.

"Kookaburra!" he cried, "that is just the sound I want. Can you laugh louder than that?"

Kookaburra opened his beak wide and let out such a peal of laughter that Punjel had to block his ears to stop being deafened.

"Wonderful!" he cried again. "Everyone will be able to hear that noise in the farthest corners of the world. Kookaburra, before the sky fire is lit each morning Baiame will hang a star in the eastern sky. Will you watch for it, and laugh your happy laugh when you see it?"

"Of course I will," said Kookaburra. "I am happiest when I am laughing."

Punjel flew up to the sky, and told Baiame what he had done.

"Good!" said the Great Spirit. "When I put the morning star in the east, listen and tell me whether you can hear Kookaburra giving the dawn call."

But there was no need for him to ask Punjel to listen. He could hear it himself, like everyone else except those who are stone deaf.

THE BLUE FISH AND THE MOON

Who can tell how the moon was made? How did he first set out on his long journey across the sky? Did Bahloo the Moon God live in the Dreamtime with Baiame and Yhi and all the spirits of the heavens? Who can tell?

But there is a tale that is told of Nullandi, the Happy Man, and Loolo, the Miserable Man, who both lived before the moon shone, when the nights were dark and friendless.

"My heart is like the dark," Loolo said to his wife, as they lay in the shelter of the fence and huddled close to the fire to keep the heat in their bodies. "The night is unfriendly. When we die our spirits will walk through an unending night of darkness, the winds will blow through the empty spaces of that night, and they will shrivel up and die, and we shall be no more."

His only answer was the sobbing of his wife as she buried her head in her arms.

From Nullandi's fire came sounds of laughter.

"See the darkness!" he said. "It rests our eyes after the fierce light of the sun by day."

"You are foolish, husband," his wife replied. "How can we see the darkness? There is nothing to see. It is as though we were to place our hands over our closed eyes."

"That is because you do not look," Nullandi said. "Look into the fire, wife. Look into the fire, children. See the flames leaping there. Keep on looking. Now look into the dark. What do you see now?"

"We see flames in the darkness," they cried together. "Why is that, Father? Are there many fires all over the world?"

"No, they are in your heads. It is more important that they should be there than in the world. Can you still see them?"

"They are growing dim, Father."

"Then look up into the sky. What do you see there?"

"We see many many sparks up there. What fire do they come from?"

"They must be sparks from the fire that Baiame has lit. We cannot see it yet, but when dawn comes we will see its yellow glow."

"But why is the sky covered with sparks, Father?"

"I cannot tell you that. You must wait till you are old men and women, and your spirits take the long trail to Bullima. Then you will learn many mysteries that only the spirits of the dead learn when they become alive for ever more. See, I will become Baiame for you."

He took a log from the fire and waved it through the air so that it became a circle of flame, and the sparks flew out like living creatures.

"Do it again," the children shouted when Nullandi threw it back on the fire.

"No," their father said sternly. "That was just a kind of joking and I should not have done it, because no man can be like Baiame. Now go to sleep and in the morning the warmth of his fire will wake you to a wonderful world of light and colour."

*   *   *   *   •

"What were you laughing at last night?" said Loolo. "With your laughing and my wife crying I could not get to sleep."

"Why was your wife crying?"

"I was telling her when death comes it will be like the darkness that falls after the sun has set."

"That is not really so," Nullandi said seriously. "We cannot tell until the time comes, but I believe that death will be only for a little time . . . so short that it will be like shutting our eyes and opening them again."

"You are a foolish man," Loolo said, and gave a croak that faintly resembled laughter. "What do you think will happen to you?"

"I know that the Great Spirit has not made us for nothing, to be like a flower that blooms for a day and fades away, or like a twig that is consumed in the fierce heat of the fire. He has made us because we are his children, and when our time comes he will give us an even better place to live in than this beautiful world."

"This is not a beautiful world. Often we are thirsty and hungry. We have to work all day to get food to keep our bodies alive. When it is all over that will be the end of us. The sparks will all go out, and only darkness will be left."

Nullandi picked up his spear and began to sharpen the blade.

"You can think that if it makes you happy, Loolo. For me, I'm off to hunt for wallabies while my wife gets some waterlily

50

roots for our evening meal. Listen to me: you are making your wife miserable with all your talk. If you want to be a blue fish at the bottom of the sea when you die, you can be a blue fish for all I care. But leave your wife alone and let her be happy."

"You leave your wife alone too, Nullandi. Let her make up her own mind. What do you think will happen to you when your body lies dead on the plain and the dingoes come and eat your flesh?"

Nullandi thought for a while. "I don't really know, Loolo. I am content to leave it all to Baiame. But I tell you this: if there are many people like you in the world who dread the dark, perhaps Baiame will make me a light to comfort them."

*　　　*　　　*　　　*

The long years rolled by. Nullandi and Loolo grew old. When they had no strength left, they lay down and died, and Loolo became a blue fish which lived for a little while at the bottom of the sea. Then he was eaten by another fish and his bones lay on the muddy bed of the sea until they crumbled and fell to pieces. That was the end of Loolo.

But Nullandi the Happy Man went up into the sky, to the home of Baiame, where the Great Spirit turned him into the round and shining moon. Nullandi turned the darkness of the nights to silver light, and even when he waned and became as thin as a sliver of bark, men knew that he would grow again, just as their own spirits might die for a little while, and then come to life and live for ever.

So Nullandi the Happy Man became Bahloo, the cheerful God of the Moon.

WAHN AND THE MOON GOD

WAHN the Crow had long been envious of Bahloo, because the Moon God was the maker of baby girls.

"Let me help you. I'm very good at making babies," Wahn begged him.

Bahloo was suspicious of his friend, and with good reason, for when at last he consented, reluctantly, because of the great number that were needed, Wahn produced babies which grew up to be noisy and quarrelsome. They inherited Crow's own disposition.

On one occasion the two baby-makers quarrelled. Wahn wanted to take the spirits of men and women who had died and put them back into the bodies of unborn babies.

"We cannot do that," Bahloo protested. "Every baby born into the world must fulfil its own destiny."

"But think how wonderful it would be to give people a chance to live their lives all over again. They would learn by the mistakes they made the first time."

"Nonsense, Wahn. You haven't thought about it properly. The good spirits have all gone to Bullima, and the others are having a bad time at the hands of the Eleanba Wunda. No one would want to inflict the lost spirits on poor little new-born babies."

"Bahloo, you know very well that some spirits go and live in the bodies of living men and women. I know where to find them."

"They won't go and live in the bodies of my babies," Bahloo said firmly. "If you don't forget the whole silly idea I won't let you help make my girl babies, ever."

Wahn hopped off in a huff. While he was hunting for grubs a pleasant thought occurred to him. He hurried back to his friend.

"Forget what I said about the babies, Bahloo. Full bellies are more important than new ideas. I have found a tree with hundreds of grubs in the bark. You never saw anything like it in your life. I need your help."

Wahn gave Bahloo his hooked stick and said, "I've already got a bag full of them. It is your turn now. Take this hook and climb up the tree. I will stay down below and catch them as you throw them down to me."

Relieved that Wahn had forgotten his peculiar ideas about babies, Bahloo climbed into the tree and began to fossick in the crevices of the bark with the hooked stick.

"Where are they? I can't find any," he shouted.

"Higher up," Wahn called to him. "I've taken all the lower ones. You'll have to climb further into the branches."

Bahloo climbed higher and found a plentiful supply of grubs, which he pulled out of their hiding places, and threw down to Wahn. Every time he caught one, Crow put it into his bag and breathed on the trunk of the tree. There was magic in his breath and the tree grew quickly, inching its way upwards. There were many grubs, and by the time Bahloo had gathered the last of them, the tree had lifted him far into the sky. He looked down. Wahn was so far away that he seemed like an ant on the ground. The Moon God cupped his hands and shouted, "Where am I? What has happened?"

The only reply was a faint cackle of laughter from Wahn.

*   *   *   *

Bahloo remained in the sky for a long time, and while he was there, Yhi, the Sun Goddess fell in love with him. Bahloo knew all about her. She had many lovers and Bahloo would have nothing to do with her, but he had nowhere to run and hide except in the empty spaces of the sky. Sometimes he was eclipsed, but always he managed to escape.

Although Yhi will never be satisfied until she captures the Moon, the rejection of her advances has made her angry. Knowing that Bahloo's ambition was to return to earth, she instructed the spirits who hold up the edges of the sky to turn him back whenever he attempted to slide down to earth.

"If you let him escape," she threatened them, "I will take away the spirit who holds up the earth. It will sink down, down, down into darkness – and you will go with it."

Bahloo became desperate. In his absence Wahn was having the time of his life, making babies by the hundred, every one of them noisy and quarrelsome. So Bahloo disguised himself as an emu and walked boldly past the spirits of the sky. It was night time. Back on earth, he crept inside his gunyah and whispered to his wives.

"Be quiet," he said. "It is Bahloo. I don't want my brothers to know that I am here. Have they been worrying you?"

The youngest wife giggled.

"We have seen a lot of them while you have been away."

"I thought so," Bahloo said grimly.

He went outside and brought in a log which was the home of a spirit called Mingga. He put it on the ground and told one of his wives to cover it with a possum skin so that it looked like a man sleeping on the floor.

"Now come with me," he whispered.

They followed him outside and into the bush. He did not stop until he came to a place where they would not be likely to be discovered, and there they set up their camp.

Shortly after they had left, Bahloo's brothers crept expectantly into the deserted gunyah.

"Strange," one of them whispered. "The women are not here. But who is that, rolled up in the possum skin?"

"It must be Bahloo! He has come back," another said. "This is the chance we have been waiting for."

He raised his club and brought it down with all his force on the end of the log where he thought Bahloo's head would be.

"That's the end of brother Bahloo," he said, and kicked the log viciously.

He staggered back with an agonized shout and hopped about on one foot, nursing the other in his hands.

Another brother twitched the skin back and realised that they had all been tricked by the Moon God. They followed his trail, but Bahloo had changed back into an emu, and they were never able to find him again.

In the meantime Bahloo had settled down happily in his new camp, and continued his task of making female babies. After a while he was joined by his friend Bu-maya-mul, the Wood Lizard, who was responsible for creating boy babies. Bu-maya-mul had little regard for girl babies. He tried to change Bahloo's girl spirits into boys, but the Moon God stopped him, saying, "I know you respect hunters and warriors, but after all, they need wives and daughters. Leave them alone."

When a number of baby spirits were ready they gave them into the care of Walla-gudjail-uan, the spirit of birth, who has the responsibility of placing the unborn spirits where they will be found by the right mothers. The favourite food of Walla-gudjail-

He staggered back with an agonised shout.

uan is mussels. Sometimes the baby spirits tease her by taking them away. Then she grows angry and threatens to hide them in places where they will never be found. Fortunately there is another spirit, Walla-guroon-buan, who takes pity on them and puts them in hollow trees, streams, and caves where they are sure to be found. These places are usually associated with different totems. When a woman comes close to the baby spirit's hiding place, she knows at once what its totem is.

The Moon God and the Birth Spirits had such an important part to play in the birth of the child that mothers and expectant mothers were careful not to offend them. If a woman stared at the moon, Bahloo would be annoyed and would send her twins. This was a disgrace that could not be lived down.

It was customary for mothers to stand under the drooping branches of a coolabah tree, which was a favourite hiding place for the baby spirits. A new baby is said to have a coolabah leaf in its mouth when it is born. This must be removed at once or the child will die, and its spirit will go back to the tree.

If the spirit baby was unable to find a mother, it wailed dismally until it was turned into a clump of mistletoe, the flowers of which were stained with the baby's blood.

But powerful though the Birth Spirits may be, it is Bahloo who is responsible for creating the bodies of all the girl babies in the world. If he is late in rising, the women say, "Bahloo is busy making girl babies." When he appears above the horizon he smiles down benignly on all women, for he knows he is the greatest influence in their lives.

WAXING AND WANING MOON

Moon was so fat that he was quite round. He was a good-natured man. He had only one sorrow which sometimes dimmed his face as though clouds were passing across it. Looking down at the earth he saw many attractive young women, and he longed to take one of them to cheer him on his lonely journey through the sky. Time after time he went to places where he could see camp fires burning cheerfully, and begged the girls to come with him, but they did not find him attractive. As soon as he appeared they ran away and hid in their gunyahs.

Moon would not give up, but he was so bright that he could be seen coming from a distance. The older people took to hiding all the eligible young women before Bahloo could reach their encampments.

One night he strolled down a valley where his light was hidden in the deep gorge. Coming round a bluff he saw two young women sitting by the bank of the river. They looked up at him with interest.

"It must be Bahloo, the Moon," one whispered to the other. "We have been warned against him, but I would like to see him."

"So would I," the other responded. "Let us stay here and find out what he looks like. Everything looks so beautiful where he is walking."

Moon quickened his footsteps when he saw that the girls did not run away. He broke into a shambling trot, at which they both began to laugh.

"His arms and legs are like twigs," one of them gasped. "Quick, let us take the canoes across the river before he catches us."

They jumped into two canoes that were moored to the bank and paddled across.

Moon fell on his knees and pleaded with them.

"You did not run away at first. Why have you left me now? You are beautiful. I will do you no harm. If you come and live with me in the sky you shall be so happy."

The only answer was their mocking laughter.

57

"It is good to live in the sky," Bahloo persisted. "Remember the Seven Sisters."

The girls looked at one another and felt ashamed. Every young woman admired the Seven Sisters who were turned to an immortal constellation of stars.

"Perhaps we were cruel to him," one girl said. "Let us go back and help him."

They paddled back to Bahloo's side of the river and jumped ashore.

"Choose which canoe you want. Then you can paddle to the other side and we will follow and bring the canoe back."

Bahloo smiled to conceal his thoughts. It was not the canoes he wanted but the young women themselves.

"Alas, I have not learned to paddle," he said. "Get into the canoe with me and show me what I should do."

"You get in, Bahloo," one of them said. "You are so fat that you will fill it and there will be no room for us. We will tow you across."

Moon got in gingerly and sat in the bottom of the canoe. The girls jumped into the water, caught the sides of the canoe in their hands, and swam beside it, pulling it across the river. Moon looked over the side and saw their hair streaming in the water and the moonlight dancing on their slim backs. He had never seen the female form so close before. Putting his arms over the side he began to stroke and tickle them. They warned him that if he did not stop they would scream for help.

"Scream as much as you like," said Bahloo rudely. "No one will hear you. We are too far away from your camp."

One of the girls dived under the canoe and joined her friend on the other side.

"Now!" she said.

They put all their weight on the side of the canoe. It tipped over, and with a despairing shriek Bahloo sank into the water. Deeper and deeper down he went, his light dwindling until nothing was to be seen except a silver sliver at the bottom of the water.

The girls hurried home and told what had happened. Some of the older people were glad because Moon would no longer be able to annoy the young women; but others were alarmed at the thought of the dark nights that would follow.

"Moon was good to us," they said. "Without him, every night

will be dark and dangerous. No one will dare to walk beyond the circle of firelight."

In their perplexity they asked Wahn the Crow for his advice.

"Perhaps it is a good thing," he told them. "Perhaps it is a bad thing. But the nights will be different from now on. I will tell you what will happen. Bahloo is not dead. You can still see a tiny piece of him, and it is shining brightly."

They peered down into the river.

"Not there," Wahn said impatiently. "That is only his reflection. Look up in the sky."

Sure enough, a thin slice of light was to be seen. It was so thin and pale that it left no shadows on the ground.

"He will get bigger again," Wahn went on. "Now he is ashamed, but after a while he will grow more confident. In the end he will be as round as he was before, and again he will try to attract the girls. If they take no notice of him he will grow sad and become small once more. And this will happen now, and for ever and ever more."

And Wahn was right.

THE HUSBAND AND WIVES WHO BECAME STARS

THE widow's body was streaked with bands of red and white where the blood had trickled over the lines of mourning pipeclay. She continued to gash herself with a flint knife as she wailed her grief by her husband's grave.

"Why have you taken my husband?" she cried to Nepelle, the ruler of the heavens. "Why have you not given me a son to comfort me in my sorrow?"

Nepelle heard her cry of anguish.

"Go to the woman quickly," he said to his servant Nurunderi. "Take this child with you and give it to her. Her love will find fulfilment in him, and her grief will be assuaged."

Nurunderi took the child spirit in his arms and descended to earth. He placed the boy under a bush and hid in the scrub to see what would happen. Presently, as the widow lay on the ground exhausted with sobbing, she heard the cry of a baby. Raising herself on her hands, she looked round until she saw a small form in the shadow cast by the bush. She hurried over to it. When she saw that it was a real baby, left ownerless in the desert, she gathered him to her breast and soothed him, until he laughed and put his tiny hand up to her face.

Some inner voice told her that the child should be called Wyungara meaning "He who returns to the stars". The boy grew to adolescence, tended by his foster-mother, and fulfilled all her desires for him. He was tall and straight, learned in all the lore she had taught him. In due course he went through the initiation ceremonies of manhood with credit to himself and to her.

Wyungara was hunting one day when he heard the cry of an emu. He crept stealthily through the scrub with his spear held lightly in his hand, ready for instant use, and came to an open space. No emu was there, but a beautiful girl looked steadily at him and then turned her head slowly away.

"Who are you?" he asked.

"My name is Mar-rallang. You are Wyungara. I have heard of you."

The young man put down his spear and went up to her. They

asked questions of each other. They spoke of many things until the sun sank low in the sky and it was time for the girl to go home.

The following day Wyungara went in the same direction and heard, from a nearby marsh, the mating call of a swan. He had been hoping to meet the girl again, but the hunter's instinct was too strong for him. He parted the reeds gently and saw, standing in the water, not a swan, but another young woman.

"What is your name?" he asked.

"I am Mar-rallang."

He looked at her in surprise.

"Yesterday morning I saw a beautiful girl. Her name was Mar-rallang."

"I know. She is my sister. We are so much alike that we are both called Two-in-one."

While talking to the younger Mar-rallang, Wyungara found that the hours passed as swiftly as on the previous day. In the weeks that followed Wyungara spent many hours with the two charming sisters. When he was with one he forgot the other. They were so alike in disposition, so appealing and gentle, that he realised that he was in love with them both. There was only one solution to his problem. He asked them both to become his wife.

His foster-mother's brother raised many objections to the marriage, but Wyungara was insistent. When he saw that his uncle would never consent, he took the two Mar-rallang girls away to a distant part of the country. The three lived happily together. The young husband was so skilful at hunting, and the girls so industrious at finding roots and grubs, that they were well fed and lived together in harmony, content to share each other's love.

*　　　*　　　*　　　*

Nepelle called Nurunderi to him.

"Why has Wyungara married the daughters of earth?" he enquired. "Does he not know that the spirits of heaven may not be joined with the daughters of men?"

"No one has told him," Nurunderi replied. "He was only a baby when I left him at your command to comfort the widow."

"They must be separated at once."

"How can that be done? Shall I bear his spirit back to you and leave the women desolate?"

He held his spear firmly in one hand and helped them climb the shaft with the other.

"No; you will separate them by fire."

Nurunderi returned to earth. He found the encampment of the lovers and set fire to the dry bushes there. They sprang into crackling life. The flames leapt from one bush to another, and from tree to tree, until the camp was ringed with fire.

Wyungara was asleep, but as the smoke drifted over the shelter fence he woke and sprang to his feet. Through the curtain of smoke he could see the red and yellow flame blossoms. He picked up his spears, caught one of his wives under each arm, and burst through the ring of fire. Then, with his heavy burden, he plunged into a lagoon. The reeds by the bank were dry and caught fire, forcing him to wade further and further into the water, and to submerge himself and his wives from time to time.

The rushes in the middle of the shallow lagoon were green, but they withered in the heat and caught alight. The whole surface of the marsh became one dancing carpet of flame, and the smoke lay as thick and heavy on the water as a kangaroo-skin rug.

"There is no hope for us here," Wyungara gasped, "but I will save you."

He thrust the butt of his longest spear firmly into the mud.

"Great ruler of the sky," he called, "save these women. They have done no wrong. Take their hands and lead them to safety."

The flames licked his body and singed his hair, but he held his spear firmly in one hand and helped them to climb the shaft with the other.

"Hold fast!" he shouted. Then, putting forth all his strength he hurled the spear up into the air. It sped as quickly as a meteor in the night sky. It seemed like a star that had mistaken its direction and was fleeing from earth. It dwindled into the distance and was lost to sight.

Wyungara sank back into the water, content to face death now that his wives were safe. But the heart of Nepelle had been softened by the flame of love that was stronger than the searing heat of the marsh rushes.

The spirit of Wyungara was lifted gently from the lagoon and placed in the sky beside the wives he had loved more than his own life. Nepelle has granted them eternal life and love together in his heavenly home, where they shine steadily – three stars, united for ever.

NURUNDERI, THE TWO GIRLS, AND THE EVIL ONE

NEPELLE, the ruler of the heavens and the father of all spirits, had sent Nurunderi to be his messenger to men and women, to teach them the wisdom that would make them fit to be his children. Nurunderi travelled through every part of the continent until he came to South Australia, where he made his home between Lakes Albert and Alexandrina. Many of the tribesmen were afraid of him. Some ran away and hid in the scrub. When they refused to come out he knew they were not fit to receive the Father Spirit's commands, so he changed them into birds. Those who ventured out and listened to him became skilled in hunting and bushcraft, and wise in all the secrets of nature.

Of all men the Narrinyeri tribe were the most attentive and therefore the most learned. (At least, that is what the Narrinyeri people say.) Nurunderi was so pleased at his reception that he shifted his camp into their territory and waited until Nepelle was ready to tell him that his work was over. From his permanent camp he was able to make excursions to the lakes whenever he required a supply of fish.

On one such expedition he was passing two grass trees standing close together when he heard a doleful cry. Wise as he was, Nurunderi did not know that the voices were those of two sisters who had caused a great deal of trouble to the souls of men as they made their last long journey to the land of spirits. Plants and trees, which were the friends of mankind, had tried to capture the sisters and put an end to them, but they had all failed until one day the grass trees on the banks of Lake Albert had caught them while they were asleep, and imprisoned them. Day after day the girls called to men to release them, but in vain.

They were aware of Nurunderi's presence and were filled with excitement. If only they could persuade Nepelle's own messenger to rescue them!

Nurunderi, whose whole life was devoted to helping others, could not resist their pleas.

"Where are you?" he asked. "I hear your voices but I cannot see you."

"We are imprisoned in the grass trees you are looking at. An evil spirit has confined us here. We cannot free ourselves and live the normal life of women until a great and good man such as you comes and rescues us."

Now at this time Nurunderi was old and tired. His long task ended, he was waiting for the Great Spirit to take him to his eternal home. He had never touched a woman, and had spoken to them only when he had words of advice to give them. He reflected for a while. The element of human nature which guides and often misdirects the wisest of men prompted him to reflect on the joy of companionship that he had missed during his long life. An overwhelming desire to see these women, whose voices came so sweetly and plaintively from the grass trees, swept over him. It was easy to persuade himself that it would be a good deed to release them, even though he realised in his innermost being that there must have been some good reason for their imprisonment.

He made up his mind.

"By the power that is invested in me by the Great Spirit himself I tell you to come out and show yourselves as women."

The words had hardly been spoken when the two young women stood in front of him. Their eyes were fixed demurely on the ground to hide a mischievous sparkle.

"We are grateful for your help," they said. "Our only thought now is to help you, to cook your food, to find roots and grubs to make your meals more tasty when you return from hunting."

Nurunderi was pleased with their reply.

"Come with me," he said.

They followed him back to his wurley, giggling when he was out of hearing, and looking sideways at each other. That evening the old man enjoyed his meal as never before. When the moon rose, Nurunderi raised himself on his elbow and looked at the women who lay on either side of him. Unusual feelings of love and protection rose in him. Contentment filled him with a sense of well-being, as though he had found something he had been seeking all his life and had never discovered until that moment.

Weeks passed by in this idyllic manner. There was no work for him to do except fishing and hunting, no message to give to his people. The only thing that troubled him was the occasional thought that Nepelle might soon take him away from his camp and his women. Such forebodings came only when he was alone. During the evening the little glade where the camp was located rang with laughter. At night there was company and the touch of his hand on warm, living flesh.

Nurunderi became so fond of the girls, who had now become his wives, that he could not bear to leave them behind, even when he went across to the lake to fish.

"You can help me there as well as in camp," he told them. "Take the small hand-net and try to catch the fish close to the bank."

He waded out to his waist to catch the larger fish with his spear, while his wives hauled the small net through the shallows.

"See what we have caught!" one whispered excitedly to the other. "Three tukkeri!"

"But they are only for men. We are not allowed to eat them."

"Why shouldn't we? The old man will never know. I don't see why men should always keep the best food for themselves."

"All right. Let's put them in our bags and cover them with rushes so the old man won't see them."

They called to their husband, "We are going back to camp now. There are no fish here. We'll dig some yams and have the fire ready for you when you bring your catch home."

He waved his spear to show them he had heard, and went on with his fishing. The young women ran back to the camp, built up the fire, and baked the fish they had caught.

"No wonder the men keep it to themselves," the wives said as they sank their teeth into the succulent white flesh. "This is better than wallaby meat or the big, coarse fish old Messenger catches for us. We'll go back another time and get some more."

The gentle breeze carried the smell of the cooked fish down the slope of the hill and across the water. Nurunderi straightened himself and sniffed suspiciously.

"Tukkeri! Surely my wives are not cooking the forbidden fish?"

He waded ashore hurriedly and ran towards the camp. When he arrived he found the fire burning. Everywhere there was a strong smell of cooked fish and tukkeri oil, but of his wives there was no sign. They had seen him coming and had gone down to the edge of the lake by another path. They pulled an old raft from its hiding place in the reeds and paddled towards the far side of the lake.

Nurunderi was aghast. For the first time he realised that young women do not mate readily with an old man, and that he had been deceived by them. Shading his eyes, he looked across the lake and saw the black dot in the middle of the water. It was all that could be seen of the raft and the runaway wives. Pausing only to make sure that he had all his weapons, the old man ran to his canoe and set out in pursuit.

It was dark when he reached the far side, but he could see where the women had landed, and was satisfied that he could follow their trail in the morning. He lit a fire, cooked food, and examined his weapons again before going to sleep. Among them was a plongge, a short weapon with a knob at one end, used to inflict bruises on anyone who broke the tribal laws. He fingered it with a grim smile on his face, and lay down to sleep with the weapon cradled in his arm.

All the next morning he followed the two sets of footprints, but lost the trail when it came to stony ground. He made several casts, trying to cut the track where it was likely to ccme out on soft ground, but though he searched throughout the afternoon, he could not find it again.

Dispirited and lonely, he made his camp fire in the late afternoon and prepared for the night. While he was half awake, half asleep, Puckowie the Grandmother Spirit came to him, and warned him that danger was near. In the early morning he was fully on guard, but he could see no sign of an enemy. The only living thing in sight was a wombat. Learned man that he was, still he did not recognise that the Evil One himself had taken this shape to deceive him.

Nurunderi was hungry. He stalked the wombat and killed it. When he drew his spear from its body, blood poured on to the sand. He carried the animal back to his overnight camp and was making up the fire ready to roast the flesh, when he remembered that he had left his spear behind. He hurried back and saw a strange sight. The wombat's blood had congealed and was stirring in the sand. Nurunderi watched it gather itself up until it took the form of a man lying prone on the ground. After a long time the face and features were fully formed. The man was alive, but appeared to be sleeping.

"Perhaps he will be a friend to me, and will help me in my search for those wicked women," thought Nurunderi.

He left his spear behind as a gift and went into the bush to make another for his own use. When he returned the man and the spear had gone. Nurunderi could see the shallow depression where the body had been lying, but there was no sign of any footprints leading away from it. He sat down to consider the matter. Friends always leave footprints. It is only an enemy who destroys his trail, but in this case Nurunderi could think of no way in which it could have been disguised. He was worried. The recollection of Puckowie's warning came back to him, and he kept a careful watch.

Before long he heard a sound which came from the further side of a large sandhill. He sidled round it and saw the figure of the Evil One, who had now resumed his normal appearance.

"Are you the man who came from the blood of the wombat this morning?" asked Nurunderi.

"It may be that I am; it may be that I am not."

Nurunderi looked at him more closely.

"You are that man," he said. "That is my spear you are holding."

"Then you may have it back," the Evil One replied, and swung it backwards, ready to hurl it at Nurunderi.

"Wait!" the Messenger cried. "I gave you that spear in case you should need it. It was an act of friendship. I want you to help me."

The Evil One laughed sardonically.

"What help do you think I can give you?"

"I am looking for my wives. They did an evil deed and then ran away. I want to find them."

"Why?"

"So that I can give them the punishment they deserve."

The Evil One laughed again.

"Then you will get no help from me, Nurunderi. I know who you are. You are the teacher Nepelle sent into the world to help men. You are old and you have offended against his law. You are at my mercy. I am the Evil One."

Nurunderi's heart sank. He regretted his weakness in marrying the young women. He realised that he had put himself at the mercy of the enemy of Nepelle. He tried to divert the other's attention.

"You can't be the Evil One. He would never enter into the body of a wombat!"

"I can take any form I want," the Evil One retorted. "But in this case I admit that I was a prisoner of the wombat. I tried to attack you many times, but the good spirits prevented me, and

68

shut me up in the body of a wombat. Then you forgot Nepelle's teaching and fell under the spell of two foolish girls. They deceived you. When they fled it was I who made them come this way. You killed the wombat and released me from my prison."

"Then you should regard me as your friend."

"No, you are not my friend. And you have forfeited the friendship of Nepelle. You are just a lonely old man who is about to die at the hand of the Evil One!"

He hurled the spear at Nurunderi like a bolt of lightning. The teacher leapt aside, but not quickly enough. The spear pierced his leg. He stooped and drew it out.

"Now you are at my mercy," Nurunderi cried in triumph. He threw the spear back with all his might, straight into the heart of the Evil one.

The old man cried aloud in gratitude to Nepelle, thinking that the Father Spirit had forgiven him, and prepared to resume his journey. He walked for several hours, until it dawned slowly on him that he was making no progress. His heart sank again. He recognised the same sandhills, the same trees and, when he turned and looked back, the same body of the Evil One lying on the ground. He crouched down and watched it closely. He saw that birds, small animals, and insects which approached the body were unable to escape.

"The spirit of the Evil One is still alive," he thought, "even though I have killed his outward form. I must destroy the body completely and all will be well."

He gathered scrub and dry sticks and built a huge funeral pyre. He dragged the body on to it and waited until it was consumed by the flames. Then he turned to leave the haunted place. But still he found himself unable to escape. A careful examination of the ground showed that the blood of the man had soaked into the sand. Nurunderi raked the embers across so that the blood was burned, and at last he found he was free to depart. The animals and insects, suddenly released, danced round him trying to express their gratitude.

Many leagues lay behind him when he came to the bank of the Murray River. Two sets of footprints showed that his wives had come this way. The tracks stopped at the water's edge, and he knew that they must have crossed by means of a canoe or raft. There was no way for Nurunderi to cross. He prayed to Nepelle, and to his relief the earth trembled, heaped itself up, and a long tongue of sand and rock stretched out across the river, forming a bridge which he crossed at a run.

"It is a sign of forgiveness!" he said.

The next day he reached the sea. The ashes of a camp fire lay on the sand. Shells and the remains of a meal showed that the young women were still eating forbidden food. Nurunderi sat down on the sand and wept. His tears flowed together and ran in rivulets, soaking into the ground and forming a pool which overflowed and trickled into the sea. The pool remains in that place, but because of the love of Nepelle for his erring teacher, the water is no longer salt. It has become clear and fresh, and sustains the spirits of the departed who are seeking the land of eternal life.

The following morning, as soon as it was light, Nurunderi saw a peninsula at a little distance from the shore. It was connected by a long, narrow strip to the land, but it was evident that at flood tide the higher ground at the end would be cut off from the shore by the water. The keeper of the isthmus was Ga-ra-gah the Blue Crane, who guarded the approach. The young women sat close to the shore, talking to the Crane. Far away though they were, Nurunderi realised that they were using their powers of persuasion to induce the keeper to let them cross. Nurunderi shouted and saw them turn and look at him. He beckoned, but they turned and spoke even more earnestly to Ga-ra-gah. One of them put her arms round his neck. Blue Crane stepped to one side and they began to run along the causeway.

"This is your opportunity!"

It was faithful old Puckowie whispering in his ear.

"Help me, Nepelle," cried Nurunderi. "In your wisdom you know what should be done to the wives whom I have loved so well and so foolishly. They are young. Remember this, and forgive me for my wrong-doing which has been so much greater than theirs."

"They are entering the Spirit Land," Puckowie whispered again. "It is the will of Nepelle that you should chant the wind song. Quickly!"

Nurunderi threw back his head and began to sing. A puff of wind caught the words and blew them towards the peninsula. The waves leaped to hear them. The wind caught their crests and blew them to a fine spray which drenched the racing girls. The sea lifted itself from its bed, surged over the land, and swept the

The waves swept the young women from their feet.

young women from their feet. The wind howled across the sea until the waves broke over their heads and they were lost to sight. The tears ran in streams down Nurunderi's cheeks as he sat watching and grieving for them.

The wind died away quickly. The sun shone out on a calm sea between the shore and the little island which had now become the Island of the Spirit Land. At a short distance two rounded rocks rose above the water.

"They are your wives," Puckowie said. "Nepelle has turned them to stone, and will not allow them to go to the Spirit Land."

The tears dropped from the old man's chin.

"They do not deserve that," he whispered brokenly. "They were so young, so beautiful. They did not understand what they were doing. Nepelle is all-forgiving. He will not let his servant suffer."

He threw himself into the water. His body was seized in the grip of a current which swept him down to the bottom of the ocean, where he met the spirits of his young wives. All three clung together, and felt themselves lifted up through the water, into the clear air, up through thick folds of clouds until they reached the very heavens, where Nepelle lets them shine as stars to show that he has forgiven them.

It was because Nurunderi loved his wives so greatly that they were forgiven and allowed to live together in the starry sky; but their petrified bodies remain in the sea as a warning to all women never to eat forbidden food.

EAGLE-HAWK AND THE WOODPECKERS

THE yaraan tree soared up into the sky. It was as tall as five trees.* The topmost branches were so far away that they could hardly be seen, and indeed there were times when they were hidden from sight by low-lying clouds. It was here that Mullian the Eagle-hawk lived with his wife Moodai the Possum, his mother-in-law Moodai, who was also a Possum, and Butterga the Flying Squirrel.

One man and three women, and every one of them a cannibal! Mullian was taller and stronger and braver than his women. When they cried, "Mullian, we are hungry!" the mighty Eagle-hawk would climb down from his home, armed with a spear which was too heavy for any other man to carry. He would follow the trail of any two-legged man until he caught up with him.

Thud! Mullian's spear would crash into his body, and that was the end of the unfortunate man. Leaving the lifeless body impaled on his spear, Mullian would throw it over his shoulder, walk back to the yaraan tree and run swiftly up the smooth trunk with the grisly meal dangling at the end of his spear.

When he reached the little humpy on the branches far away in the clouds, the fire would be burning brightly. The women would dismember the body and cook it on the hot stones.

For a long time no one knew that Mullian was killing the men who lived on the ground, but one day he was seen running swiftly with the body of a young woman transfixed by his spear.

"What shall we do?" the men asked each other. "It is not right that Mullian should be allowed to kill men and women."

"Wait till he comes down and we'll ambush him," someone suggested; but there were plenty of men to advise against such a foolhardy idea.

"Twenty men could not overcome Mullian," they said. "They would die, and nothing would be achieved but an extra large meal for his women-folk."

* One version of the legend states that the tall tree, which grew by the Barwon River, was actually composed of five different trees – gum, boxtree, coolabah, belar, and pine. The progress of those who climbed the tree could be followed by the chips of bark which fell down.

"Then someone had better climb up the yaraan tree and set fire to his humpy."

A little old man who was noted for his prowess as a hunter burst into a cackling laugh.

"Oh yes, climb up the tree and set fire to his humpy," he mocked. "Put wings on your feet and soar like a bird. Or cover them with gum and walk up the trunk like a fly."

"The Bibbis can do it," called a voice out of the darkness.

Two strong, active young Bibbis who belonged to the Woodpecker tribe jumped into the firelight.

"Ho ho! We are the men to do it," they shouted, and they danced round the fire. Their arms and legs jerked up and down as though they were climbing the tree.

"That's how we will climb the tree."

The old man laughed again.

"Very good, you Bibbis, but how will you set fire to the humpy?"

"Like this," said a squeaky voice from above them. Murra-wunda the Climbing Rat sprang out of an overhanging branch and landed inside the circle of men. As he flew through the air he left a trail of smoke and flame behind him. When he stood up they saw that he was holding a lighted twig between his teeth. He had stolen it from the fire while everyone was looking at the old hunter.

"Good, Murra-wunda, good. You may come with us," the Bibbi men said approvingly.

Early next morning the three eager young men began to climb the trunk of the yaraan tree. They were frightened when the tree shook, because Mullian was descending on one of his hunting trips, but they hid on the other side of the trunk and he did not see them. All day they climbed. When night fell they were less than halfway up. They camped for the night on a broad branch, fearful lest Mullian should discover them on his way home; but Eagle-hawk must have had to forage far afield for food, for he did not pass them during the hours of darkness.

The following morning they reached the platform where Mullian had built his home. The women were busy preparing vegetable food as a relish for the meal they expected Mullian to bring them. Murra-wunda and the Bibbis crept into the humpy unseen. Climbing Rat had nursed the smouldering twig carefully. He tucked it into a dark corner where it would

74

keep on smouldering until the red ember touched the grass wall.

"Now we shall see the sight of a lifetime," Murra-wunda whispered. "Come on. If we don't get down quickly we'll be in trouble."

They slid over the edge of the platform and climbed down the trunk much more quickly than they had gone up. Safe on the ground once more they waited until Mullian had gone past. In spite of his load he swung himself up effortlessly from branch to branch, and dwindled in size until he seemed as small as an insect. The tiny black dot reached the aerial home and disappeared from sight.

The climbers called to their friends to come and watch. Soon the tree was surrounded with a circle of upturned faces. Unaware of the expectant gaze of the men below, Mullian tossed the body he had brought to Butterga and the two Moodias and went into the grass shelter.

"Something is burning," he called.

"It's only the cooking fire," Butterga said.

Mullian was not satisfied.

"The humpy is full of smoke," he said. "Come and see if you can find out what's wrong."

The women crowded inside and began to cough. The smoke grew thicker and they could hardly see each other. A red glow sprang to life in the far corner, and with a roar the whole wall burst into flames. The women fled to the opening in the far wall, but Mullian was ahead of them. The hut creaked and sagged a little. His broad shoulders were caught in the doorway.

Now the flames licked against the roof, which flowered into a blaze of yellow flame. To the watchers far below it seemed as though the yaraan tree had put forth a beautiful flower, but for Mullian and his wives it was the flower of death.

Mullian's arm was burnt off at the shoulder. With singed hair and bursting skin the women fell unconscious to the floor. The flames roared as they consumed the bodies. Soon nothing was left on the bare branch but the charred bones of the four cannibals.

Strong in death as he had been in life, the spirit of Mullian soared away from the yaraan tree taking the soul of one wife with him. Moodai the mother-in-law and Butterga the Flying Squirrel were left behind, but up in the sky Mullian took his place as Mullian-ga, the Morning Star. By his side is a faint star which is his

75

arm, separated from his body, and a larger one which is Moodai his wife.

The fire burnt down the trunk of the yaraan tree and along the roots until nothing was left. The earth fell in when the roots were consumed, leaving channels along which water flows, in time of flood, into the great hole where the barrel of the tree once grew from the ground.

THE SEVEN SISTERS

It was in the Dreamtime that girls decided that they should go through severe tests to show that they were ready for womanhood and marriage, just as the young men had to prove themselves for manhood. They went to the elders of the tribe and told them what they had decided. The leading men and the old ones sat late that night nodding their heads and speaking slowly. In the morning they summoned the girls to the council. They told them that they approved their decision and commended them for their wisdom.

"But what is it you want to do?" they asked.

"We want to show that our minds are not ruled by our bodies. We believe that women, as well as men, should be able to overcome fear and pain. Then our sons will be brave and strong in the years to come. Give us the same sort of tests as the boys," they pleaded.

The wise men looked at each other questioningly. Only grown men were allowed to know what boys had to endure during the initiation tests.

"We shall make new tests," they said after they had thought about it for a long time. "Girls could never stand the ordeals that boys have to go through."

The young women stood firm.

"In days to come we will give birth to boys who will be subject to the rites. It is only fitting that we, who will be their mothers, should know what they will have to go through when they are older. They will be bone of our bone, flesh of our flesh. If we conquer fear and pain, they will be strong when their time comes."

"Very well," the elders said. "We would never willingly have made you suffer; but if you can endure to the end you will win our respect, and we shall think the more of our women."

It was no light thing that the girls had undertaken. For three years they were taken to a place where no one else was allowed to go. The elders taught them the law of the tribe. They gave them only a small portion of food at sunrise and another at sunset.

Their bodies became lean and sinewy, until they felt that they had learned to control their appetites.

"Now we are ready," they said.

"No," the elders replied. "For three years you have endured your training. Now the time for the testing has come. The first test will show whether you have learned the first lesson."

They were taken on a long, difficult journey for three days. They went through dense bush where thorns and sharp stakes scratched and tore their flesh; they crossed burning plains and high mountains, and in all that time they were not permitted to touch food. On the morning of the fourth day the elders caught kangaroos and wallabies, and gave each girl a flint knife.

"Cut your food with this," they said. "Take as much as you want to satisfy your appetites."

To the relief of the elders the young women took only enough meat to satisfy their immediate hunger. If they had obeyed their instincts they would have taken the whole joint to distend their stomachs after the long fast, but they had learnt the lesson well.

They returned to camp and the second series of tests began.

"This is to see whether you have overcome pain," they were warned.

One by one they were made to lie flat on their backs on the bare ground. A wirinun took a pointed stick, thrust it between a girl's lips so that it rested on a front tooth, and hit the butt of the stick with repeated blows until the tooth was knocked out.

"Are you ready to lose another tooth?" she was asked.

"Yes."

A second tooth was knocked out, but the girl made no sound. The others submitted themselves to the ordeal without protest.

" Now stand in a row," the wirinun commanded. With a sharp flint he scored heavy lines across their breasts until the blood flowed down their stomachs and dropped on to the ground. Ashes were rubbed into the wounds to increase the pain, but they endured the double agony without a murmur.

"Now you may lie down and go to sleep," they were told.

They stretched out on the bare ground and sank into a sleep of exhaustion, forgetting for a little while their aching gums and the wounds in which ashes stung as they healed the jagged cuts. Several hours later one of the girls woke and smothered a scream before it reached her lips. She felt something moving across her body. She tensed her muscles until they were as hard as wood. Every part of her was covered with crawling insects. They slithered across her lips, wormed their way into her nostrils and ears, and over her eyelids, but she remained silent and motionless; and so with every girl, until daylight came to release them.

The tests continued until it seemed that there was no end to them: there was the ordeal of the pierced nose, in which they were required to wear a stick, which kept the wound from healing, through the septum. Every time it was touched it was agony to the wearer as it tore further through the flesh. There was the ordeal of the bed of hot cinders; and others that degraded the body and could be overcome only by steadfastness of mind and spirit.

"It is over," the elders said at last. "You have endured every ordeal, every test of pain, every torture, with fortitude and cheerfulness. The elders of your tribe are proud of you. There now remains the last test, the conquering of fear. You have gone a long way towards it. Do you think you can survive this as well?"

"We can!" cried the girls with a single voice.

The ordeal came at night. The old men went to the isolated camp where the girls were to sleep without the comfort of fire, where the wind moaned eerily in the trees, and the spirits of darkness and evil seemed to hide in every bush. The elders chanted spine-chilling tales of bunyips and maldarpes, of the Yara-ma-yha-who and the Keen Keeng, of monsters such as the Whowhie, Thardid Jimbo, and Cheeroonear, and of the Evil One himself. Then they stole away, and the girls were left all alone.

Horrible screams came from the surrounding bush and continued all night, as though the encampment was surrounded by spirits and monsters. The old men enjoyed themselves as they endeavoured to fill the girls' hearts with fear; but the young women who had passed through pain to the ultimate test of womanhood were able to call on their hard-won reserves of courage and endurance.

Morning came. The whole tribe came out to greet them and congratulate them on the triumph of mind over body. On that day even the gods and spirits of the high heaven were present. The girls, now entered into full womanhood, were snatched from the midst of their friends and taken up to the sky where, as the Seven Sisters of the constellation of the Pleiades, they shine down

The old men endeavoured to fill the girls' hearts with fear.

serenely on the world, encouraging every successive generation to follow their example.

*   *   *   *

But there is another tribal tale which gives the names of the Seven Sisters as Meamei. They were the custodians of a unique treasure, the gift of fire, which they kept hidden in their yam sticks. They cooked their food with it and lit the fires that warmed them at night. When the weather was cold, men and women came to them and begged for the fire; but the hearts of the Meamei were as hard as mountain rocks.

"This is our possession," they boasted. "We will not share it with anyone."

Amongst those who had been repulsed by the sisters was Wahn the Crow. Others had gone away disappointed, but it was not in Wahn's nature to accept a rebuff. He knew there must be some way of getting the fire away from the Meamei, so he hid in a tree and watched everything they did. Soon he discovered that they were fond of eating white ants. They spent a great deal of their time searching for them, and when they had gathered a quantity, they ate them for their evening meal.

Wahn went off to a little distance and caught a number of poisonous snakes, which he sealed inside a termite nest. He hurried back to the Meamei and said excitedly, "I have found an enormous termite hill. Come with me. I'll show you where it is."

The Seven Sisters follows him, licking their lips in anticipation. When they reached the ant hill they broke it down with their yam sticks. To their dismay a number of hissing snakes glided out and darted at them. The sisters struck wildly at them with their yam sticks, till the ends of the sticks broke off and the fire fell on the ground. Wahn crept into their midst, picked up the fire, and carried it away.

It was after this that the Seven Sisters went up into the sky and became the constellation of the Pleiades. The gift of fire was now in the possession of Crow, who guarded it as jealously as its previous owners. Mankind had expected that he would make it available to everyone, but Wahn had a much more cunning plan.

"I am now the custodian of fire," he told them. "It is a sacred trust conferred on me by Baiame – as a reward for my own courage and cleverness," he added hastily. "I am not permitted to share it with you, but I am anxious to help you. If you bring your food to me, I will cook it for you."

The people applauded his generosity, and Wahn kept his promise. He cooked their food when it was brought to him, but he always kept the choicest pieces for himself.

"Why don't you hunt for your own food?" they asked him.

Wahn reproached them.

"You are ungrateful," he said. "I cook your food for you. The least you can do is to supply my modest requirements. The custodian of fire has no time to go looking for food."

The people complained to Baiame. The Great Spirit was angry when he heard what Wahn was doing. He told the people not to be afraid, but to take the fire away from Wahn by force.

So they gathered together and rushed Crow's camp. As they drew close he threw the burning logs at them to drive off the attackers, who snatched them up and carried them away to start their own camp fires. Wahn was left alone. He chuckled to himself when he thought how easily he had escaped; but he had forgotten that the all-seeing Father Spirit could see everything that happened in the world he had created.

Baiame cursed the Crow.

"May you be as black as the charred wood of your fire," he thundered. "You do not deserve to be a man."

He pointed at Wahn, whose body began to shrink. His legs became like little sticks, his face elongated, terminating in a beak, and feathers sprouted from his arms. There he stood: no longer Wahn the man, but Wahn the Crow – black as the burnt logs that fall from the fire.

*   *   *   *

Before the Meamei sisters left the earth they went into the mountains and made springs of water to feed the rivers, so that there would be water for men and women for all time. A young hunter Karambal was sorrowful when he heard the Meamei sisters were leaving because he had fallen in love with one of them. When he found the girl alone one day he carried her off to be his wife. But the other sisters sent cold wintry weather to the earth to force the hunter to release their sister. After this they made their departure into the sky in search of summer, to melt the snow and ice.

It is at summer time every year that they appear, bringing the hot days with them. After the hot weather they travel far to the west, and winter comes to remind men that it is wrong to carry off women who belong to a totem that is forbidden them.

After his experience with the Meamei, Karambal went in search of another wife. He thought he had learnt his lesson, and was determined to choose one of the right totem. When he found the woman he wanted he was again unfortunate, for she was already married to a great warrior whose name was Bullabogabun. With soft words Karambal induced the woman to leave her husband and go away with him.

Their life together was short and sweet. Bullabogabun followed their tracks and speedily overtook them. Karambal's love was less than his fear. Abandoning the woman, he climbed a tall tree which grew near the camp and hid in the branches. Bullabogabun saw him crouched there, and lit a fire at the base of the tree. The branches caught fire, and then the trunk, which blazed like the torch of a giant in the midst of the plain. Karambal was borne up by the hungry flames and rode on them into the sky, close to the Seven Sisters. Forgetting all that he had learned, he still pursues them through the sky – Karambal, who became the star Aldebaran, the pursuer.

THE BRUSH TURKEYS OF THE SKY

In the Dreamtime there was a large plain where no one lived except a flock of brush turkeys. They were free to roam wherever they wanted, and they had no enemies. Life would have been very pleasant if it had not been for Old Grandfather Brush Turkey, who was still strong and vigorous, and larger than all the other birds. He had never been popular with the rest of the flock, and had withdrawn into himself, often absenting himself for long periods.

There was an outcry when it was discovered that one of the younger birds was missing.

"Where can she have gone?" everyone asked. "We saw her at the dance last night, but now there is no sign of her."

One of the birds plucked up courage and went to look for Grandfather Brush Turkey.

"Have you seen our little one?" he asked.

"How should I know?" the old bird answered gruffly. "None of you take any notice of me. Why should I notice you?"

The young bird went away sorely puzzled, for he had seen feathers and a trickle of dried blood on the ground, but had not dared to ask more questions.

The matter was forgotten for several days, and then another bird went missing. The hunters examined the ground cautiously. They saw signs of a body which had been dragged through the bushes, more feathers, and a pathetic heap of bones.

"It is old Grandfather Turkey," they told the rest of the flock that night. "He has become a cannibal. He waits until we dance in the moonlight. Then he pounces on one of the younger birds when it is overcome with fatigue, and drags it away and kills it."

"What shall we do? We cannot permit the old Grandfather to do this to our loved ones."

"What can we do?"

"We can go and kill him."

"Who dares to go?"

There was a long silence. It was obvious that something should be done to remove the danger, but no one dared to attack the oldest and biggest and strongest of the Brush Turkeys.

In the absence of any bird with sufficient courage to rid them of the peril, they had to endure the loss of the young birds.

"It would be easy to forego our dances," a mother bird said one day. "It is only when the youngsters become tired during the dance and fall over that Grandfather is able to carry them away and kill them."

They all agreed with her, but the next night they were dancing again under the bright moon. The moonlight was in their blood, and if they stopped dancing they would no longer be brush turkeys.

But this state of affairs could not go on indefinitely, or the whole flock would diminish and be lost in the silence of the desert.

Another conference was called.

"There is only one thing left to us," said one of the leaders. "We cannot fight; nor can we stay here waiting to be killed. We must go away to some place where Grandfather cannot find us."

"When shall we go?" came a chorus of voices, because everyone agreed with him.

"We shall go now," he said unexpectedly. "We could think about it for a long time and talk about it; perhaps old Grandfather would overhear us, and he would follow. Last night he stole one of our finest girls, and now he will be lying asleep somewhere so full of food that he will not be able to move."

A long procession set out. They tried to conceal their tracks so that the cannibal turkey would not be able to follow; but how can a great company of birds go walkabout without leaving traces of their passage?

Two days later, when morning came and his appetite was revived, Grandfather Brush Turkey realised that the desert was silent. He fluttered into the branches of a tree and looked about. Nowhere could he see the rest of his flock, who should have been browsing on the plain. He hurried to their dancing ground and saw the beaten circle where the dances had been held, and a clear trail that led towards the mountains. Fluttering his wings, he ran along it until he came to the mountains. It was more difficult to follow the trail over the stones, but here and there he found a telltale mark, or a feather that had dropped to the ground. Even when the flock had waded down the bed of a stream he could read the signs in the disturbed leaves and the feathers caught in bushy twigs.

Presently he came to an outcrop of rock where there was a clear

85

view of the plains on the further side of the mountain. Shading the sun from his eyes with one wing, he stared intently until he saw the distant specks which told him where his flock had camped.

The old bird smiled inwardly. He waited till dusk before going near the camp and hiding in some dense bush.

"The mountain air has sharpened my appetite," he said to himself. "And these bushes are wonderfully placed to give cover, and yet so handy that I can pounce on to the dancing ring without being seen."

He settled down to wait. He had no way of telling that when the flock had reached the new encampment, the birds had been visited by two large brush turkeys who had flown down to them from somewhere in Baiame's realm in the sky.

"Why have you come here?" the two birds asked the turkeys of the plain. "What is the matter with your home over the mountains?"

The brush turkeys gathered round them and all began to talk at once. From the babble of sound the visitors learned of Grandfather Brush Turkey and what he was doing to the flock.

They looked at each other understandingly and said, "We understand. Baiame tells us that what you have done is right. Do not fear. Tonight you must have your dance as usual. Don't take any notice of anything that may happen."

Grandfather Brush Turkey remained hidden in the bushes, watching the dancers intently in the soft light of the moon. Behind and a little to one side the two Sky Brush Turkeys were hidden, watching old Grandfather Brush Turkey.

As the night went on the dancers grew more excited; their songs and their dancing feet went quicker and quicker. One of the young birds fell to the ground. Grandfather Turkey sprang to his feet, pushed his way through the brush, and stooped over the body. But at that moment a huge bird towered over him and struck him such a blow that he rolled over on the ground. Grandfather Turkey lay on his back and looked up with an expression of dismay on his old, wrinkled face. Another great bird came from behind, there was a soft sound of a second blow, and the cannibal lay dead on the rim of the dancing floor.

The birds went on dancing, taking no notice of what had happened, until the sky visitors called them.

"That is the end of your troubles," they said. "Old Grandfather will never kill your young birds again."

The whole flock gobbled and clucked with admiration and relief. From their midst the huge birds rose, flapping their wings majestically, and mounted up into the sky. As a reward for their services to the smaller birds of earth, Baiame stretched out his hand and placed them in the sky where, as guides for the spirits of the heavens and for men on earth, they became two specks of light that point to the burning stars of the Southern Cross.

THE DANCING OF PRIEPRIGGIE

LIKE sparks from a burning branch when it is struck on the ground, so the stars flew aimlessly through the dark sky. In a little valley in Queensland men and women danced their nightly dance, led by Priepriggie, the singer of songs, the whirler of bullroarers, the skilled huntsman, the wirinun with the flying feet. They sang his songs and danced his songs, while the stars left fiery trails in the sky, in a confusion of light and bewildering chaos. Above there was no order or rhythm, but in the little valley the chanting and the dancing footsteps blended as Priepriggie's people followed him round the magic circle. Their hearts thumped in the rhythm, and when the singing was over and they sank exhausted to the ground, they murmured to each other, "Great is Priepriggie. If he wished he could even make the stars dance to his songs!"

Men and women who spend the long hours of the night dancing, and who sleep till dawn, need food to sustain their bodies. The women had their tasks, and the men were hunters; but of all who sought for food, Priepriggie was the most successful. He was first up at dawn, and this morning he stole through the pearly grey mist by the river bank until he came to the huge tree where the flying foxes hung from the branches. They had returned from their nightly flight, and were sound asleep.

His footfall was as light as the glint of sunbeams on the grass, and not a twig stirred, not a drop of dew fell from the leaves as he made his way towards the tree. The flying foxes hung in clusters from the bare branches. There was little food for a man or woman in a flying fox, but their leader was many times the size of his followers, and it was the leader whom Priepriggie was seeking in order to provide his people with a meal that night.

Closer still he moved, until at last he could see the huge body of the leader of the flying foxes, surrounded by his wives and attendants. Priepriggie fitted the butt of his spear into his woomera, and drew it back, inch by inch, until his arm was fully stretched behind him. Then, with one convulsive thrust, with every ounce of body and muscles behind it, the throwing stick swept forward and the spear sang through the air. It pierced the body of the

Like a cloud of flies they lifted him up and bore him away.

great flying fox and pinned it to the tree trunk. A moment later there was a deafening roar as the flying foxes woke and spread their wings. They flew out of the tree like a cloud of smoke and circled round, waiting for their leader.

He did not come. Presently they saw his body against the trunk, with the haft of the spear still vibrating. With another circling of the tree they saw Priepriggie crouched on the ground, his woomera in front of him. Like a cloud of flies they descended on him, lifted him up and bore him away. Higher and higher they mounted until they disappeared from sight.

That night men and women searched for the singer of songs, but they could not see him anywhere. Their bellies were empty, because their hunting had not been successful, and a sadness descended on them.

"Without Priepriggie we are helpless," they cried. "If we dance his dance, perhaps he will come back to us. Perhaps he is lost, and is waiting to hear our songs."

They broke into a shuffling dance, but it had no life in it. Suddenly they stopped. They heard the sound of someone singing. It came from a long distance, and seemed to come from the stars.

"Listen! It is the voice of Priepriggie," they said.

The song grew louder; a compelling rhythm beat through their heads, and set their blood running faster.

"Look! The stars are dancing."

The random, darting stars had arranged themselves in order, and were dancing to Priepriggie's song. The men and women joined in. Their feet flew over the ground, the song rose from deep in their bodies and burst out of their throats. The new dance of Priepriggie was danced on earth and in the sky.

The song was over. The dance was finished. They lay back and stared in amazement. Right across the sky the stars were resting in a ribbon of light. The dancers of the heavens were lying where they had fallen when the corroboree of the skies ended. Though men mourned the loss of Priepriggie, they rejoiced because the Milky Way was spread above them to remind them that Priepriggie could charm the stars of heaven as easily as the feet of men.

Legends of Animals

THE LAST OF HIS TRIBE

He crouches, and buries his face on his knees,
   And hides in the dark of his hair;
For he cannot look up to the storm-smitten trees,
   Or think of the loneliness there –
   Of the loss and the loneliness there.

The wallaroos grope through the tufts of the grass,
   And turn to their coverts for fear;
But he sits in the ashes and lets them pass
   Where the boomerangs sleep with the spear –
   With the nullah, the sling and the spear.

Uloola, behold him! the thunder that breaks
   On the tops of the rocks with the rain,
And the wind which drives up with the salt of the lakes,
   Have made him a hunter again –
   A hunter and fisher again.

For his eyes have been full with a smouldering thought;
   But he dreams of the hunts of yore,
And of foes that he sought, and of fights that he fought
   With those who will battle no more –
   Who will go to the battle no more.

It is well that the water which tumbles and fills,
   Goes moaning and moaning along;
For an echo rolls out from the sides of the hills,
   And he starts at a wonderful song –
   At the sound of a wonderful song.

And he sees, through the rents of the scattering fogs,
   The corroboree warlike and grim,
And the lubra who sat by the fire on the logs,
To watch, like a mourner, for him –
   Like a mother and mourner for him.

Will he go in his sleep from these desolate lands,
    Like a chief, to the rest or his race,
With the honey-voiced woman who beckons and stands,
    And gleams like a dream in his face –
    Like a marvellous dream in his face?

Henry Kendall

HOW THE ANIMALS CAME TO AUSTRALIA

LONG before there were men or animals in Australia,* the only living things that had eyes to see the vast continent were flocks of migratory birds. When they returned to their homeland far to the east, they told the animals, which at that time had the form of men and women, of the unending plains, the tree-covered mountains, the wide, long rivers, and the abundant vegetation of the great land over which they had flown. The reports created such excitement that the animals assembled from far and near to hold a corroboree and discuss the matter. It was decided that, as the land appeared to be so much richer and more desirable than their own, they would all go and live there.

The big problem was how to reach the land of promise. Every animal had its own canoe, but they were frail craft, well suited to the placid waters of lakes and streams, but not to the ocean that lay between the two lands. The only vessel that could contain them all was the one that belonged to Whale. He was asked if he would lend it to them, but he gave a flat refusal.

The animals were determined to migrate, no matter what difficulties had to be overcome. They held another secret meeting at which they enlisted the aid of Starfish, who was Whale's

* This legend is also related in *Aboriginal Fables and Legendary Tales* by the same author. It is included in the present compilation because it may be regarded as the basic story of the arrival of the animals in Australia when they were still men. In this legend and others that follow, we see how the actions of men led to the characteristic forms of the animals which succeeded them, in a reversal of the evolutionary system. The first printed version was recorded by R. H. Mathews in the journal *Science of Man*, and in his book *Folklore of the Australian Aborigines* he referred to it as the origin of the Thurrawai tribe.

closest friend. Starfish agreed to help, for he was as anxious as the others to make the journey.

"Greetings, my friend," he said to Whale.

"Greetings," Whale replied in his deep, rumbling voice. "What do you want?"

"There is nothing I want, except to help you. I see your hair is badly infested with lice. I thought that as I am so small I could pick them off for you."

"That's extraordinarily kind of you. They do worry me a bit," Whale admitted. He placed his head in Starfish's lap and gave a sensuous wriggle of contentment. Starfish plucked off the lice in a leisurely fashion.

While the cleaning task went on, the animals went on tiptoe to the shore, loaded all their possessions in Whale's huge canoe, and paddled silently out to sea. The faint splash of their paddles was drowned by Starfish as he scratched vigorously at the vermin.

After a while Whale became restless, and began to fret.

"Where is my canoe?" he asked. "I can't see it."

"It's here, right beside you," said Starfish soothingly.

He picked up a piece of wood and struck a hollow log by his side. It gave out a booming noise.

"Are you satisfied now?"

Whale sank back again and submitted himself to his friend's attentions once more. The sun was low in the sky when Whale woke up for the second time.

"I am anxious about my canoe," he said. "Let me see it."

He brushed Starfish aside and rolled over so that he could look round him. There was a long furrow in the sand where the canoe had been pulled down the beach, but of the canoe itself there was no sign. Whale turned round in alarm and saw it on the distant horizon, almost lost to sight. He turned on Starfish and attacked him so fiercely that the poor fellow was nearly torn to pieces. His limbs and torn flesh were tossed aside contemptuously. His descendants still hide among the rocks and in salt water pools as their ancestor did that day, and their bodies bear the marks of the fury of Whale when he turned against his friend. But little Starfish had not submitted to punishment without some resistance, and in his struggles he managed to tear a hole in Whale's head, which is also inherited by the descendants of their huge ancestor.

Whale raced across the ocean with water vapour roaring from the hole in his head, and began to overtake the canoe. The terrified animals dug their paddles deeper in the water and strained every muscle to make the canoe go faster, but it was mainly through the efforts of Koala that they managed to keep at a safe distance from their infuriated pursuer.

"Look at my strong arms," cried Native Bear. "Take your paddle strokes from me." The gap grew wider as his powerful arms made the paddle fly through the water, and ever since his arms have been strong and muscular.

The chase continued for several days and nights, until at last land came in sight – the country they had longed for. At the entrance to Lake Illawarra the canoe was grounded and the animals jumped ashore. As they disappeared into the bush the canoe rose and fell on the waves. Brolga, the Native Companion, was the only one who had the presence of mind to remember that they would never be safe while Whale was free to roam the seas in his canoe, for at any time he might come ashore and take up the pursuit again. So Brolga pushed the canoe out from the shore and danced and stamped on the thin bark until it was broken and sank beneath the waves. There it turned to stone; and it can still be seen as the island of Canman-gang near the entrance to Lake Illawarra. Ever since that day Brolga has continued the dance that broke up the canoe.

Whale turned aside in disgust and swam away up the coast, as his descendants still do. As for the animal-men, they explored the land and found it as good as the birds had said. They settled there, making their homes in trees and caves, by rivers and lakes, in the bush, and on the endless plains of the interior.

HOW FLYING FOX DIVIDED DAY AND NIGHT

In the first corroboree at the beginning of time, birds and animals mixed happily together and joined in the dances. The tribes vied with each other. Cockatoo, who was vain, sidled up to Eagle-hawk, the leader of the birds, and said, "There is no doubt that birds are better performers than animals, is there?"

"No doubt at all," said Eagle-hawk.

Cockatoo bustled off and told all his friends that Eagle-hawk had said that birds were better than animals. Before long Kangaroo, who was the natural leader of the animal tribes, was told what the birds were saying. He went to Eagle-hawk to remonstrate with him, but the bird man was so stubborn that the two began to quarrel. Tempers rose, others joined in the argument, and in a short space of time blows were struck, and a battle began. The animal-men fought against the bird-men; the only ones who were uncertain about the dispute were Flying Fox and Owl. They conferred together.

"The sensible thing to do is to join the winning side," Owl advised his friend.

"But how do we know who will win?"

"We will not move hastily. Let us wait for a while in the shade of this tree. We can rest, and when we are sure how the battle is going, we will know what to do."

They reclined in comfort, watching the birds and animals swaying backwards and forwards as their fortunes ebbed and flowed. Weapons flashed and were dulled with blood. Gradually the animals were forced backwards. Cheered by their success, the birds redoubled their efforts.

"Come on," shouted Owl. "We are bird-men. To the defence of our brothers!"

They made themselves conspicuous, and with their support the birds seemed to be overcoming their opponents.

But in the rear of the animals Kangaroo was mustering a fresh band of highly-trained warriors. They stole behind the trees and burst unexpectedly into the ranks of the birds, who reeled under the shock. The animals who had been so hard-pressed rallied their forces, and in a short time the position was reversed. The birds had to defend themselves against the animals who were bitterly avenging the deaths of their friends.

"You made a mistake," Flying Fox hissed.

"Don't worry," Owl replied. "Everyone makes mistakes. It is a wise person who realises it."

He turned round and belaboured the birds with his nullanulla, and Flying Fox reluctantly followed his example. As the tide of battle raged to and fro, Kangaroo and Eagle-hawk found themselves facing each other. They were so weary that they could hardly raise their clubs. Eagle-hawk dropped his to the ground.

"What are we really fighting about, Kangaroo?" he asked. "If I offended you by my boasting I am sorry for it."

"You were boastful," Kangaroo said thoughtfully, "but perhaps you had good cause. Certainly it is not worth fighting about. Let us be friends as we were before."

They called to their followers to cease fighting. Once again Flying Fox and Owl found themselves in an awkward position. They had fought for the birds, and then for the animals, and now they knew that no one would trust them. They went off and hid in the bush. The light paled, and presently the darkness became impenetrable.

"This is good," Owl remarked. "We can both see in the dark; but the other birds and animals need light. They'll never find us now."

But they were puzzled that it should be so dark when it was many hours till sunset. They did not know that Yhi had been so grieved at the fighting that she had hidden her light from her creatures. The darkness that had brought relief to Owl and Flying Fox had brought distress to others. They could not see to gather food, nor even to find their homes, or their dead relatives. They stumbled over stones and blundered into trees, while there seemed to be no end to the all-pervading blackness.

Two dim shapes met with a shock.

"Who are you?" asked one of them. "I am Emu."

"I am Kangaroo."

"Kangaroo, you are wise," Emu said. "Tell us what we must do to save ourselves."

"I have been thinking about it. We must light fires – many fires. By their light we shall be able to find food and cook it, and we can warm ourselves, and know that we are men again."

Birds and animals scurried about picking up dead wood, and

soon the cheerful glow of firelight flickered on the sandy ground among the bushes. It was a strange, shadowy world: outside the circles of light the gloom seemed more intense than before. The animals dragged big logs to their encampment, and the smaller birds were kept busy fossicking for chips and dry twigs, but it was not long before the supply of wood was exhausted.

Kangaroo called everyone together to discuss the matter. No one had any solution to the problem until one of the smaller lizards said, "Why don't we ask Owl and Flying Fox to tell us what to do? They might have the answer to our problem."

"It would do no harm to ask them, but where are they?" Kangaroo asked. "Ever since they proved themselves traitors they have been hiding, and we could never find them now in the darkness outside the firelight."

"I think I know where they have gone," little Lizard said. "I'll try to find them if you like."

"Very well," Kangaroo said with a smile. "Off you go."

Lizard scuttled off into the darkness.

"Where are you, Owl? Where are you, Flying Fox?" he kept calling. Presently there was an answering cry, and he saw Owl sitting up on the branch of a tree.

"What do you want, little Lizard?"

"We want you and Flying Fox to come to our meeting and tell us how to get the light back again. Listen!"

In the stillness they heard a dismal wailing.

"That is Dingo and Curlew. They go on like that all the time. They are waiting for the sunlight."

"Oh, no," Owl said. "If we went with you we would be killed. Don't you know that we have offended everybody?"

"No one will touch you," Lizard said earnestly. "We are too sad and frightened. All we want is someone to tell us how to get rid of the darkness."

"Very well then, we will take the risk." Owl raised his voice. "Come, Flying Fox," he called.

Together the three men, bird, animal, and lizard, went back to the main camp, which could be identified only by the dull glow of the dying embers.

"Is it you, Owl and Flying Fox?" asked Kangaroo.

"Yes. We have come to see what you want."

"Do you know how to dispel the darkness?"

"Yes."

"Will you help us, then?"

Owl gave an evil chuckle.

"Why should we help you? We have no love for you, and you only want us for what we can give you. Darkness is a good thing – good for hunting, good for living in. You had better get used to it."

"But . . ." began Flying Fox.

"Don't be silly," Owl said quickly. "You know very well that the birds and animals wouldn't do anything for us. Let us go at once."

Kangaroo and Emu tried to catch them, but like two shadows, they vanished into the darkness. Behind them rose a sad cry, "O Uncle, give us back the light. O Uncle . . ." The voices died away; but as despair settled on the gathering, Flying Fox suddenly appeared among them again.

"I cannot leave you like this," he said. "I have been influenced by Owl far too much. I am half bird and half animal, so I am kin to everyone. I will help you. Can someone lend me a boomerang?"

"Here you are," half a dozen voices said eagerly.

Flying Fox chose one that the little Lizard held out to him, balanced it carefully, and threw it towards the north. It flew up and over the earth like a streak of light, turned in a wide circle, and came back over their heads from the south. Flying Fox caught it deftly and threw it to the east. When it returned from the west, Flying Fox prepared to throw it for the third time. Emu could tolerate this game no longer. He caught Flying Fox by the shoulder.

"We asked you to bring back the light, Flying Fox," he said roughly. "Why do you keep throwing the returning boomerang? Anyone could do that."

Flying Fox shook himself free.

"I am doing what I promised. I am cutting the darkness in two. I will give the light to you, but I will keep the darkness for myself."

He threw the boomerang to the west. They watched it speeding like a meteor, curving gently at the end of its flight, circling towards the north, then to the south, and finally to the east. As it came towards them it brought the light with it – light which flooded the plain and shone on their anxious faces.

"There you are," said Flying Fox. "Remember that the darkness came because your hearts were evil, not mine. It was you

He threw the boomerang to the west.

who fought against each other. It was Lizard who braved the terrors of the night to find me, and it was he who gave me the boomerang. For that he will always carry the sign of the boomerang on his neck. I will take my share now and leave you to enjoy the warm sunshine," and with these words he left them, taking the darkness with him, and hid it in the cave where he had made his home.

The selfishness of Owl has never been forgotten by the birds who have descended from the bird-men. At night he is safe but if he ventures out in the early dusk, he is mobbed by the other birds. But if Flying Fox flies out of his cave while it is still light, he knows that he will be safe. No one will molest him because of the memory of how he brought the sun to the world when men had despaired of ever seeing it again.

THE IMPRISONMENT OF NARAHDARN THE BAT

NARAHDARN the Bat was a man who enjoyed darkness, and the evil that is performed in darkness. He had married Wahlillee and Goonaroo, the daughters of Bilbie the Rabbit-eared Bandicoot. They were industrious young women who employed all their time in gathering food. Narahdarn lived a life of luxury, seldom going out on the hunting trail, but growing fat and indolent on the food that his women brought to him.

For a long time they pandered to their husband, but at last they grew tired of working so hard and decided that it was better to have no husband than one who lived off his wives. They made long strings of dried reeds and clothed themselves in them so they rattled with every movement they made.

Wahlillie and Goonaroo waited until Narahdarn was away visiting friends in another tribe, and hid themselves beside the path they knew he must follow on his return.

After a while Narahdarn and his dog came unsuspectingly along this path. The women jumped out with blood-curdling screams, with the reeds flying round them in a cloud and clashing together. Narahdarn reeled back, turned, and fled with his dog. He could not see very well in the daylight, and bruised himself by banging into tree trunks. He dared not turn round, for he was frightened of the apparitions, and he was fast growing weak and tired. Suddenly he crashed into a tree, saw that it was hollow, and squeezed himself through the opening, followed by his dog.

The women looked at each other, and the same thought occurred to them simultaneously. They scooped mud from the ground and plastered it over the opening. Then they stood on guard till it dried, and Narahdarn and the dog were safely imprisoned in the tree. The man heard their laughter dying away in the distance, and began to scrape the mud with his fingernails, but it had become as hard as the timber of the tree in which he was imprisoned.

Shut up in the dark with little room to move, the hours and days seemed like an eternity. His biggest problem was hunger and thirst. The only food that could sustain him was the flesh of his dog, but Narahdarn could not bear the thought of eating his only

The women jumped out with blood-curdling screams.

friend. Instead, he told the dog to tear the flesh of his arm, and when it had done so, the man drank his own blood to quench his thirst.

Many days passed by. The dog died and lay still at his feet. Then Narahdarn heard the sound of wood being chopped nearby. He shouted, and the sound echoed in the narrow confines of his prison. The sound of axe blows stopped. The woodcutter felt the hairs on his scalp rising as words came indistinctly from the tree.

"Who are you?" he asked, his voice trembling.

"I am a man. I am imprisoned in this tree. My name is Narahdarn."

"What are you doing in there?"

"I was caught when I sought shelter. Please help me."

"How can I help you?"

"Look at the dried mud on the trunk, friend. I have no tool to scrape it away, but you could break it down with your axe."

"How do I know that you are not an evil spirit that will do me harm if I release you?"

"Spirits cannot be shut up in trees. I am a man, weak and at the point of death, for I have been here many days."

The woodcutter was convinced that it was the tone of man who was close to death. He summoned up his courage, and soon the mud filling crumbled under the blows of his axe. Then he leapt back in alarm. It was scarcely the figure of a man who came out of the narrow prison. It was a skeleton that lived and moved. From its arms hung rags and tatters of skin that flapped as he walked. The woodcutter dropped his tool and raced for home to tell a tale that no one would believe.

Once he was free Narahdarn's heart was black and heavy with vengeance. He rested for a few days to recover his strength, and to allow his wounds to heal. His body began to fill out, but his mind was an empty dish in which ugly thoughts rolled and clashed unceasingly.

With the axe that the woodcutter had left behind in his haste, he cut two long stakes and pointed them at both ends. Taking them down to the river, he drove them deep into the bed below the bank at the place where his wives usually fished, and returned to his own camp. Wahlillee and Goonaroo were making preparations for the evening meal when their husband appeared suddenly in front of them.

He grunted as though nothing unusual had happened, and said, "I am hungry. Go and catch some fish for me."

The young women rushed off in a panic.

"What shall we do?" Goonaroo asked her sister. "He will kill us!"

"I don't know," Wahlillee replied, "but first of all let us catch some fish. That may put him in a good mood, and we can make plans when he falls asleep."

They jumped into the water with their nets, and were immediately impaled on the hidden stakes.

Presently Narahdarn came sauntering along the bank. He pulled Wahlillee out of the water and threw her body on the ground. With rather more interest he watched Goonaroo, who was still struggling feebly in the water, trying to release herself from the stake which had gone through her throat.

Her husband sat down to watch, nodding approvingly when she managed to release herself and struggle to the bank. The breath whistled through the hole in her throat. Her fat body grew still plumper, her legs and feet shrank, her arms turned into wings. In despair she tried to call out to Narahdarn, but her voice whistled in her throat and sounded as though she was saying "Goonaroo! Goonaroo!" She flapped her wings and flew across the water, disappearing into the twilight. And still we may hear the call of the Whistling Duck as she calls her own name – Goonaroo, Goonaroo.

Narahdarn remained alone in the deserted camp. The death of his wives was not the sweet revenge he had anticipated. Now he had to hunt for meat and vegetables, and cook his own food. No laughter now by the camp fire at night; no comfort in the warm body of a woman by his side; not even the friendship of his dog.

One day he was visited by Bilbie the younger, the brother of his wives. Bilbie looked round the untidy camp with distaste.

"Where are my sisters?"

"I don't know. They went away and left me."

"It was your laziness that drove them away," Bilbie said. He left the camp and called the people of his tribe together.

"Narahdarn is living alone," he told them. "Wahlillie and Goonaroo are not with him now. If they had left him of their own accord they would have come back to us."

"What do you mean, Bilbie?" someone asked. "If Narahdarn says they left him, where could they have gone?"

104

There was a little silence. Far away they heard the voice of Goonaroo the Whistling Duck.

"They are dead," Bilbie said suddenly. "I know it. Narahdarn has killed them."

There was a chorus of grunts. A young man stood up and waved his spear.

"What are we waiting for? Our sisters have been killed and we sit round the fire like old men brooding over their troubles."

Others jumped up to join him. Darkness had fallen when the men reached Narahdarn's encampment. He was sitting by the fire when a spear thudded into the ground at his feet. He whirled round and saw his wives' kinsmen coming stealthily towards him. He sprang from side to side, trying to escape the spears that hurtled from every direction. In a frenzy of fear he leaped higher and higher, and the torn skin of his arms flapped against his body.

Bilbie aimed a murderous blow at him. Narahdarn jumped even higher in the air, his arms waving. As his body dwindled and his head and legs grew small, he remembered what he had done to Goonaroo. Like a dark, evil shadow, he fled to the shelter of the trees. He was no longer a man flying through the dark, but Narahdarn the Bat. His refuge was the hollow tree where the spirit of his dog awaited him, and in hollow trees he has remained through all the years.

He is Narahdarn, the Bat, the spirit of death, who flies by night and sleeps by day.

WHY PLATYPUS LIVES ALONE

WHEN the first men became animals, the country was so thickly populated by birds, lizards, and snakes, that it became impossible for them to live together in peace. There was not enough food, so the weaker ones died of starvation if they did not meet a sudden death. While birds preyed on reptiles, reptiles on animals, and animals on birds, not one of them was safe. To drop off to sleep was to run the danger of never waking again, or to feel the bite of sharp teeth, the spearlike thrust of a beak, or the poison fang of a snake before life ebbed quickly away.

At length, remembering the corroborees that they had held while they were still men, they all met together to discuss what should be done. The snakes spoke first.

"We are tired of being hunted by birds and animals. Only this morning several of our people were eaten by the kookaburras. Snakes have as much right to live as anyone else. We are an inoffensive tribe."

"But you rob our nests," the birds accused them. "If the eggs escape you, you take our fledglings. Our nests should be left alone."

There was an outcry from the animals.

"Do you respect our children? It is when they are young and defenceless that you kill them without thought of the sorrow you are bringing to us."

"Enough!" shouted the leader of the snakes. "We all have the right to live, snakes as well as anyone else. We have debated the matter in our own tribe. There is only one solution to the problem."

"What is it? What is it?"

"You must go away and leave us in peace. The land belongs to us reptiles. There is no place here for birds and animals."

A chorus of derisive laughter rose, led by Kookaburra.

"If anyone leaves, it will be you reptiles."

"No, it will be you. We are a humble people. We creep along the ground and try to make ourselves inconspicuous, but we have a weapon that is denied to you. Long years ago the Crow gave us poison fangs. We would not like to keep on using them on you."

Such a babble of voices now arose that no one could be heard, and the meeting broke up in disorder.

Of all the reptiles, the frilled lizards were the most vicious. Their leaders called them together to discuss what had happened at the corroboree.

"The snakes made threats, but they talk too much. The animals and birds need a real fright. The snakes are only making them fighting mad. We have no poison fangs, but we must remember our totem. There is no need to tell you what to do."

The totem of the frilled lizards was the wild elements of nature: thunder and lightning, wind and rain and storm. Leaving the other people of the lizard tribe behind, they swarmed up the nearest mountain until they reached the summit where they were close to the spirits of the storm. They painted their bodies with a mixture of fat and red ochre, and lined them with bands of white clay; they were a fearsome sight. Then they gashed themselves with stone knives until the blood ran down their bodies and mingled with the painted designs, and they sang the song that conjures up the storm.

So many frilled lizards sang that weird song that black clouds raced across the sky and pressed heavily on the mountain top. Lightning flashed in the gloom and thunder rolled down the long valleys. Then came the rain . . . driving spears and splinters of silver that slashed into the trees and dug pits in the dry ground. The pits filled with water, overflowed into runnels that grew to streams, and streams into rivers that spilled into lakes. The lakes rose until the tops of tall trees were lost beneath the surging water.

The birds fled from the storm, while the reptiles and animals crouched in caves, shivered under the poor shelter of trees, or climbed the mountainside to escape the advancing water. With a final peal of thunder the storm rolled away. For many days and nights the storm spirits had hurled their weapons against the defenceless earth. Blue skies returned and the sun shone until the land steamed, and bedraggled animals stretched out to feel the unaccustomed warmth.

They searched for their friends among the fallen trees. Everywhere they went they found pathetic bodies of platypuses, who were so slow-moving that they had been unable to escape from the flood waters. Before the storm they had been the most numerous of all animals. Now not a single one could be found.

107

The Frilled Lizards sang the song that conjures up the storm.

Several years passed by. The birds returned, and as children were born to the animals, the strength of the tribes increased; but there were still no platypuses. Even those who had been impatient with them in the past regretted their loss. Others sorrowed, and sought everywhere to see if there were any survivors. Hope revived when far-ranging Cormorant came one day with a report that he had seen platypus tracks in the mud at a place somewhere between the Blue Mountains and the sea. A carpet snake, returning from a visit to distant relatives, also related that as he was watching a pool he had seen a hole under water which led into the bank, and which he recognised as the entrance to the burrow of a platypus.

There was great excitement at the news. Animals of all kinds met together to talk about it. The only absentees were the frilled lizards. Everyone knew that they had been responsible for the flood which had destroyed the poor little platypuses. They had been told that they would not be welcome at the gathering. The lizards puffed out their frills in vexation and wore frowning faces, which they have never since managed to get rid of.

"What totem do the platypuses belong to?" someone asked.

Everybody seemed to join in the discussion. Because they had ducks' heads and laid eggs, the birds claimed that platypuses were really birds; but the lizards and snakes had an equal claim because they too were egg-layers. Kangaroos, possums, wallabies, and many other animals maintained that as platypuses had bodies covered with hair, as well as tails, they undoubtedly belonged to the animal family. No one could resolve these contradictory statements, especially when the fish joined in and pointed out that platypuses spent a good deal of their time under water.

"We need to hear what they have to say for themselves," one of the leaders said. "If someone will volunteer to go beyond the mountains, it may be that they will find the platypus family that Cormorant and Carpet Snake have reported."

It was agreed that this was a good plan. As Carpet Snake knew where the place was, he agreed to make the journey. To everyone's satisfaction he returned a few days later with an old and venerable platypus, who was at once surrounded by an eager throng of animals, birds, and reptiles, anxious to do all they could to show how glad they were to see him.

When the excitement died down, a space was cleared, and the old platypus began to speak. At first his voice was low and

109

unsteady, because he was not used to company, but gradually it grew stronger and he could be heard by all his listeners.

"My friends, you have asked me to tell you what people we belong to. Ever since the great flood we have been isolated. We have felt that no one wanted us; but as you assure me that you are all my friends, we shall be glad to come back.

"We come from an ancient race, renowned for their wisdom, and we claim kinship with you all. Our first ancestors were reptiles. Later we belonged to the family of birds. Lastly we became animals."

The platypus was interrupted by a buzz of conversation; he raised his paws and silence fell once more.

"Where is Theen-who-ween?"

They looked at each other in bewilderment until Emu strode to the front.

"Why is *he* coming forward?" they whispered to each other. "His name is Pinyali."

Emu addressed Platypus.

"You have called me by the name that was given to my fathers, but is known to no one of this present generation except myself. Great is your wisdom and knowledge, Platypus."

Emu embraced him and said, "Tell me, O wise one, what is your totem?"

"The totem of the Platypus is the Bandicoot. What is your totem?"

"Our totem is the Snake."

"Then, as I have already told you, we are all kin."

"No, no," Emu said hastily. "We would welcome you into our family of birds. Your young men should marry Emu girls."

Platypus looked at him sadly.

"You tell me that the totem of a bird is the Snake, and I say that our totem is an animal. I will consult my uncle Bandicoot."

"But Bandicoot is my uncle," Emu said, more puzzled than before.

"It is as I say. The platypus is akin to you all, yet he cannot marry you. We are alone. It has been planned from the beginning of time, and we must accept the decision of Baiame the Great Spirit."

He made his way through the crowd, which parted in front of him, and walked slowly and sadly back to his home. When he got there he found the friendly bandicoots waiting for him.

"We shall never leave you," they told him. "We are your people, and you are ours. Show us your sons."

Then the bandicoot girls married the young platypus boys when they reached manhood and passed the initiation ceremonies. Everyone left them alone, except the water rats, who were jealous of the bandicoots. The water rats attacked the combined tribes, but were driven back by spears and other weapons, and many of them were killed.

So Platypus, who is of no tribe, yet of every tribe, lives alone, on land and in the water; and thanks the ancient gods who made him as he is.

HOW KANGAROO GOT HIS TAIL

Mirram the Kangaroo and Warreen the Wombat, walking on two legs as men, were friends. They lived together, but each had his own way of doing things. Warreen built a gunyah, a little house made of bark, to protect himself from the rain, a place where he could light a fire and sleep in comfort on cold nights. Mirram was much more of an outdoor man. He loved to lie out in the open at night where he could see the stars shining through the leaves of the trees and feel the wind on his face. Sometimes he persuaded Warreen to leave his gunyah and spend the night with him, but Wombat never felt really happy unless he was curled up inside his hut.

During the summer the friends lived happily together, but it was different in the winter. One night a bitter wind blew across the land. Mirram huddled up against the trunk of a tree and tried to keep warm by rolling himself into a ball; he was still proud of the way he could face the weather while his timid companion hid under the bark roof of a stuffy hut. He laughed a little at the thought of Warreen crouched in the tiny gunyah.

After a while it began to rain. Not a light shower, but sheets of icy water that were driven by the wind, soaking him from head to foot. It was no use trying to shelter under the trees. The branches were lashing like snakes in the wind, adding to the raindrops that were hurled under them by the wind. The thought of Warreen's cosy little gunyah suddenly became very attractive.

He imagined what it would be like inside, with the bark walls lit by the flames of the fire, and the lovely feeling he would have as he stretched out in front of it, warm and dry. He could bear the thought no longer. Fighting his way against wind and rain, he came to the gunyah and knocked against the wall.

"Who is it?" asked a sleepy voice.

"It's me, Mirram. I'm wet and cold. May I come in?"

Warreen laughed. "Oh no, it can't be you, Mirram. You like sleeping out in the fresh air. It must be someone trying to imitate your voice. I'm scared."

"Open the door," Kangaroo called sharply. "This is no time for playing. I'm frozen."

"But you like it that way," Warreen replied. "Remember, I offered to help you build a gunyah for yourself, but you said it was silly to hide from the wind and the rain. Besides, there's no room in here."

Mirram forced his way through the narrow doorway.

"I'm here," he said. "What are you going to do about it?"

"If you must come in, put the door back after you. Stand over there in the corner. You're wet, and you're waking me up."

Mirram sniffed.

"Move over," he said, his teeth chattering with the cold. "I must get dry before I can talk."

"But I don't want to talk. I want to go to sleep again. If you stand against the wall you'll soon get dry, but don't come near me."

He stretched himself out in front of the fire and went back to sleep. Mirram was crowded into a corner where there was a crack in the bark. The rain poured through it, and whenever he moved the draught seemed to follow him. When his front was dry he turned round to let the fire warm his back. Warreen snored gently, and the fire died down until there was only a dull red glow from the embers.

Bitter thoughts circled round inside Mirram's head. He beat his arms against his body to keep warm. When morning came he hobbled outside, picked up a large stone which was half buried in the mud, and staggered back to the hut. Warreen was stretching himself lazily and looking round to see where Mirram had gone. Kangaroo stepped inside, raised the stone at arm's length, and smashed it against Warreen's head, flattening the front part of his skull.

"There!" he said, "that will teach you to neglect a friend. You'll always have a flat forehead now to remind you of your unkindness. I'll tell you another thing too, friend Wombat. From now on you'll always live in this dark, damp hole you call your home."

From that day Kangaroo and Wombat never spoke to each other. Warreen planned revenge. He cut a big spear and made a woomera to help him throw the spear much better than he could manage with his tiny paws.

He had a long time to wait, but at last his opportunity came. Mirram's back was turned and the woomera was in the right position. He threw it with all his might. The spear whistled through the air and struck Mirram at the base of his spine.

"There!" shouted Warreen, as Mirram let out a yell of pain and fright. "That'll teach you to knock me about!"

Kangaroo tugged at the spear, but he could not move it. Wombat laughed and laughed until he rolled right back into his burrow.

"You've got a tail now," he said as he disappeared from sight. "Mirram has got a tail, and no home to go to. Serves him right!"

THE CAT KILLER

KINIE-GER was on the hunting trail, and terror stalked through the land. Kinie-ger had the body and limbs of a man and the head of a cat. He was a voracious eater. No one would have held that against him, for both men and animals must live on flesh as well as vegetable food; but Kinie-ger was an insensate killer, destroying living things for the pleasure of seeing them die. No one was safe from him. Tiny children, young people and old folk, all were afraid when Kinie-ger was abroad.

The men did their best to protect the weaker members of their tribe, standing on guard throughout the night, but they were unable to maintain a watch throughout the day, for there were many other things to be done. If everyone had stayed within the limits of the encampment all would have been well, but the younger folk would not submit to too much restraint. Apart from this it was necessary for young and old alike to spend time hunting for food, which could not always be obtained close to the camp. Many lovely girls never returned to their parents. Their mangled bodies were found only when a search was made for them.

The men of the Kangaroo tribe took counsel together and determined to hunt Kinie-ger down and put him to death so that the shadow of fear might be lifted from their people. Going out in small parties, armed with spear, boomerang, and nullanulla, they spread out over the plain, beating the bushes, but all in vain. The wily Cat-man had seen them coming and hid himself where no one could find him.

Another Kangaroo council was held. The wisest men said that only by combining with other tribes could they hope to put an end to Kinie-ger. It took many days to gather all the tribesmen together, but at length a great encampment was formed. Many armed men went out, determined not to return until they brought with them the lifeless body of Kinie-ger.

Three days later the last of them straggled back, dejected and ashamed, for of Kinie-ger they had found not the slightest sign.

"Perhaps he is not an animal at all," someone suggested. "Maybe he is a spirit sent to punish us."

There were some who thought that this might be true, but

others said, "The work that has been done on the bodies of our women and children is truly the work of an animal. No spirit would flay the skin from their bodies and eat the flesh."

"We are powerless against Kinie-ger," an old man said. "He can do as he wills with us. When we seek him he can vanish like a spirit, even though he is an animal-man. There is only one way to find him."

"What is that?" several men shouted.

"If we can find him, we can kill him," the old man went on.

There were cries of annoyance. "Tell us what thoughts are in your head, old man, or it will be you that is killed."

The old man took his time. He looked up at the sky, scratched himself reflectively, and at last said, "We cannot do it by ourselves. Let us ask Eagle-hawk and Owl."

He held up his hand.

"Listen. There is wisdom in my thoughts. Eagle-hawk can see from afar. Nothing can hide from him except by night. In the dark Owl will stare with his big eyes, and we shall find Kinie-ger. If we can find him we can kill him," he said again triumphantly.

The advice was talked over and found good. Eagle-hawk and Owl promised to help, and plans were made. There was to be no premature move.

The Kangaroo tribe waited through the dry weather until the ground was parched and leaves hung limply from the trees. Everyone was consumed by thirst. On a hot morning under a cloudless sky, when the whole land was covered with a haze of dust and smoke from distant fires, the men went to every water hole but one.

"The time has come," the old man said.

He led Eagle-hawk and Owl to the last water hole, and the three of them dug a pit, into which Owl and Eagle-hawk jumped so that they were hidden from sight, while the old man returned to the camp.

The land lay silent, quivering in the heat which rose in shimmering waves above the earth. Owl and Eagle-hawk were silent too, listening for the sound of footsteps. In the late afternoon they heard a soft pad, pad, padding, and then the sound of someone lapping water. Eagle-hawk peered cautiously from his hiding place. Slowly the two birds' heads rose above the ground, and two pairs of eyes stared intently at the water hole.

Kinie-ger was lying flat on his stomach, his weapons by his

116

side, lapping thirstily at the unguarded water. Owl and Eagle-hawk climbed stealthily and silently out of the pit, tiptoed to the water hole, and plunged their spears into the back of Kinie-ger.

The stars had appeared by the time the bird men brought the news of the killing of Kinie-ger to the Kangaroo tribe. Through the darkness a laughing, chattering, shouting crowd of men, women, and children ran to see the body of the hated Cat-man. Before they reached it they saw a star rising from the water hole, moving steadily up into the sky, where it remained shining brightly.

Kinie-ger was no longer by the edge of the water hole. All they could find was the body of a small grey animal covered with white spots. Every head was turned towards the old man who had planned the death of the Cat-man. He grinned fiercely and shook his waddy.

"This is Kinie-ger," he said. "The courage of Owl and Eagle-hawk has brought about his death, but I have rid you of his spirit, which will never come down from the sky. There it is," pointing dramatically up at the new star, "and here is all that remains of the Cat-man – this little animal."

"How do we know that this is really Kinie-ger?" someone asked.

The old man bent down and showed them the white spots in the grey fur.

"Those are the wounds that Owl and Eagle-hawk made with their spears. Every time you see the little Kinie-ger, the cat that has taken the place of the Cat-man, you must remember the spear thrusts that killed him. You must remember Owl and Eagle-hawk in gratitude, because you need no longer fear the death that pounces from the bush when you are alone. And you must remember that it was my magic that set you free of fear."

Legends of the Birds

BAIAME AND THE CROW

WAHN was the most famous of all the men of the Dreamtime. He was clever and could mimic the cries of animals and birds. After he became fully grown he grew lazy and conceited, expecting other people to work for him while he rested in the shade and amused the women of the tribe or played tricks on his friends. The other hunters became impatient with him and finally drove him away from their camp.

Wahn gathered up his belongings. He placed some food in his dilly bag, a rope of hair, a firestick, and a magic kangaroo bone. Taking his spears and a throwing stick which had not been used for many moons, he journeyed a long way until he came to a water hole beside some tall gum trees. It was a perfect place for a camp. He built two long rows of miamias with branches, and thatched them over with grass. Late one afternoon he lit a fire and climbed into the branches of one of the gum trees. As darkness fell he watched the hunters going back to their own tribes. Some of them looked curiously at the new camp with the many miamias.

When it was nearly dark a lonely hunter who was carrying a wallaby on his back was attracted to the fire. Wahn slipped down the tree, entered one of the huts, and began to cry like a baby. He peeped through the cracks and smiled when he saw the hunter standing still to listen. He flitted from one miamia to another, making a different sound in each: in one, the noise of husband and wife quarrelling; in another, of water boiling in a pot; in another, running water; in another, the notes of birds; and in the last hut, the plaintive song of a young woman singing to her lover.

Neilyeri, the hunter, stood in the doorway of this last hut, looking for the girl whose voice had so enchanted him. Wahn came out of the miamia.

"What are you looking for?" he asked innocently.

"I heard a girl singing."

Wahn looked at him sideways. "There is no girl here."

"But I heard the sound of many people, and a girl singing."

"I tell you there is no one here. See for yourself."

The two men looked in every miamia. They were all empty. Neilyeri scratched his head.

"Why are there so many miamias?" he asked. "Who made them? Why are they all empty?"

"So many questions!" Wahn laughed. "I built them myself so that people will have somewhere to sleep when they come to visit me. Why don't you stay here? We can cook the wallaby you are carrying and then go to sleep."

"No, I am going home," Neilyeri said hastily. He felt there was something strange about these empty miamias. He ran away, but stopped abruptly when he came to the end of the double row of miamias. Outside the circle of firelight everything was black. There were no stars, and no way to find a path to his own camp.

"Don't worry," said Wahn, coming up to him and taking the wallaby off his shoulders. "Come and warm yourself by the fire."

No sooner had the hunter spread his hands out to warm them than Wahn gave him a push which sent him plunging into the middle of the fire, where he was burnt up till nothing was left save a few charred bones.

"This is the life!" Wahn said as he raked away the ashes and put the wallaby to roast on the hot stones. The meat, together with leaves and roots that he had gathered, lasted him for several days.

After a week had gone by, all the food was exhausted. Wahn lured another hunter into his camp at nightfall, pushed him in the fire, and cooked the meat the hunter had brought with him.

This went on for a long time. Wahn was never discovered, because he was careful to choose hunters who came from different tribes. But one day men gathered together from many different parts of the plain for a corroboree.

"Where is Neilyeri?" someone asked.

No one knew where Neilyeri was, nor the other hunters who had disappeared one by one. It dawned on them that there had been many disappearances, and they began to connect them in their minds.

An old man swayed backwards and forwards as he sat on the ground and crooned,

> What shall we do?
> Who will be next?
> What shall we do?

Others joined in and soon many men were all singing together, "What shall we do?"

A tall figure strode into the circle.

"What shall we do about what?" he asked with a smile.

Everyone stopped singing and shouted, "Baiame! It's Baiame!"

And indeed it was Baiame, the Great Spirit, who had been born before time began.

"What can Baiame do to help you?" the Great Spirit asked. "I have come to you as a man because I knew you needed me."

He listened to the tale of the hunters who went hunting and never came back. He thought for a while and then said, "Stay here. I am going away. For a little while you will see no stars at night, but when they shine again you will know that I have gone back to my home in the Milky Way. Then the hunters may leave their camps in the morning knowing that they will return safely at night."

Suddenly he was gone.

Now Baiame stood alone in the middle of the plain with a wallaby slung over his shoulders. Many tracks led towards a camp where there were two rows of miamias, but there were no footprints leading away from it. He walked slowly towards it and heard the sound of a baby crying, the voices of men and women, the notes of birds, the sound of running water, and lastly the sad song of a young girl mourning for her lover.

Baiame strode out of the gathering darkness into the firelight.

"What are you looking for?" asked Wahn.

"I heard a girl singing."

Wahn looked at him sideways. "There is no girl here."

"But I heard many people, and a girl singing."

"There is no one here. See for yourself."

"It doesn't matter," Baiame said wearily. "I'm tired. Let me sleep in one of your miamias."

"Very well," Wahn said. "But first come to my fire and warm yourself. Bring your wallaby with you."

Side by side they walked towards the fire. When they came close, Wahn stepped behind the Great Spirit. Baiame stooped suddenly, caught Wahn by the ankle, swung him round like a churinga on the end of a string, and hurled him into the fire.

The flames leaped high, and Wahn grew smaller and smaller, and sank down into a little heap of ashes. Baiame bent over and blew on them. They swirled and whirled in the flames and fluttered out of the fire and up into the branches of one of the trees.

Baiame looked up. A bird perched on the bough of the tree and cawed at him. The ashes had turned into a bird, a bird who a little while before had been a man mocking the cry of a baby and the song of a young woman, a bird who was now Wahn the Crow, watching Baiame going back to his home in the sky.

WHY THE PELICAN IS WHITE AND BLACK

THOUSANDS of people were drowned in the great flood of Tiddalick. They were swept away like straws in the raging waters. Some clung to trees, but the water rose so high that they were torn from their refuge.

Only a few men and one woman managed to escape to a hilltop which, when the flood was at its height, became a small island. They watched the water swirling past and wondered whether it might have been better to have met a quick death by drowning instead of dying slowly of starvation.

One morning, to their relief, they saw a canoe in the distance. As it drew closer they could see that it was being paddled by Booran the Pelican.

"Help! Help! Come and help us," they cried.

"Yes, I will help," he replied at length, "but as you can see, my canoe is small. I can take only one of you at a time."

The woman came forward eagerly, but Booran ordered her back. "I will take the men first."

One by one he took them across the lake to the distant shore. When the canoe left with the last of the men, and the woman was left alone on the island, she was frightened. She knew that when Booran returned he would take her for his wife, and she had no desire to marry Pelican.

She covered a log with her possum skin rug, and rolled it near the fire so that it looked as though she were lying asleep on the ground. The flood was receding and the shore was not so far away as when Booran had first arrived. She slipped into the water and swam away in the opposite direction.

Pelican came back and pulled his canoe well up the bank. He fluttered towards the remains of the encampment and chattered excitedly to himself when he espied the sleeping form of the woman wrapped in her rug. There was no finesse in his approach. He went up to her and kicked her in the ribs, and then staggered back in agony as his claws came in contact with the hard wood.

Pelican Booran tore the rug away and realised that he had been duped. His excitement turned to anger. He danced with rage,

*Booran lay lifeless on the floor, his beak pointing
pathetically to the sky.*

swore vengeance on the woman and her friends, and daubed himself with white clay in imitation of warriors who paint themselves for the corroboree. Jumping into his canoe, he paddled furiously to the shore of the lake. There was no sign of the men, but along the shore came another black Pelican – one who was much bigger and stronger than Booran.

He looked in astonishment at the white streaks on Booran's black plumage and realised that the strangely marked bird was likely to make trouble. Before Booran could defend himself he rushed forward and impaled him on his beak.

Booran lay lifeless on the shore, his beak pointing pathetically to the sky, his feathers torn and bedraggled and patchy with the white pipeclay. And ever since that day when the flood of Tiddalick receded, the plumage of the Pelicans has been a mixture of black and white.

THE CANNIBAL COOK

THERE are black Magpies with splashes of white on their tail feathers and wings, and Bell Magpies which have drab, grey plumage. Moograbah was the name of the Bell Magpie, long before he was turned into a bird, while he was still a man.

Moograbah was famous for his cooking. Where others would make an unappetising mess, Moograbah could cook a delectable meal to make any man's mouth water. Cakes that he baked with grass-seed were eagerly sought after, and men came from long distances to barter valuable goods for them. What was not realised for a long time was that the cakes were only a kind of bait for human beings. When visitors came to his camp, he fed them with his cakes until they fell asleep. Then Moograbah crushed their heads with his club and roasted them on the same fire that he had used to cook the grass-seed cakes.

It was only when too many coincidences had occurred that men began to talk. Relatives had been seen going through the bush towards Moograbah's camp, and had never returned. Suspicion crystallised into certainty. A strict watch was kept, and one day the cook was seen devouring his horrible meal. The word spread like fire in the brush. Men gathered together from a distance to discuss such a serious matter.

"It will be better to take him by stealth rather than by numbers," they decided. "If we fight him some of us are bound to be killed. Who will volunteer for the task?"

"I will," said little Gidgeereegah and his big friend Ouyarh. "We will pretend that we want to eat his cakes, and then we'll take him unawares."

"You will have to be very careful," they were told. "It is not only Moograbah that you have to overcome. He has two wives and two strong sons."

"We will be careful," they said, and went away to prepare themselves for their visit. Gidgeereegah painted himself all over with bright green and yellow and red, while Ouyarh tied his yellow hair into a knot. They walked round each other admiringly.

K They closed their eyes and pretended to be asleep.

"Moograbah will think we are important visitors," they told one another. "He will suspect nothing."

They took their waddies and spears and went straight to the camp. Bell Magpie saw them coming and went to meet them.

"What do you want?" he asked with a grin.

"We have heard of your famous cakes from many people."

Moograbah held out his arms as a sign of welcome.

"You have come at the right time. The fire is burning and the grain has been ground."

He welcomed them into his gunyah and busied himself with his preparations. After a while he carried the hot cakes in to them. Gidgeereegah and Ouyarh ate one or two and hid the others behind them, fearing that they might contain herbs which would put them to sleep.

"Do you like my cakes?" asked Moograbah.

"They are the best cakes we have ever tasted. Now we are sleepy."

"Lie down then, both of you. I have put kangaroo skins on the floor for you. When you wake up I will have more food ready."

They closed their eyes and pretended to be asleep. Moograbah came to the entrance with his sons and pointed at them, speaking softly.

"I have never seen such fine-looking men. Look at their beautiful garments, and the splendid topknot on that one! They will make good eating and an ornament to my cooking fire. I will lie down beside them in case they wake up suddenly. When I call you, bring your spears and we shall have a great feast tonight."

Moograbah lay down and closed his eyes. It was hot in the gunyah and he was drowsy with the heat of the fire. When he began to breathe heavily his two visitors opened their eyes and got cautiously to their feet. They drew back their spears and thrust them through the cannibal's heart.

"Now for the sons," said Ouyarh. "Do you remember what Bell Magpie's voice sounded like?"

"I do," Gidgeereegah said grimly. Imitating the voice of the dead man, he called, "Come at once. They are dead. I need help."

The two young men came in, one after the other, and were promptly knocked on the head. The visitors carried them outside, made a pile of dry leaves and twigs, and laid heavy logs over it. The bodies were placed on top.

128

"There are still the wives," Ouyarh said. "They too have eaten human flesh, and must share the fate of their husband and their sons. We must destroy every shoot of this evil tree."

When the women came home to prepare the evening meal, they were killed and their bodies added to the pile. A burning twig from the cooking fire was applied to the dry leaves. The flames roared up in the dusk, and before the sky was covered with stars the bodies of the cannibal cook, his sons, and his wives, had crumbled to ashes.

The fire died down. Suddenly in the midst of the red embers there was a flapping of wings and a bird, covered in grey ash, rose from the glowing pile and soared upwards, calling its own name, "Moograbah", as it went.

That was how the grey Bell Magpie came by his drab plumage. Gidgeereegah and Ouyarh were also transformed into birds, but for them it was badge of victory. The colours of their clothes were retained in their feathers: Ouyarh the Cockatoo has a brilliant yellow crest, while Gidgeereegah the Budgerigar, or Warbling Grass Parrot, clad in the soft grey cloak he wore, has patches of colour on his face.

Moograbah still calls to them, hoping they will eat more of his cakes and put themselves at his mercy; but Ouyarh and Gidgeereegah ignore him and go about their own business quietly and peacefully, for their task is ended.

THE FATE OF SOLDIER BIRD AND HIS FAMILY

THE Mullians, or Eagle-hawks, went out to hunt the emus, carrying their net with them. It was five feet high and several hundred yards in length. As they left the camp they saw Deegeenboya the Soldier Bird sitting by himself sharpening the point of his spear.

"Come along with us, Deegeenboya," they called, because they felt sorry for him. Soldier Bird was old and had great difficulty in getting enough food for his two wives and daughters.

"Thank you," the old man said in a quavering voice. "You are kind to spare a thought for me. Don't wait for me – I will come as quickly as I can."

The Mullians ran on until they came to a place where they knew the emus were nesting. Moving quietly, and without speaking, they thrust long poles into the ground and tied the net to them. It was built with converging arms, with the third side open, and a length of net lying loose in order to close the trap when they were ready.

Leaving two of their number by the net, the others spread out in a wide circle which enclosed the trees where the emus were nesting. There was a gap in the line opposite the open side of the net. When everyone was ready, they rushed forward, shouting at the top of their voices. The startled birds ran out from the trees and fled from the advancing men, straight into the net. As the hunters passed the nests they gathered up the eggs and put them carefully in their bags. When they reached the net, the men who had remained by it had already closed the opening, and six birds were trapped and were running frantically from one side of the enclosure to the other.

They were soon killed, and made into two pies, one small and the other large. The eggs were baked in the ashes of a fire and eaten while the emu flesh steamed slowly in a big earth oven. When it was opened the birds were taken out and a delicious odour of cooked meat rose on the still evening air. Old Deegeenboya, who had arrived shortly before, wiped the saliva from his chin and said to the leader of the Mullians, "I will help you carry the birds back to camp."

Mullian-ga put his hands on his hips, threw back his head, and roared with laughter.

"Oh Deegeenboya, your shrivelled shanks would give way before you'd gone half a mile."

"Please, Mullian-ga. I did nothing to help you catch the emus, but at least I can carry one of the birds home."

"Very well, we'll let you carry one of them, but you'll have to hurry to keep up with us."

The young men put the smallest bird on Deegeenboya's back, lifted up the others, and began the long trek back to camp. Deegeenboya was soon left behind, but Mullian-ga went back and appeared suddenly beside him.

"You have done very well, old man," he said. "Let me take your burden now."

"No, no," Deegeenboya pleaded. "I don't want to be a burden to you. Even though I am old, it is a challenge to my manhood. If I succeed in carrying it back to camp perhaps you will give me a leg of the bird to feed my family."

"We will certainly do that," Mullian-ga said. "But I warn you that if you are too long we shall have to come back to help you."

When Mullian-ga had gone on, Deegeenboya permitted himself a crafty grin. Not far away a large stone was lying on the ground, and by its side was the trapdoor that led to the home of Murga-muggai, the Trapdoor Spider, who was a friend of his. He hurried over to it, raised the door, and called down the tunnel, "Are you there, Murga-muggai? It's me, Deegeenboya."

"Come in, Deegeenboya. What have you got there?" he asked as Soldier Bird came backwards down the tunnel, dragging the body of the emu after him.

"Murga-muggai, my friend," he said, panting a little, "I want you to help me. The Mullians have given this bird to me. I want to get it home before they arrive. If you will let me go down your tunnel I will get there without being seen."

"You are quite right," Trapdoor Spider said. "The other end comes out close to your gunyah, but I don't think you can carry such a heavy load. Let us cut it in half and then it won't weigh so much."

Deegeenboya sighed. He knew that he would have to give half his treasure to Murga-muggai in payment for using the tunnel.

*　　　*　　　*　　　*

131

While Deegeenboya was talking to his friend, Mullian-ga left his companions.

"Take the emus on to the camp," he said to his men. "I feel uneasy about Deegeenboya. He is a very old man and he may be in trouble."

He turned back and searched for Soldier Bird. There was still sufficient light for him to see the old man's trail. It led up to an isolated stone and then disappeared. The trapdoor was half concealed by the stone and he did not notice it.

He ran back to his men and said, "Something strange is going on. I think Deegeenboya has deceived us. Bring the birds along as fast as you can. I am going on ahead."

When he arrived at the camp he went straight to Soldier Bird's gunyah and saw Deegeenboya's children climbing a tree. He examined the place carefully and saw the trapdoor at the other end of Murga-muggai's tunnel, close beside the tree. The light dawned in his mind. It was as though a dry piece of wood had flared up among the dull embers of the fire when he saw the trick that the old man was playing on him. The anger in his heart burned as fiercely and clearly as the light that had come to his understanding.

Mullian-ga stood under the tree and called out to the older girl.

"Your father asked me to come ahead to see whether you were all right. What are you doing up there?"

"We are having such fun in the tree," she replied. "We were pretending to be birds. We've built a nest up here."

"You might fall out," Mullian-ga said. "Anyway it's time for little girls to go to bed. Jump down and I will catch you in my arms."

She drew back in alarm. "It's too far. I might hurt myself. We'll climb down."

"It's not so very far," said Mullian-ga. "It's much more fun to jump. You will really be a bird then, flying through the air. See, I'm waiting to catch you."

The girl jumped straight at him, but Mullian-ga stepped to one side and she crashed to the ground and lay still. Her little sister began to cry, but Mullian-ga soothed her.

"She will be all right soon," he said. "She didn't jump in the right place."

But the girl continued to sob, holding tightly to the tree.

Mullian-ga became impatient and shouted at her so loudly that she was startled. She toppled over, clutched desperately at the leaves, and fell headlong down, bouncing off a lower branch and falling to the ground with a piercing shriek.

Deegeenboya's wives heard the cry and came rushing from the camp to see what had happened to their daughters. Mullian-ga concealed himself behind the tree. As the women came past the gunyah and bent over the bodies of their children, he thrust his spear through their bodies and those of the girls and dragged them all to the foot of the tree.

Then the Eagle-hawk leader sat down to wait, with his eyes fixed on the trapdoor. After a while it trembled and was thrown back. Mullian-ga lifted it clear.

"Thank you," Deegeenboya said, thinking that one of his wives had come to help him. He climbed out of the tunnel, closed the door, and turned round.

"It was kind of you to bring the bird all this way for us," Mullian-ga said grimly.

Deegeenboya started.

"I was glad to help," he said nervously. "My friend Murga-muggai let me use his tunnel because it was easier to come that way."

"Very kind of him; but it is the last time you will use it, I promise you. I see that half the bird has vanished already, and by the time you and your family had finished with it, it would have disappeared completely."

"Oh no, Mullian-ga! We were going to give it back to you, but you did promise that my family could have a little bit. Where are they?"

"Here."

Mullian-ga showed him the bodies of his wives and daughters.

"There is no place in my camp for thieves. Your family has already paid the penalty. Now it is your turn."

Deegeenboya's thin legs shook so violently that they could not support his old body. He sank to his knees and begged Mullian-ga to spare his life, but Mullian-ga the Morning Star, the bold leader of all the Mullians, had no pity in his heart for the aged one who had tried to deceive him. His waddy crashed down on the old man's head, and he fell down beside his womenfolk.

*　　　*　　　*　　　*

There was a bustle and a stir by the camp fire, and an excited chattering as the Mullians brought in the cooked birds. After the feast everyone joined in the dancing and singing. No one spared a thought for the old man or his wives and children who lay stiff and cold beyond the circle of firelight. They had met the punishment that is visited upon all thieves.

WHY CUCKOO HAS NO NEST

Of all the birds that Nungeena the Mother Spirit made, the one with the loveliest voice was Cuckoo. And of all birds, the most conceited was Cuckoo. It was his voice and his vanity that brought about his downfall, and the manner of it was this.

Marmoo the Evil Spirit had tried to destroy Tya, the world that Baiame had beautified, by sending a plague of insects, grubs, and beetles to devour it. Baiame and the friendly spirit Nungeena had thwarted his evil plan by creating birds which ate up the insects.

Marmoo went back to his wife and asked her what he should do next. She gave a wicked chuckle.

"Baiame has given beautiful voices to the birds," she said. "They know that you are their enemy, but if you tell them what wonderful songs they sing, they will become your friends."

"You silly woman," Marmoo said, "what good will that do me? I don't want to be their friend. I want to destroy them."

The woman rubbed her arm where Marmoo had struck her and said resentfully, "No you don't. You are jealous of Baiame. What you really want is to hurt him. If you will only listen to me, I will tell you what to do."

"Go on, then," Marmoo said curtly. "Tell me."

"If you praise them and tell them what beautiful voices they have, they will listen. I know. I am a woman. You should tell them how proud Baiame must be. Say that the way to please him is to keep on singing. Tell them that the only thing Baiame wants is to hear them sing."

Marmoo lifted his hand threateningly. His wife shrank back.

"If you hit me again I won't tell you. Listen, you bad-tempered man. The birds will be so pleased that they will sing all day long. They won't even have time to build their nests. And if they have no nests there will be nowhere to lay their eggs. And if there are no eggs there will be no birds to eat the insects. Now do you see?"

A crafty smile spread over Marmoo's face.

"Trust a woman to think up a good way of doing a bad thing," he said. "Yes, my dear, it's worth trying."

He went to the birds and praised their songs. They listened to him eagerly and nodded their heads in agreement; but when he went on to say that all Baiame wanted was to hear them sing all day long, they laughed at him and said, "Oh no, Marmoo. You are quite wrong. Baiame loves to hear us sing, but he wants us also to build nests, and make love, and lay eggs, and hatch them, and provide food for our fledglings. Singing is for love-making and joy; but there is work to do as well."

They flicked their tails and flew away. Only Cuckoo remained.

"You have a voice that is worth all the others put together," Marmoo said, and Cuckoo believed him.

There are many different kinds of cuckoo in Australia. The one who had listened so intently to the Evil Spirit called all the members of the cuckoo tribe to a meeting with Marmoo.

"There has never been such a chorus of beautiful voices as I can hear today," Marmoo told them. "I have heard the songs of birds in the early morning, and at midday, and again in the evening; but they were nothing to compare with yours."

The cuckoos fell silent, eager to hear more.

"I want you to sing all day long, because then you will help to make Baiame's world a place where men and animals and even spirits can live happily for ever."

"But we have other things to do beside singing," said one of the smallest cuckoos. "There are nests to be built so that we can lay our eggs; and when the eggs are hatched there is no time for singing, because we are busy all day long feeding the young birds. You have no idea how much a fledgling cuckoo eats."

"Oh yes, I have," Marmoo replied. "I want to talk to you about that. You all admire the Great Spirit Baiame and the Mother Spirit Nungeena. Have you ever seen them building nests and feeding their young? Of course not! They are content to leave the hard work to you."

"That is true," another cuckoo said. "Why should we work while they are playing? I think it would be much better if we sang to them. I'm sure it would be much better for them, and they would praise us for giving them so much pleasure."

In their vanity all the cuckoos agreed, and flew off, singing with full throats and hearts bursting with pride. Marmoo grinned to himself and went back to the other birds to try to persuade them

136

to follow the example of the cuckoos. He failed. They were too busy flying backwards and forwards with grass, moss, feathers, and twigs with which to build their nests.

The night-loving Mopoke had been curled cosily inside a hollow tree. He had been woken by the chatter and song of the cuckoos and had heard what Marmoo had said. As soon as it was dark he flew off to the bower where Baiame lived and warned him that the evil Marmoo was acting suspiciously, and trying to get the birds to do something harmful.

"What it is I don't know," he said. "All that he is asking is for them to sing their songs, and that is a pleasant thing to hear. But he has some dark purpose behind it, I know."

"I know too," Baiame agreed. "I know what it is. Summon all the birds here to talk to me."

The next day a vast flock of birds flew to the mountain and settled round the Great Spirit, anxious to hear what he had to say to them, for they knew he loved them all.

"Is everyone here?" Baiame asked.

"The cuckoos haven't come yet," Mopoke answered, for he had been peering intently at the gathering throng with his huge eyes.

Presently they all heard the sound of birds singing. The cuckoos arrived in a compact group and sat on the outskirts of the crowd.

"It is you I want to speak to especially," Baiame called. "Why were you so long in coming?"

"We were singing," said the largest cuckoo impudently, singing the words instead of speaking them. "We are going to spend all our time singing. Why should we build nests and waste the sunny days fetching and carrying and feeding our young and catching silly insects for you?"

"There are many reasons," Baiame said gravely. "If all the birds did that there would be no fledglings, and in the end there would be no birds to sing. Work is a good thing. I know. Have I not worked hard to make the world beautiful for you and me? All the work will be undone if you do not eat the insects that are trying to devour Tya, the land of Baiame."

The cuckoo tossed his head and sang defiantly, "The cuckoos do not care. The cuckoos will be the singing birds while all the others do your bidding."

Baiame smiled sadly and said, "I am sorry for you. Your heads have been turned by pride. Your sweet voices must be taken away from you."

The cuckoos began to sing louder than ever, but stopped in dismay. Their voices sounded harsh even to themselves. The sound that came from them had become a crazy chorus of croaking and twittering and squeaking. The other birds turned on them and drove them away to the waste lands of the north.

"Don't ever dare to come back to our lovely land," they cried. "If you do we will drive you away. Birds that will not work do not deserve to live in Baiame's land. We will see that the insects are kept at bay. We will even feel sorry for you when our children lift their heads out of our nests and we know the joy of mother love and father love."

Winter passed by. Yarrageh, the Spirit of Spring, blew across the land with her soft breath. In the arid lands of the far north the cuckoos longed for the land of Baiame and the companionship of the other birds. They forgot that they had been warned never to return. They flew to the trees and bushes where the rest of the birds were building nests once more.

The cuckoos laughed to themselves. "How silly they are to waste their time. They never have any fun. We're much better off, even if we have lost our voices, because it is good to play in the sun all day long and sleep at night."

Presently the nests were finished and the mother birds sat warming the dainty eggs they had laid. Whenever they flew off to get food the cuckoos would cluster round to admire the delicate white and pink and brown and speckled eggs.

"It is time we laid our eggs," they said, "but where can we put them?"

"There are the nests all ready and waiting for you," whispered a voice. Marmoo the Evil Spirit had returned. "I am your friend. I've helped you all the time, even though you didn't know it. Go on," he said to the biggest cuckoo. "Throw out one of the eggs in this nest and lay yours in its place. The mother bird will never know the difference."

The biggest cuckoo did what Marmoo had told him. Then they all hid in the leaves of a nearby tree to see what would happen. Presently the mother bird came back. She did not notice that one of the eggs had been changed, and sat down and spread her soft wings over the nest.

"See!" Marmoo whispered again. "You don't need to look after your young birds. The other birds will do it for you."

The cuckoos flew out of the tree and laid their eggs in every waiting nest. They felt no love towards their offspring. When the young cuckoos hatched out, they proved to be as selfish and inconsiderate as their parents, demanding more food from their foster-parents than all the other birds in the nest.

It is only because the birds that were loyal to Baiame do not recognise the cuckoos in their nests that they continue to feed them, as they have done for countless generations.

WHY EMU CANNOT FLY

DINEWAN the Emu was the leader of the bird tribe. They all looked up to him because he was large and strong. His huge wings carried him great distances, and his wife had nearly a score of children each year. No wonder that he was feared and respected. And, as was only natural, he had enemies, chief of whom was Goomblegubbon the Bustard or Brush Turkey.

The Brush Turkey was a large bird too, but no one obeyed his orders as they did with Dinewan. He envied Emu's power of flight and the way he could run swiftly across the plain without tiring. Goomblegubbon told no one but his wife that he had determined to do some lasting injury to Dinewan. It took him a long time to perfect a plan that satisfied him. He waited until he knew that Dinewan was going out on the plain to feed, and made sure that he was there well before Emu. He held his wings close to his sides, ruffled up his feathers, and squatted on the ground where the grass was rich and long.

Dinewan alighted nearby and began to browse on the grass.

"Good morning, Dinewan," Brush Turkey said.

"'Morning," Emu said, barely pausing as he took big beakfuls of grass.

"I have some splendid worms here if you would like them."

"No. Never eat them."

"Did you have a good flight out here?"

"M-m-m-m," said Dinewan, not even stopping eating.

Goomblegubbon waited until Emu had eaten enough and was feeling in a better mood.

"Dinewan, as a friend there's something I would like to say to you. You are so strong and handsome, and everyone admires you so much, that they don't like to say anything to you."

Emu looked at him curiously.

"It's a strange thing for you to be so concerned with my welfare, Goomblegubbon."

"I assure you it's for your own good, otherwise I wouldn't dare to address the chief of all the birds."

"Speak up then," Dinewan said, a trifle impatiently.

"Well, what I want to say is that I'm surprised that you fly through the air when you want to go anywhere."

Dinewan looked at him incredulously.

"What on earth and in the sky do you mean, Goomblegubbon? Are you out of your mind? I have the most powerful wings of any bird, better even than Mullian's. How else would I go?"

"Walking."

"Walking? Like slow, ugly Goanna? Pull yourself together, Goomblegubbon, and talk sense for a change."

"I am talking sense, Dinewan. Just as I said, no one but a friend would tell you these things. You see, flying is something that any bird can do, even the weakest and commonest ones. Any bird can fly. It's only men, and strong birds like you and me, who are able to get about by walking. It's a sign of distinction to walk. Look!"

He ruffled out his feathers still further, keeping his wings pressed closely to his body and strode quickly round Dinewan on his strong legs.

"See how steadily I go . . . how fast I can travel? I've given up using wings altogether. Your legs are longer than mine and much stronger. Imagine Curlew or Cockatoo trying to catch up with you on their tiny legs! That's why they have to fly, but it's scarcely becoming for the great leader of the birds to compete with them in the air."

Dinewan took a few steps forward and said thoughtfully, "You may be right, Goomblegubbon. I must talk this over with my wife."

He spread his wings, and then hastily clapped them to his sides, and began to stride across the plain towards his home. Goomblegubbon laughed as the little cloud of dust grew smaller, and he flew off to tell his wife all about it.

The next day the two birds met again.

"I have followed your advice, Goomblegubbon. I'm sure you are right. My wife and I chopped off our wings with a stone tomahawk last night. It was rather painful, but my leg muscles are growing stronger already. I'll race you to that bush."

Brush Turkey laughed derisively.

"I never thought you could be deceived so easily, Dinewan. Your brains must be as small as a fledgling's. But if you want to I'll gladly race you to the bush."

Emu sprinted across the sun-baked ground, the earth coming from his flying feet in little spurts of dust. Goomblegubbon waited until Emu had nearly reached the bush, then spread his wings, and flapped noisily through the air, alighting well ahead of Dinewan. The larger bird stopped suddenly.

"I thought you said it was only common birds who used their wings?" he exclaimed. "I thought you said you had taken off your wings?"

Goomblegubbon laughed louder than ever.

"What a simpleton you are, Dinewan. I said nothing of the sort. What I did say was that I had given up using my wings. That was yesterday, but today is another day, and tomorrow is another day again. I'm afraid you will have little authority with your people from now on. They will hardly respect a bird who is not a bird, one who is unable to fly. I expect it will be Mullian who will become the new leader – or it might even be me! To be a leader you must have two things you lack: wings, and brains!"

Slowly the truth dawned on Dinewan. He ran forward and struck at Goomblegubbon with his powerful legs. With another gobbling laugh Brush Turkey flapped out of his reach and flew back to his home to tell his wife how he had humiliated the chief of the birds.

A whole year went by. Dinewan never said anything to Goomblegubbon about the loss of his wings, and this puzzled Brush Turkey. Emu's legs grew stronger, and soon he was able to run as fast as the other could fly. The strangest thing of all was that Dinewan seemed to become more and more friendly with him as the days and months passed by. At first Goomblegubbon was suspicious; but at last he came to the conclusion that Emu was even more simple than he had thought.

It was summer again. Everywhere the young fledglings were twittering and crying for food. Their parents were kept busy from sun-up to sun-down supplying them with things to eat. One morning Dinewan took his two biggest children out with him, leaving the remaining fourteen in their mother's care. The eldest children ran after their father, their little legs twinkling as they tried to keep up with him. Goomblegubbon and his wife were foraging in the scrub, surrounded by a noisy brood of children.

"Busy?" asked Dinewan.

"Busy!" Goomblegubbon said. "We have to work all day long to keep all their bellies full. We're trying to get them to hunt for their own food, but we haven't had much luck so far."

"Yes, they're rather scrawny, aren't they? The trouble is that there are too many of them. They don't get a chance to grow big."

Goomblegubbon spread his wings and flapped noisily through the air.

"What do you mean? You have plenty of children of your own."

"Not now," Dinewan said airily. "We have disposed of most of them."

"But why?" cried Turkey's wife.

"Well, we came to the conclusion that the only way to have strong, healthy chicks was to keep the best of them and get rid of the others. Look at them," he said proudly. "See how much bigger they are than your brood. The Dinewans of the next generation will be real birds."

"There is something in what you say," Goomblegubbon said thoughtfully. "What do you think?" he asked his wife.

She had been walking round the Emu chicks looking at them from every angle.

"Yes, Dinewan might be right. There's no doubt that the young Emus are a credit to their mother."

"Think about it," Emu said, and strode off with the two chicks running after him.

"We can't let Dinewan have the laugh on us," Goomblegubbon said. "Come, wife. We will pick out our two biggest and kill all the rest. If we feed them to the eldest children they may grow even stronger than the Emu chicks."

*　　　*　　　*　　　*

He met Emu on the plain the following day.

"I have taken your advice," he said. "Here are my two biggest Goomblegubbons. The others have gone. What do you think of these bonny birds?"

Dinewan began to laugh, and a shaft of fear shot through Goomblegubbon's heart.

"What are you laughing at, Dinewan?"

Emu called to his wife and she came out of the scrub leading a brood of sixteen young chickens.

"What a simpleton you are, Goomblegubbon," he said, using the words that he had remembered for a whole year. "A bird's strength lies not in his ability to use his wings, but in the number of his offspring. I am sorry for you, my friend, but perhaps it will teach you that Bustards are even more foolish than Emus."

That is why Emus have many children but cannot fly, and why Bustards lay only two eggs each year.

THE DANCE OF BROLGA

BROLGA was the best dancer in her tribe, but to say this is to do her less than justice. She seemed not to be made of flesh and blood, but of the very spirit of the dance. Her back was straight, but it could bend like a tree in the wind, and her feet were as dainty and full of life as butterflies. Her hands were like little leaves that flutter in the breeze; and when she danced round the camp fires men thought that the Spirit of Earth had returned to them. There was a song in her every movement, and with her steps she charmed the hearts of men and women. There were no dull tasks for Brolga. To see her was enough, and other women were glad to take their yam-sticks and dig for roots to provide her with food.

Brolga ate very little. Her whole life was given over to dancing. It seemed that honey, and water, and the cool night air were all she needed to keep her restless spirit in her body. There was dignity and grace in every movement. The gay dancing of leaves on trees, the swift movement of insects, the sinuous slithering of the snake, the bubbling joy of running water, the slow, majestic rising of sun and moon, the soft shining of stars: all these could be seen as she danced.

Even the winds caressed her, and the Wurrawilberoos longed to possess her for themselves. The Wurrawilberoos were the boister-ous whirlwinds that raised dust devils on the plains and pestered the camps of men and women. They were greatly feared, and were only kept at bay by the sharp spear points of the hunters and their frenzied shouting when the dust devils invaded their gunyahs and camp fires.

Brolga sought no man and feared no whirlwind. She was equally at home on the dusty plain and in the flickering light of the camp fires, and her dancing feet led her wherever she fancied.

Her mother went fossicking with her yam-stick one day, and Brolga danced along with her, weaving round the older woman a web of intricate pattern that failed even to disturb the dust. Far away rose the gaunt bones of a mountain range, where two exuberant Wurrawilberoos lived amongst the valleys. They saw the shimmering pattern that Brolga was weaving, far away from

The Wurrawilberoos snatched them up and carried them off.

the protection of the warriors of her tribe. Shouting to each other in glee, they raced down the mountain slopes and out across the plain.

The two women were smothered in spinning dust and before they had realised what was happening, the Wurrawilberoos had snatched them up and carried them off to their hiding place. As they whirled round they laughed to think how easy it had been to capture such a rich prize.

"This creature of air and movement I will keep to dance for me," one of them said. "The old woman is well-nourished and tender. She will make a good meal as we sit by the fire looking at Brolga dancing for us tonight."

"That's all very well," grumbled the other Wurrawilberoo. "She is as light as a feather, but this old woman is heavy, and I have her stone axe to carry as well."

"Give it to me. I'll make Brolga carry it."

He took the sharp axe and tucked it into Brolga's waistband, but when his attention was distracted she dropped it on the ground.

Burdened as they were, it took the Wurrawilberoos a long time to reach their home.

"Hurry up. I'm hungry. Where is the axe?"

The other Whirlwind, whose fingers were busy caressing the young woman, felt for the axe in her girdle.

"It's gone!" he exclaimed. "Girl, where have you put it?"

Brolga laughed.

"You will not find it in a hurry. I dropped it on the sand many miles away."

The Wurrawilberoos glared at each other.

"Go and fetch it," said the one who had carried the old lady. "It's your fault that it is lost."

"And leave you with Brolga? That's the last thing I would do! You might run off with her."

"If you won't trust me, I won't trust you. We had better go together."

As soon as the whirling Wurrawilberoos had roared off down the valley, Brolga caught her mother's hand and together they climbed to the crest of the mountain, descended another valley, and raced across the plain, where they could see their own camp fires twinkling in the gathering darkness. The young woman tugged at her mother's hand and kept looking over her shoulder.

147

Before long she saw two swirling clouds of dust and knew that the Wurrawilberoos were after them.

"Faster, faster," she urged.

The old woman was too exhausted to hurry. She sank to her knees and begged her daughter to go on without her.

Brolga did not waste breath in words. Summoning all her strength, she lifted her mother up in her slender arms and staggered on. Her feet were no longer light as a breath of air upon the sand. They sank deep, and her progress was painfully slow. She called out, and the hunters heard her. As they sprang to their feet they saw the furious whirlwinds about to leap on the two women. They ran out into the dusk, shouting at the top of their voices, and stabbing at the wind with their spears.

They were in time to save Brolga's mother; but the girl stumbled and was swept from their sight in the swirling dust.

The triumphant Wurrawilberoo retreated with his prey; and that was the last that was seen of Brolga until one day, long afterwards, a tall and stately bird walked up to the encampment.

To the amazement of the watchers in the camp it began a dance so beautiful that it reminded them of the dearly-loved girl they had lost.

"It must be Brolga!" someone cried. There was no doubt about it. Here were the same grace and poetry of motion, the same rhythm, the same abandonment to utter ecstasy of movement.

"Where have you been?" they cried, but she could not reply. She pointed with her beak towards the sky, and they realised that the Wurrawilberoo had made his home somewhere in the blue heavens, leaving the dancing girl behind in the form of Brolga, the Native Companion.

*　　　*　　　*　　　*

Perhaps it is an injustice to accuse the Wurrawilberoos of capturing the women, for there is another tribal tale which says that they were taken away by two cannibals. They made their escape and returned to their own people, but the cannibals came back at nightfall and stole them away a second time. When the tribespeople discovered their loss they called on Wurrawilberoo, the beneficent Spirit of the Whirlwind, to help them.

The Spirit rapidly overtook the cannibals and whirled round them until they were forced to cling to trees to keep their feet.

They dropped their burdens, but the one who was carrying Brolga muttered a spell.

The thud of racing feet was heard and they saw the hunters running swiftly with their spears levelled at them. Wurrawilberoo was not to be denied his prey. He increased his efforts, the trees were lifted out of the ground with the cannibals still clinging to them, and hurled into space. Neither the trees nor the cannibals were ever seen again.

The old woman lay in a heap on the ground. They lifted her up and carried her back to camp, but they could see no trace of their dearly-loved young woman. The spell that had been cast on her had turned her into a graceful bird which tried, but failed, to speak. Then it danced majestically before them, and they knew that in Native Companion they would always have a dancing girl to watch and admire.

WHY MALLEE BIRD LAYS HER EGGS IN THE SAND

WAYAMBEH, a descendant of the original Wayambeh, who was turned into a tortoise, married Kookaburra. It was a strange mating, with an even stranger consequence.

Tortoises lay their eggs in the sand close to streams and billabongs, leaving them to hatch out for themselves, whereas kookaburras are like all sensible birds: they build nests and keep the eggs warm with their own bodies.

Kookaburra argued with his tortoise wife.

"It's not right," he protested. "Whoever heard of anyone burying eggs in the sand, just as if they were rubbish to be disposed of? Don't be so silly, Wayambeh. Do the sensible thing. I'll help you build a nest and then you can do your duty as a mother in the proper way."

Tortoise darted her head from side to side in exasperation.

"I don't know why I ever married you, you silly bird. A fine figure I would make climbing a tree!"

"If my mother could lay her eggs in a nest, surely it's good enough for you?"

Wayambeh danced with rage, her shell jumping up and down on her back.

"Can't you get it into your thick head that I can't fly, I can't climb trees, I can't build nests, and if I sat on my eggs I would break them?"

She waddled down to the stream. Kookaburra flew overhead keeping a sharp eye on her; but once she settled down she remained motionless for so long that he grew tired of watching and flew off to get some food.

Presently Ouyouboolooey the Black Snake came by. He was an old friend of Wayambeh. She was glad to confide in him. Ouyouboolooey was a sympathetic listener. And it was at this moment that Kookaburra returned.

He gave a cry of rage, swooped down, caught Black Snake by the neck, flew to the top of a tree with him, and dropped him on the ground. Ouyouboolooey's back was broken. While he lay writhing in his death struggles, Kookaburra opened his beak and gave a great laugh: *Goor-gour-gah-gah!* and from that exultant, chattering laugh he gained his true name, Goorgourgahgah.

Although his wife was innocent of any liaison with Ouyou-boolooey, she was terrified of her husband's anger. She scuttled off swiftly on her short legs, but her time of egg-laying had come and could not be delayed. The instincts of a long line of ancestors were not to be denied, no matter what her husband might think. So she scooped a hole in the mud with her hind legs and laid six white eggs in it, covered them over, and smoothed the mud with her lower shell.

She had an interested spectator – Woggoon, the Mallee Fowl.

"Why do you lay your eggs there?" she asked. "It seems a silly thing to do."

"Nothing of the sort," retorted Wayambeh. "It's much more sensible than laying them in a nest high up in a tree, or even in the grass, and sitting on them to keep them warm."

"If we didn't keep them warm the chicks would die of cold."

"Ah, that is true. They must be kept warm. You see, that is why I lay mine in the mud. They are close to the surface where they are kept warm by the sun. We don't have to hatch them out, so you can see how much trouble we are saved."

"I see," said Woggoon thoughtfully.

She flew away and spoke seriously to her husband.

"I'm not going to lay my eggs in the nest this year," she told him.

He laughed.

"Then where do you propose to lay them, my dear? Perhaps you thought of burying them somewhere!"

"That's just what I am going to do," she retorted.

The argument between husband and wife raged all night long, but by morning the male bird was worn out and gave in. He even took part in the experiment, helping her to make a mound of leaves, sticks, and sand, and scraping a hole in which to bury her eggs.

Once the eggs were laid they were covered over. The two birds were not completely satisfied that Wayambeh's method would be successful. Day after day they visited the nest but saw no signs of the fledglings emerging. At last the female could stand the suspense no longer.

"My chicks are dead!" she wailed. "They should have hatched out long ago "

She scratched the soil from the mound. To her dismay she

151

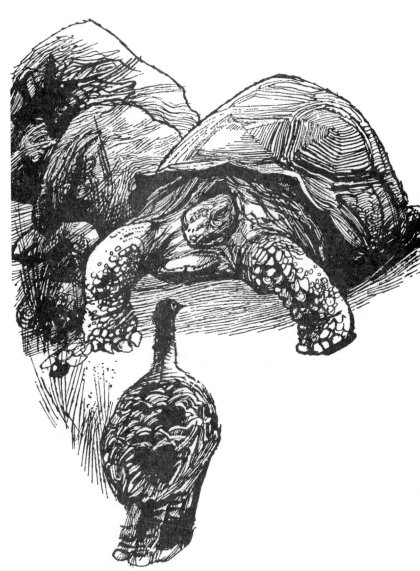

Tortoise darted her head from side to side in desperation.

found only a few broken shells where her lovely eggs had been. But at that moment she looked up and saw the gladdest sight of her life. Coming towards her were several adorable little Mallee Fowl chickens whom she recognised at once as her own. The great experiment had proved successful. Ever since then Woggoon has followed Wayambeh's example and has laid her eggs in leaf-mould so they will hatch in the warm earth.

Legends of River, Lake and Shore

THE FROG WHO CAUSED A FLOOD

IN Central Australia and the western districts of New South Wales there are frogs which survive droughts by distending themselves with water until they are as round as balls. Then they bury themselves and wait for the rains to come again. In dry weather the aborigines dig up the frogs and drink the water with which their bodies are filled.

These little frogs may well be descended from Tiddalick, an enormous frog which lived in the far off days when men first came to Australia. Who can tell how big he was? Did he tower over the hills, and did the earth shake when he moved his feet?

There came a day when Tiddalick was thirsty. He drank the water of the nearest river until it was quite dry, and nothing was left but black mud at the bottom of a long trench. He roamed further afield in search of water, for his thirst was not yet quenched. Wherever he went billabongs, lakes, and streams disappeared into his vast mouth, until there was no more water left in all the land.

Animals and men gathered together in great distress. Every drop of water was contained in Tiddalick's swollen stomach. By this time he had drunk so much that he was unable to move.

There was still no sign of rain. The only way that water could possibly be obtained was to get it back from Tiddalick. Spears and boomerangs were useless, because the monster frog would not feel them however hard they were hurled at him.

"We must make him laugh," said Goorgourgahgah the Kookaburra. "If only we can do that, then he will have to hold his hands against his sides and the water will pour out of his mouth."

"*Come on, Tiddalick, you big, fat, overgrown, squelchy frog.*"

"Very good," said Kangaroo. "You try and make him laugh. You're the best laugher in the bush."

Goorgourgahgah perched on a branch close to Tiddalick's head, and his chattering laugh rang out again and again.

"Goorgourgahgah, Goorgourgahgah," it went, and his beak clattered incessantly. "Come on, Tiddalick, laugh, you big, fat, bloated, squelchy frog. If you could see yourself squatting there like a bursting pot, you'd laugh till you cried. Goorgourgahgah, Goorgourgahgah!"

Tiddalick moved his head very deliberately and looked at Kookaburra with round, wet, mournful eyes. There was not even the shadow of a smile on his wide and doleful face.

"I give up. I can't laugh any more," Kookaburra cried. "Who will try next?"

They all tried. Some of them danced and turned somersaults, and the men told funny stories, but their exertions made them even more thirsty, and Tiddalick seemed to have gone to sleep.

The last to try was Noyang the Eel. He was their final hope. He turned himself into a hoop, he wriggled and rolled over and over on the sand, and even stood upright on his tail, spinning round like Wurrawilberoo the whirlwind.

A tiny smile began to creep slowly over Tiddalick's face and a river of water splashed out of the corner of his mouth. Men and animals rushed forward and drank before it disappeared into the dry sand. Noyang went on spinning on the point of his tail, faster and faster, till he could scarcely be seen.

Tiddalick started to chuckle. The grin spread further across his face, and more water slopped out. Deep rumbles came up from his belly, and soon he was laughing so helplessly that he put his hands to his sides and rocked to and fro. His mouth opened wide and a great smooth tide of water came gushing out. It swept the men and animals away, and soon Tiddalick was a poor, shrunken little frog, while as far as could be seen a shining lake of water spread over the land.

WHY FROGS CROAK AND LYRE BIRDS SING

THE name by which the green frog was known to animals was "Son of the Clear-running Stream". This is the legend which tells why such a beautiful name was given to him by the Lyre Bird.

There was a little stream on the western slope of the Blue Mountains which feeds the Murray River. It was cooled by overhanging trees, warmed by sparkling sunlight, and tickled into ripples by the friendly breeze. It sang an unending song of joy, and wherever it raced over pebbles in its bed or tumbled from one step of the mountain to another, thousands of little bubbles came popping to the surface. All playful little streams are full of bubbles, but only in this one tiny river was each bubble alive. They were the crystal homes of tiny water spirits which looked out from their clear cages and danced in tune with the song of the stream.

Only one river with water spirits living in the bubbles; only one bubble with a water spirit which longed so much to play with the floating twigs and the dancing sunbeams that it wished and wished until at last it turned into a living creature: a tiny little green frog. But he could not escape from his crystal prison. It bobbed up and down in the water, swirled round in the eddies, and sometimes sprang right out of the water in its struggles, falling back with a musical splash, sinking to the bottom, and bursting up into the sunshine again.

When evening came the stately Lyre Bird stepped down to the stream to drink. He was used to seeing the dancing bubbles, but on this special evening of spring he noticed that one of them seemed different to the others. It was bouncing higher, and was not as clear as air. Inside it, something green glinted in the twilight. Lyre Bird released a trill of sound like the tiny notes of a Bellbird. The bubble danced even more excitedly. Watching it closely, Lyre Bird sang the songs of many birds, mingled with the happy notes of running water.

After a while he grew tired of seeing the bubble dancing and prepared to go home, but a spirit voice sounded in his ear. It was the Great Spirit himself who had taken pity on his tiny water spirit.

157

"Go on, sing!" Lyre Bird said.

"Keep on singing, Lyre Bird," said the Great Spirit. "It is one of my little ones you are seeing in that bubble. Your song is bringing it to life, and soon the bubble will shatter and it will be released and become a living creature of the stream."

Filled with importance, and with a feeling of tenderness, Lyre Bird sang until he felt his throat would burst. And at last, as the sun rested on the hills, the bubble was gone and a tiny creature with a green body and arms and legs swam up through the water and sprang on to a broad leaf. Its sides palpitated, and its mouth opened and shut, but no sound came out of its open mouth.

"Go on, sing!" Lyre Bird said; but the little frog could make no sound.

"Teach him to sing," said the Great Spirit, and Lyre Bird stood on the bank singing on and on into the night, until at last the little frog opened his mouth very wide and gave one tiny croak.

"That's enough for tonight," Lyre Bird said to him. "Stay there and I will come back tomorrow and give you another lesson."

In the morning the frog was waiting there on the leaf when Lyre Bird came down to the stream.

"Good morning, Son of the Clear-running Stream," he said to the frog. "I want you to listen carefully today, and do your best to copy me."

By the end of the day the frog could sing a few notes. Day after day Lyre Bird went back, and at last became proud of his tiny pupil. The time came when the Son of the Clear-running Stream surprised him. He had come down to his favourite place on the bank and was looking about for the frog, when he heard his brother's voice in the bushes behind him. He swung round, but no one was there. He turned back and saw the frog holding his sides and trying not to laugh.

"You wicked little fellow," he chided him. "So you've learned to throw your voice too. The time has come for the others to hear you."

He sent out messengers calling all the birds and animals to come to the stream to listen to the water spirit singing his song. It was a selfless act. Lyre Bird was more proud of his pupil than he was of his own singing.

It was a wonderful occasion. By nightfall all the birds and

animals had assembled and a silvery moon made a fairyland of the stream and the glade through which it flowed.

"Wake up," called Lyre Bird. He knew that when the little green frog was asleep, it was at home with the other water spirits. Presently a small head and two bulging eyes appeared above the water.

"Here he is," Lyre Bird said, and they all began to laugh at the funny little creature which hopped on to a leaf and puffed out his tiny chest.

"What is it?" they asked Lyre Bird. "Have you brought us here just to see this absurd little object that looks like a bloated man?"

"Not to see him," Lyre Bird said, "to hear him."

All through that night, as the moon sailed majestically across the sky, they sat and listened to the singing of the frog who was called Son of the Clear-running Stream. In the enchantment of his voice they heard the sound of running water and tumbling waterfalls, of soft wind in the trees and raindrops thudding on the ground, the songs of the birds and the cries of animals and insects. All these sounds came from the swelling throat of the little green frog.

When it was over Lyre Bird said, "I am proud of you. You can sing better than I."

Green frog dived into the water to hide the fierce pride that shone in his eyes. "I am the best singer in the whole world!" he said to himself. "I am better than Lyre Bird!"

But it was lonely in the stream all by himself. The Great Spirit took pity on him a second time, and sent another frog to him as a wife.

"I am the best singer in the world," he said to his wife. "I could charm the moon down from the sky – if I wanted to."

"Let's see you do it," said his wife.

Son of the Clear-running Stream sat on the broad leaf close to the bank and sang and sang till he was on the point of bursting. The moon sailed serenely on and took no notice. Green Frog sang louder still and then, suddenly, his voice broke and all that came out was a harsh croak.

The sons of the clear-running stream can still throw their voices; but who wants to hear them when all they can do is croak harshly? It is the Lyre Bird, the patient teacher of the green frog, to whom men listen.

THE MIRACLE OF SPRING

It was when young Cockatoo, so full of life, splendid in white feathers and proud yellow crest, fell from the nest and lay lifeless on the ground, that living things realised for the first time that there was a mystery they could not solve.

They circled the pathetic bunch of feathers, speaking to it, trying to bring back the spark of life. A few days later, when his body had begun to disintegrate and return to the earth from which it was made, a meeting was held. Everyone was there except Narahdarn the Bat, of whom strange rumours had begun to circulate. They turned first to Wungghee the Mopoke, who sat so still and looked so wise; but Wungghee had no answer to the question, "What has happened to Ouyarh?" He turned his head slowly from side to side and looked at them with round, staring eyes, but had nothing to say.

Then Mullian spread and fanned his wings, and the waiting circle of creatures looked at him expectantly.

"Wungghee has no words that will fit this new thing," Mullian said, "but I, who am at home in the sky, can tell you what happened to Ouyarh."

He picked up a stone in his beak and dropped it in the river. There was a tiny splash, a spreading of ripples, and the stone was gone. Mullian said no more, but by his action they knew that he meant that Ouyarh had gone into another world, perhaps into another life, and that when his body wasted away they would not see him again.

The ripples had hardly died away when Wahn shook his head and squawked angrily.

"Mullian knows only a part of the mystery," he said. He picked up a piece of wood, flew over the river, and dropped it into the water.

"Watch," he said as the chip fell from his beak.

They lined the river bank. The chip sank beneath the water, but soon it emerged a little lower down the stream, bobbing in the current.

"What does that mean?" asked a Bandicoot.

"The chip is Ouyarh," Wahn explained. "Do you all understand that?"

"Yes," they chorussed.

"Ouyarh is dead. He has left us, and all we now see is his body. That is not the real Ouyarh. It is only skin and feathers, muscles and liver and entrails. The real Ouyarh stays alive. He leaves his body behind and goes into that other world that Mullian has told you about. But his spirit lives. It lives! Perhaps it stays in the other world sometimes, like Mullian's stone, but I say that it is like my piece of wood, and that it floats back to life."

There was a tumult of noise and chatter as animals and insects discussed the matter. It was another Cockatoo who called for silence.

"These may be wise words," he said, when at last he could make himself heard, "but who can tell whether Mullian is right or whether Wahn has the words of wisdom? Sticks and stones are all very well, but no one knows where the truth lies until it is proved by some living thing that Baiame has made."

Silence fell at once, for it was obvious that what Cockatoo had said was right.

Warreen the Wombat was the first to volunteer.

"I will go to the other land," he said. Then he gurgled deep in his throat and they knew that he was laughing. "It's one way to prove something. If I don't come back you will know that Mullian is right, but the only one who will know what has happened will be me."

"We'll go too," said Beewee the Goanna, Bilbie the Bandicoot, and Ouyoubooloooey the Black Snake.

"Very good," said Cockatoo. "When will you come back to us? That is, if you do come back," he added.

The volunteers conferred together.

"We shall return in the springtime, when Yarrageh fastens the flowers on the trees and carpets the grass with colour. We shall return if it is the will of Baiame that we should do so."

The meeting dispersed, and Wombat, Goanna, Bandicoot, and Black Snake disappeared into holes in the ground and hollow trees, curled up tightly, and went to sleep.

The winter months passed slowly by. Sometimes the birds and animals and insects thought of their friends who had gone into the long sleep, and wondered if their spirits would come back to earth renewed and youthful again.

But when Yarrageh spread glowing colours over mountain and plain with a lavish hand, and the daring animals returned, everyone was disappointed. They were the same old Wombat, Goanna, Bandicoot, and Snake, thinner and bedraggled. All the winter they had been living on their own fat. There was no new life, no spirit that Wahn had told them would rise from their dead bodies.

"My words have not been proved," Wahn admitted, "but neither have they been proved wrong. Nor do we know whether Mullian was right or not."

"Look at me," said Ouyouboolooey. "At least I have a new skin."

He wound sinuously among the animals, showing off his bright new scales.

"What shall we do now?" someone asked sadly.

There came a shrill piping from the insects.

"We want to help!" they cried.

The birds and animals laughed. Kookaburra's laugh went on so long that it seemed as though it would never stop. The insects were angry.

"You despise us because we are tiny; but you will never understand the mystery unless we help you."

"Very well," said Kookaburra, feeling sorry he had hurt the feelings of the little people. "I'm sorry I laughed."

He turned and spoke to the others. "The animals and reptiles failed," he reminded them. "It can do no harm to let the little ones try."

They agreed. When autumn came the grubs and insects burrowed into the soil, crawled up the tree trunks, and hid in crevices in the bark, or swam under water and clung to the stalks of water-plants.

But no one had really taken them seriously. It was a long cold winter. Some of the birds had flown away to warmer lands, and anyone who remained was so busy keeping warm and seeking food that he forgot all about the bravery of the insect people. Snake, Wombat, Goanna, and Bandicoot were fast asleep, for they had found that it was an easy way to survive the rigours of the winter season.

Yarrageh had scarcely begun another season's labour of love when the Swifts came flying down to earth, chirping excitedly, and calling the animals and birds together.

163

"We have seen something new, something new," they sang. "We have followed the path of Yarrageh, and now he has come to you, to you, to you."

The animals gathered together expectantly. Presently they saw little moving specks of colour on the ground. They were the tribe of Beetles, resplendent in flashing metallic armour. Then a sharp-eyed bird saw a grey chrysalis hanging from a tree. The chrysalis opened, a butterfly emerged, and spread its delicate wings, fanning them slowly to and fro as if to dry them in the warm breeze. Something climbed out of the river and hung from a swaying stem. Wings, almost transparent, gradually unfolded and a long shining body stiffened and came to life in the sunshine. With a whirr of wings it flew up, hovering like a rainbow above them.

Butterflies and moths and insects of every shape and size, resplendent in their new dress, fluttered and swooped and ran among the birds and animals.

"So it is true," Wahn shouted triumphantly. "These are new insects. They have been born again with new spirits and new bodies. There *is* another world, and they have come to tell us that death is not the end of life."

This was the miracle of spring; the miracle that returns every year when Yarrageh comes with warm, gentle breezes and fingers gay with colour.

THE DIGGING BONE

In the Northern Territory, where a gulf bites deeply into the land, lagoons and marshes once extended far inland. They teemed with wildfowl, and on the drier parts animals were to be found everywhere. The birds and the animals lived happily together; there was plenty of food, and they were content to share the beautiful earth and water. But with the passing years the birds became jealous of the animals and lizards who came to the edge of the lagoons to drink, and who dared to swim in the water the birds regarded as their own.

"From now on you must keep to your own place," said the birds. "There is plenty of room for you on the land. If you are thirsty you can drink from the streams and the small pools, but you must leave the marshes to us. They are our homes. We build our nests there. You trample our grass, and you crush our reeds, and you dirty our water. Keep to your own place."

The animals and lizards resented being ordered away from the lagoons which they regarded as their home just as much as the dry land.

"There is plenty of room for everyone in the marshes," they complained, "and there is very little dry land. It will be over-crowded if we have to stay there. We'll begin to fight among ourselves if we are not allowed to roam where we want. We have just as much right to the marshes and the lagoons as you."

"Keep out! Keep out!" screamed the birds. "They are ours, not yours. Keep out!"

Then the animals and lizards banded together. They advanced on the lagoons like an army, swarming on the edges, breaking down the reeds, treading unwittingly on the nests of the wildfowl. The birds rose up in clouds and attacked them with beak and claw. The air was thick with flying feathers, and fur, skin, scales, and blood floated across the marsh water.

The battle seemed to go on endlessly. Hundreds of birds and creatures of the land rose to take the place of those who were killed. From every part of the marshes hoarse shouts, high-pitched screaming, angry roaring, and the clash of weapons indicated that the fighting would never stop until all the living creatures were dead.

The only ones who took no part in the quarrel were Kangaroo, Emu, and Willy Wagtail. They met together and camped as far as they could from the contestants, but they could still hear the uproar of battle and the distant screams.

"We must do something to stop this bloodshed," said Mirram the Kangaroo. "It is sheer selfishness that has brought these troubles on us."

"I am a bird, but I am ashamed of my people," said Deereeree the Willy Wagtail sadly. "Selfishness is deep inside us. I don't know how we can take it out."

"Fighting won't do it."

"Ah, but there is one thing that can be done. If we could take the marsh lands away from the birds there would be nothing left to fight over."

"But what would happen to the birds?"

"They would find another place somewhere."

"How could we possibly take the marsh lands away from them? There are only three of us. Even if we were as many as the reeds in all the lagoons, we would only cause more fighting, and that is just what we want to avoid."

"There is one way we could do it," Deereeree said excitedly. "If we could let the sea into the lagoons, the birds would be left without a home. That would bring them to their senses."

Dinewan the Emu spoke for the first time. "Yes, that's all we would have to do," he remarked sarcastically. "Perhaps you can scratch a channel with your little claws, Deereeree?"

The bird hung its head, and Kangaroo rebuked Emu.

"If we quarrel amongst ourselves, Dinewan, nothing will be done. Let's build a shelter and go to sleep. Perhaps the Great Spirit will send us an answer in our dreams."

In the morning they looked at each other hopefully.

"In my dream," Deereeree began, "I was on an island in the marsh. A tidal wave rolled in from the sea and flooded the lagoon. I stood on the highest part of the island, because that was all that was left of it, and as far as I could see there was water everywhere."

"That's a lot of help!" Dinewan sneered. "I dreamed I was on a flat plain and everywhere the birds and animals and snakes were fighting each other. They fought so long that none of them

Emu dug with his strong claws and uncovered other bones.

were left alive, and the plain was covered with bones. And that's just what will happen unless we do something about it," he added savagely. "Perhaps Kangaroo had a wonderful dream that will tell us what to do about it?"

"No, I had no dream, Dinewan. All night I lay awake. I kept thinking about a bone I found yesterday. It may well be that Baiame has put this thought in me for a purpose. Let us go and look at it."

The two birds followed Kangaroo to the place where the bone was lying on the ground. Emu dug with his strong claws and uncovered other bones. They were all pointing in the same direction.

"There is a reason for this," Deereeree twittered.

"Then tell us what it is," croaked Dinewan.

Mirram picked up the bone he had first discovered.

"There is magic in it," he shouted excitedly. "I can feel it inside me."

He dug one end of the bone into the ground and pushed against it. It moved of its own accord, with Mirram holding on to one end and the birds running after him. It followed the direction in which the other bones were pointing, leaving a deep trench behind it. There was a sudden roar, and when the friends looked back they saw white-capped waves and a torrent of water rushing down the channel that the bone had made.

"This is the tidal wave I saw in my dream," cried Deereeree.

The three friends ran faster, and the water raced behind them, filling the trench, spilling into the marsh lands, flooding the lagoons until they overflowed, and all the trees and rushes were submerged. The lizards and animals fled to dry land as fast as their legs would carry them. The birds rose up in a vast cloud and flew from their homes. By nightfall not a single bird or animal was to be seen. The fertile marshes lay underneath a single sheet of water, stretching right out to the horizon.

That is how the great gulf was formed, and that was how the birds were cured of their selfishness. Ever since they have been content to share land and water with animals and reptiles.

THE RELENTLESS PURSUIT

I n New South Wales two mighty rivers flow together, and at their junction is a deep, clear water hole, which was once the home of the monster Gurangatch. Descended from a long line of ancestors, some of whom were lizards and some fish, Gurangatch was half-lizard, half-fish. He had grown to an enormous size, but the deep hole at the confluence of the rivers was large enough to accommodate him and give him freedom to move about. On account of his size he was never molested by fish nor birds, nor even by man until one day Mirragen the Cat came that way.

Mirragen the Cat-man was the most famous fisherman in all that part of Australia. With net and spear he could seek out the wiliest fish and entangle it in the meshes, or impale it on his many-pronged spear. He did not rely on skill alone, but had also a knowledge of spells which would lure the fish from their hiding places and draw them within reach of his spear. He was a traveller, too, always seeking fresh experiences, and priding himself on the many different kinds of fish he had caught and eaten. Little fish he despised. Only the biggest were considered fair game by Mirragen, and if they were large enough to provide sport as well as food, he was well content.

For a long time now he had had to satisfy himself with smaller fish from the rivers and lakes which were his usual hunting grounds, and he had become discontented.

"Remain here," he had said to his family. "You are safe in this valley, and there are plenty of roots and small game in the hills to keep hunger at bay. I am going away for a time. When I return I will bring back the biggest fish you have ever seen."

They tried to dissuade him, but he was adamant.

"Eels!" he exclaimed scornfully, when they pointed out that the river by their camp was full of fat eels. "They are lazy and easy to catch, and there is not a single one as long as my arm. They are food for babies. I am off to find a fish that is worthy of a man's skill."

When he came to the junction of the two rivers his eyes lit up and his stride lengthened.

"The very place I am looking for!" he exclaimed.

Placing his dilly bag and fishing gear on the ground, he crawled forward on hands and knees and put his head over the edge of a cliff where he could look straight down into the water hole. At first he could see nothing but green water, but as his eyes grew accustomed to the gloom at the foot at the cliff, his gaze went deeper and deeper into the water, as though he were actually swimming through it. Further down he went, and suddenly he found that he was looking into two enormous, unblinking eyes.

"Gurangatch!"

The name came naturally to him, for he had heard vague rumours of an enormous reptile or fish that lived at the bottom of a deep pool where two rivers flowed together.

He repeated the most powerful spells he had learned from the wirinuns, and slowly Gurangatch floated towards the surface, struggling in vain against the unseen power that was drawing him upwards. The sweat ran down Mirragen's face and dropped into the water, but in spite of the magic power that was being exerted, he was unable to hold the monster, which drifted down once more into the safety of the water hole.

"Tomorrow!" he thought; and he sharpened the prongs of his spear before lying down to sleep. "Tomorrow he will not escape me, even if I have to dive into the pool to transfix him with my spear. This is indeed the prize that I promised to bring home to my tribe. If I succeed, I shall be remembered for ever as the killer of Gurangatch."

*　　　*　　　*　　　*

The monster was really frightened. For many years he had lived in the pool, confident that no one could harm him because of his size, and he had not been prepared for Mirragen's magic. He knew that when the sun rose the Cat-man would be waiting for him, armed with more than magic. Sure enough, when the sun's first rays lit the top of the cliff, Mirragen's spear flashed down and rang against his scales, but they were hard enough to turn the prongs. He waited for the next move, knowing that Mirragen's net would be equally useless, but dreading some new device that he would be powerless to resist. Presently he began to feel sleepy. It did not seem to matter any longer what Mirragen did, and his mind began to drift away on a tide of unconsciousness. He was brought back to life with a shock when he felt himself begin to float upwards. There was a strange taste in his mouth, and he knew that the Cat-man had poisoned the water with a tincture of bark. It was not sufficient to kill him, but enough to sharpen his senses and make him aware of the danger that was threatening him.

"I must get away from the pool before he catches me in the clutch of his magic powers," he thought.

With a flick of his powerful tail he turned round and began to burrow into the solid rock. Leaving the home of his ancestors behind him, he swam through the ground almost as easily as if it were water. Earth, rocks, and sand were ploughed up in an immense wave, and as he wriggled through the new element, the river turned in its course and filled the channel with a foaming torrent of water.

Mirragen was not aware that Gurangatch had left, for he was hunting for more poisonous bark. When he returned he rubbed his eyes. A third mighty river was now flowing through the land, dwindling to a thread of silver in the far distance. Picking up his net and spears, he ran along the bank. Tiny landslides kept slipping in the river and he had to watch his steps lest he should slide down with them and be carried away in the flood.

As the heat of the day was ebbing he reached the end of the stream. It had changed course several times when Gurangatch had met with a solid outcrop of rock, but at last it had come to an end, and plunged underground. Mirragen debated whether he should follow it into the cave where it disappeared, but he knew that he was no match for a monster in the dark chasms of the earth. He climbed a small hill above the cave and dug down into the soil until he felt it give way beneath him. Tying several of his fish spears together, he probed the hole, hoping that the monster might be somewhere beneath. Failing in this, he dug another, and another, but succeeded only in piercing the rock with deep holes which remain to this day above the Whambeyan caves to witness to his attempts to reach Gurangatch.

But the monster had felt the spear slithering past his flanks, and realised that if he stayed there he must fall victim to the relentless fisherman. Once again he dug through the ground, and as he twisted and turned he came out into the valley where Mirragen had left his family. They saw him coming. First the mighty head broke the side of the valley, then the great body slithered down the side almost to their feet, and along the furrow the water raced in a torrent like a tidal wave confined to a narrow bed. The water foamed over the edges and splashed against the rocks, licking at the heels of the women and children as they raced for safety up the far side of the valley.

There they met a weary man who had been travelling along the crest of the ridges.

"Mirragen, husband," cried his wives, "stay with us! We are afraid. The monster is devastating the land and we have barely escaped with our lives. Even if you were to catch up with him you could not overcome such a monster. Be satisfied with the eels in our little stream and remain with us."

"There will be no eels here now, nor any little stream," laughed Mirragen. "The stream is a great river now, but it will be a long time before fish come into these waters. If I do not catch Gurangatch now I will never rest content. This is my destiny."

He ran on and on, and by nightfall he had caught up with the lizard-fish. Mirragen's body and limbs were torn by sharp rocks and he was faint through loss of blood. He plunged his spear into the monster's side, but again the spear points glanced off the scales, and Gurangatch's tail swung round and knocked him off his feet. In the gathering darkness they fought, until the rocks were worn smooth. Gurangatch slid off them and resumed his journey, but Mirragen was now too tired and bruised to follow.

Morning came and he took up the chase again.

"He is getting weary, but so am I," he thought. "If we fight again I may get the worst of it. The time has come to get help."

He turned back and went to a camp where he knew he would find some of his tribe. They were sitting down to their evening meal when he arrived, and greeted him enthusiastically.

"Welcome, Mirragen," they cried. "Have you brought some new fish for us to eat?"

The Cat-man sank down with a groan.

"I am weary and hurt," he said. "For day after day I have been following Gurangatch, and I have nearly caught him."

They opened their eyes wide.

"Gurangatch? No one could ever hope to catch Gurangatch!"

"Well, I have!" Mirragen snapped. "I cast magic spells over him. I poisoned the water where he lived and drove him out. I have been chasing him through valleys and over hills, and under the earth. He is at the point of death, and all that remains is to put an end to his sufferings. I am a generous man, so I invite you to help me and share the honour that will come to me."

"Not us!" they said promptly. "You don't look very fit, Mirragen. It looks as though you have been in a fight and have had the worst of it. We would rather stay here and eat the delicious eels we caught this morning."

Mirragen got up with an exclamation of disgust. "I will find someone else to share the glory," he said.

"You might try the Bird-men further down the valley," one of his relatives suggested.

As he stumbled off into the night Mirragen thought that this might be a good idea, especially if some of them were diving birds, for he suspected that Gurangatch had taken refuge in a water hole, and he was too tired to begin the whole sequence over again.

The Shags and Divers and Ducks were ready to help him, and they travelled with him along the trail that was so clearly marked by the newly-formed rivers, until in the morning they came to a large pool where the river ended, disappearing into the ground where Gurangatch in his struggles had formed the underground mazes of the Jenolan caves.

One of the Ducks paddled across the hole, bobbed his tail in the air, and sank down into the water. They waited a long time for him to return, but when he appeared he swam quickly to the bank, waddled ashore and began to walk back towards his home.

"What have you seen?" shouted Mirragen.

Duck flicked his tail and said shortly, "The hole is bottomless. There's nothing there."

Shag was the next to try. He fluttered over the water, closed his wings, and plummeted down into the depths. He came up with a small fish in his beak, which he brought ashore and laid at Mirragen's feet.

"Is this Gurangatch?" he asked.

The Cat-man was so exasperated that he kicked it back into the pool, and Shag fled in case he should do him an injury.

Only Diver Bird was left.

"Please try," Mirragen begged. "The others were afraid, but I know you will help me."

Diver flew high up into the air and fell towards the pool like a flash of lightning. The water closed over him. He was gone so long that Mirragen began to fear for the life of his friend, but at last he bobbed up and swam ashore.

"Gurangatch is there," Diver said, "but you will never catch him. All I could do was to bring you a little part of the monster that I could carry in my beak."

He gave a piece of flesh to his friend. It was covered with large silver scales that twinkled in the sunlight.

The Cat-man put his arm round the bird. "You are my friend," he said. "It is the end of the chase. Let Gurangatch lie there for ever. We have his flesh and we will eat it together to show him that we are the victors."

The flesh was soon eaten, but the Whambeyan and Jenolan caves, and many rivers of New South Wales, remain to show how Mirragen the Cat-man chased Gurangatch the monster in the Dreamtime and ate a piece of him as a token of victory.

KUBBITHA AND THE TUCKONIES

IN the days when there was no Murray River, Mungoongarlie the giant Goanna and his tribe lived by the banks of the Riverina. It was a good place to live until the drought came; then the river would dry up until only a few mud holes were left in its bed. The fierce sun beat down on them and sucked up all the moisture, leaving ugly cracks in the dried mud, and all the life of the valley was in danger. The animals began to die of thirst, and soon pathetic bundles of feathers and dehydrated bodies were lying on the ground.

The only creatures who seemed able to survive the great thirst were the Goannas. They had a secret supply of water hidden among the rocks; each day they went there to slake their thirst, but they guarded the secret and would never share it with others, not even with their own wives.

Kubbitha, the little Black Duck, the youngest wife of Mungoongarlie, begged her Goanna husband to allow the wives to share the water supply of the Goannas.

"And not only for us," she said. "You must have plenty of water, and if you share it with others you will have friends for life."

"I don't want friends," Mungoongarlie said. "I'm quite well able to look after myself."

"Don't you want wives? Without them you would soon be in trouble, especially when you want your meal prepared."

"Get out," Giant Goanna said roughly. "If I share the water with anyone who asks for it, the supply will dry up and then we'll all be dead. And dead Goannas don't need wives."

Kubbitha was a woman with a strong mind. She went to the other wives and said, "Mungoongarlie will never show us where the water is, but I think we might find it ourselves. When we go out to look for roots tomorrow, let us follow the tracks of the Goannas. They will lead us to the water hole in the rocks. It must be somewhere in the mountains, because that is the direction they always take."

So in the morning the women took their digging-sticks and set out across the plain. They scattered in various directions, but when they were well away from the camp they turned towards the hills. They searched all day, but in vain. The Goanna tracks were lost among the rocks, and though they poked into crevices with their yam-sticks they could find no sign of water. At last they realised that it was time to go home. They hurried back over the plain, but when their husbands asked them for food they had to admit that they had not been able to find any roots.

Mungoongarlie looked closely at his wife. His gaze dropped down to her feet.

"That is not the dust of the plain on your feet," he said. "It comes from the mountains. What have you been doing?"

"Looking for yams. I thought there might be some there."

"Then what about the other women? Where have they been?"

"How should I know? I am not their husband."

It was soon apparent that the Black Ducks had all been up in the mountains looking for water. The Goannas were angry with them.

"Listen to me," Mungoongarlie said. "Tomorrow morning all of us Goannas are going out on a hunting expedition. We will leave you one skin full of water, and that must last you till we come back. When we return we expect a big meal of roots and grubs, to go with the flesh we bring. Let's have no nonsense about looking for water. It will take you all the time to get the food ready."

They left early in the morning before sun-up, and the women gathered round Kubbitha.

"What shall we do?" they asked. "If we do not obey our husbands they will kill us, or make us die of thirst."

"We shall die of thirst anyway, unless they show us where the water is," Kubbitha replied. "You may gather food, but I shall go to the mountains again. This time I will not return without the water!"

Two of the wives came with her while the rest of them went out on their daily tasks. The three women toiled up the mountain side. The sun beat against the rocks. Where there were cracks they were filled with fine dust and over all the heat rose in shimmering waves.

"It's no good," one of the Black Ducks said at last. "Without water we shall die before sundown. We must go back to where there is some shade."

"You go back. I shall stay here. I have vowed not to return until I find water."

Her friends were glad to get off the mountain side and into the shelter of the trees, but Kubbitha kept on searching. When she realised that she would not find the water that day, she built a shelter wall of stones at the entrance to a shallow cave and lay down to rest.

Sleep would not come. Her tongue was swollen and her head was aching. She felt she might be delirious, especially when she felt a cool touch on her hand. She started up in the darkness and saw, outlined against the mouth of the cave, a tiny man.

"A Tuckonie!" she gasped.

"Yes," he said, "and you are Kubbitha."

"How do you know my name?"

"I know more about you than you think. I know what you are here for, and I have come here to help you. Follow me."

In the growing light of dawn she followed him further up the mountain, until they came to a plateau. The morning mists lay in the hollows, and there was a delicious coolness as though water was not far away.

The little man put his hands to his mouth and gave a cry.

"Cooee!" It floated across the plateau and echoed from the cliffs above. Presently more tiny figures appeared through the mist, and Kubbitha soon found herself surrounded by Tuckonies. They were friendly little creatures. They talked together in squeaky voices. After some argument the leader came back to Kubbitha.

"We have decided what to do. Go down to the foot of the mountain, Kubbitha. You will find your two friends coming to look for you. Send them back to their camp with the word that all the Black Ducks are to come to the mountain as quickly as they can."

"What shall I do then?"

"You must climb up to this plateau again. It will be hot and tiring, and you may think that you will die of thirst on the way, but we know you are brave. Believe us, we are your friends, and we are trying to help you."

Kubbitha did as she had been told. At the foot of the mountains she met her friends, who gave a cry of relief at seeing her.

"We thought you might have been carried away by the evil spirits of the mountain," they said. "Have you found the water?"

"Listen to me," Kubbitha said. "I have not found the water,

More tiny figures appeared through the mist.

but a wonderful thing is happening. I cannot tell you what it is because I do not know myself, but I am sure everything is going to be all right. The Tuckonies are helping us!"

The Black Ducks looked at each other and did not know what to say.

"Don't stand there doing nothing," Kubbitha urged. "Go back to the camp as quickly as you can. You'll be quite safe. The Goannas won't be back until later in the day. Tell all the women what has happened, and say that the Tuckonies want them all to gather here. Go quickly."

They ran back, and Kubbitha turned to the mountain again. It was only the great heart of Kubbitha the Black Duck that took her back to the plateau. She arrived almost fainting and fell against the rocks.

"Here," said the leader of the Tuckonies. He put her yam-stick, which she had left behind earlier in the morning, into her hand.

"Drive it deep into the heart of the mountain," he said; then he vanished, and all his people with him.

Kubbitha rubbed her eyes. Perhaps the sun had made her see things that were not there? Perhaps it was all a device of the Evil One to drive her mad? But the Tuckonie's words still rang through her head, so she lifted her digging stick and thrust it into the ground. To her surprise it went down through the solid rock and disappeared from sight.

"Run, Kubbitha, run," a voice drummed in her ears.

She turned and stumbled down the steep mountain side. Behind her there was hissing, rumbling sound as though all the mountain devils were at her heels. She dared not turn round to see what it was that was following her. The sounds became louder and she ran faster still. Everything was blurred in front of her and she could hardly recognise the Black Ducks until she fell into waiting arms, and heard a cry of rejoicing from them.

"Look, Kubbitha! Look at the gift you have brought from the Tuckonies!"

As the breath came back into her lungs she lifted her head, and saw a mountain stream tumbling down the mountains, piling itself up against the rocks, springing over them, dropping in smooth sheets, only to splash and rear up again, and finally to spread out across the plain at her feet in a shining band of silver. The thirsty sand tried to drink up the water, but the water flowed faster still from the unseen source above.

They turned to watch it as it swept on. Men and women and little children were running towards it, falling on their knees, and burying their heads in that blissful water. Birds and animals of all kinds mingled with them. All were drinking from the never-ending waters of the newly-born Murrumbidgee River.

Their thirst quenched, the Black Ducks returned to their camp, to find that they were on the wrong side of the new river.

"What shall we do?" they asked Kubbitha.

She laughed at them.

"We shall stay here, right where we are. Do you want to return to your husbands after what they have done to you?"

"No!" said the women with one voice. "Besides, it is much more pleasant here than on the other side. Here there are trees and green bushes, but over there it is hot and dusty."

At the end of that afternoon the Goannas returned to camp. They stared at the river in amazement, and then looked across to the other side. Mungoongarlie shouted to the wives,. "Come across and get our meal ready for us."

The only reply was a chorus of mocking laughter.

"Never more," Kubbitha called back. "You would not be kind to us; now we shall never be kind to you."

And since then Goannas have lived in hot and dusty places, while Black Ducks disport themselves in the cool waters of rivers and billabongs.

THE MONSTER OF THE MURRAY RIVER

THERE were few terrifying monsters in Australia, but one could never be sure that an innocent lake might not conceal a dreadful Bunyip. And in some rivers there were fish or lizards like Gurangatch. Whowhie, the monster of the Murray River, was three or four times the length of the tallest man. He looked something like a Goanna, but was much more fearsome. He had a long tail, three legs on each side of his body, and the head of a frog. And he was an eater of flesh. No man or animal was safe when Whowhie was about, for he had an insatiable appetite.

The only thing that saved the tribes of the Murray River from extinction was that Whowhie was so large, his body so heavy, that he could move only slowly. As he dragged himself over the ground, the earth trembled; people knew that he was coming and were able to make their escape. He lived in a huge underground cave with many tunnels which led out to the bank of the river. When he came out of his lair, his feet stirred up the sand, forming the sandhills of the Riverina district.

It was at night that Whowhie was most feared. By day even the slowest animals could escape from him, but at night men and animals must sleep. Whowhie learned the art of creeping silently through the darkness towards the gleam of a camp fire, picking up children, and older people too, without a sound and swallowing them whole. He was not satisfied with a small meal: twenty or thirty, or sixty persons at a time were not too many for Whowhie's capacious belly, and there was still room for unwary rats, wombats, wallabies, and even kangaroos as titbits for the feast.

The animal and human population of the district began to dwindle, and no one could go to sleep happily at night lest the monster should discover them in the darkness. To light a fire was dangerous, for it was a sign to him that food was waiting for him.

Sentries were posted, but Whowhie learned the art of appearing suddenly out of the darkness and engulfing them before they could shout a warning. In the finish men and animals banded together to make plans to destroy the monster. Whowhie had raided one camp and had eaten everyone in the tribe – every single person with the exception of one small, terrified boy who had escaped to tell the news to others. It was decided that all the tribes should be assembled in an attempt to kill Whowhie, and that they should be summoned immediately. Whowhie could hardly move now on account of the enormous meal he had eaten, and it was felt that there was no reason for delay.

The water-rats who lived in little tunnels in the banks of the river reported that he had left a long trench behind him as he dragged his body back to his cave. There was no doubt that he had gone to the furthest part of the cave to sleep off the effects of his meal, and it would take him a week to get back to the entrance.

Fires were lit in several places and their smoke, rising in the still air, was the signal for the tribes to come together. Those who lived closest to the monster's cave were kept busy gathering shellfish and catching fish and cooking them to feed the visitors when they arrived. All day long the warriors trooped in to the river bank, carrying their sharpest and most deadly weapons, and eager to put an end to the terror of the Murray River. That night they held a feast, with much dancing and singing, for it had been a long time since they had dared to hold a corroboree, lest Whowhie should come on it unawares. This night all would be well, for he could not stir.

Early in the morning the water-rats explored the cave and reported that they could hear Whowhie puffing and snoring in the furthermost recess, and that it would be safe to enter. Piles of brushwood were dragged inside, and heaped up at the entrance to the cave. A torch was applied and the brushwood roared into flame. Green vegetation was piled on top of the fire and soon the cave was filled from end to end with dense, choking smoke. Above the crackling of twigs and the roaring of the flames the men could hear Whowhie coughing. The sound reverberated in the tunnels and grew louder as it reached the entrance, until it was like the roaring of wind in the pines or the crashing of waves on the seashore.

Day after day the fires burned on. The coughing and roaring grew louder as Whowhie staggered towards the open air. On the seventh day the warriors gathered in a half circle round the entrance, waiting expectantly.

A cloud of smoke billowed out of the tunnel, and through it lurched Whowhie, scattering the fire with his feet. His huge eyes

Whowhie roared louder than ever, but his strength was gone.

were bloodshot, his skin blackened, his cavernous mouth opening and shutting as he gulped in the fresh air and expelled the smoke from his lungs. With one great shout the warriors fell upon him, thrusting their spears deep into his sides, beating him with clubs, and stripping the flesh from his body with their flint knives. Whowhie roared louder than ever, but his strength was ebbing fast. At length he tottered and fell, and the earth shook with the impact.

There has never been another Whowhie on the banks of the Murray River, for he lived alone without wife or family; but when the wind blows through the cave and echoes in the tunnels it is a reminder that the spirit of Whowhie lives on in the tortuous depths beneath the earth.

The Winjarning Brothers and Other Hero Stories

HOW WYJU MADE RED OCHRE

AS he drew near to the camp Wyju the traveller heard the lamentations of mourners.

"What is this?" he asked the first person he met. "What is the matter?"

"One of our children has been swallowed by a huge snake that lives in the valley."

Wyju was a kind-hearted man who spent much of his time helping others, and he was sad when he heard this.

"Have you killed it?" he asked.

"No. That is one of the reasons for our grief. You see, it was no ordinary Carpet Snake: there is a spirit in the snake, and we dare not touch it. If we did there would be no water left in our valley."

"I know how it is," Wyju agreed. "But surely, if you were to kill it, and even if the streams flowed underground, you would be able to find them again?"

"It is easy to see that you are a stranger. If the great snake were to lie straight out with his head on the ground, we could kill him and there would be no trouble with the water; but, you see, he is always coiled up. We dare not touch him then because the water would go away and we would never find it again."

"I think I know a way to make him stretch out his body," Wyju said. "Leave him to me."

Followed by the curious glances of the tribesmen, he searched till he found a mallee shrub. He dug its long root out of the ground and walked with it down the valley until he saw the carpet snake curled on a flat rock asleep in the sunshine. Taking care not to wake it, he climbed up into the branches of a tall tree which overhung the rock and lowered the mallee root until it dangled above the snake's head. Presently a few drops of water seeped out and fell on the snake; it stirred and opened its mouth so that the water fell on its tongue. Slowly it uncoiled its body and reached up towards the source of the water. When it was standing on the tip of its tail with its body as straight as a young tree, Wyju jumped off the branch and slid down the snake's body with his flint knife pressed into its belly. The snake shuddered and collapsed on the rock, and the missing child emerged unharmed from its limp body.

The tribesmen had been watching from a vantage point above the valley. When they saw that the snake was dead they swarmed down and bore Wyju back with them, giving him a tumultuous reception. The traveller was a quiet-spoken man, and his modesty only increased his popularity. News of his skill and daring spread to other tribes, and everyone spoke well of him. The uncles of eligible young women walked long distances to see him and offer their nieces in marriage. Wyju received them hospitably but excused himself.

"I am a restless man," he told them. "Though I am resting now with my friends, I am a solitary person, and no woman could keep up with me when the mood is on me. I would be a sore trial to any young woman."

He did not tell them that his journeys gave him the opportunity of helping people in distress, for it was not his custom to speak of himself.

Through the encampment there passed an endless stream of men who were travelling towards Maljarna, where a rocky hill lifts out of a vast plain. Men who came to see Wyju and were unsuccessful in getting him to marry their nieces did not turn back but went on towards Maljarna.

"Seeing that I cannot agree to your proposals, why do you not return to your own tribe?" he asked one of the visiting men.

"I am looking for a husband for my niece."

"I know; but I have already told you that I cannot accept her."

"Ah, but there is always Kirkin. I must see him for myself. I would gladly give my niece in marriage to him, but . . ."

He broke off and would say no more.

Slowly Wyju pieced together the story of Kirkin. He learned why men were so eager to visit him, and why they broke off their conversations so abruptly.

Kirkin, it seemed, was admired by men because of his hair, which was long and golden. Every morning he combed it out, and the rising sun seemed to turn it into living flame. He was always the centre of a large audience, not only of men, but of animals, birds, reptiles, and insects; all were fascinated by the sight.

The surprising thing was that they were all males. Women detested Kirkin because he was vain and boastful, and because

186

they were jealous of his golden hair. If an uncle proposed that the man with the golden hair would make a good husband, the girls and women set up such an outcry that the man was glad to get away from them.

While Wyju was being sought vainly in marriage, Kirkin was thinking that, pleasant as it was to be admired by men, it would be much more satisfying if he had a wife to cook his meals and look after him. Even his closest friends had no hesitation in telling him about the women's dislike of him, nor in contrasting it with their eagerness to marry Wyju.

"Where does this wonderful man live?" he asked sarcastically.

When he was told that Wyju had no fixed abode, but at that time was not far away, he went to see the traveller.

"Why have you not come to pay your respects to me and see my golden hair?" he asked.

"I have been content to admire your reputation," Wyju answered mildly. "All men speak well of you."

Kirkin saw that Wyju was a man not lightly to be taunted. He changed his tactics.

"And I have heard good things about you. We should be friends. Come to my camp and tomorrow I will show you how to catch a walliow," he said.

"What is that?" asked Wyju.

"It has the finest flesh you ever tasted. It's something like a kangaroo-rat."

Wyju accompanied Kirkin to his camp. As soon as he was asleep, his host went quietly into the long grass, and by the light of the moon he flattened it into the shape of a shallow coolamon, and buried long sticks in the ground. They had been sharpened, and hardened by fire. Kirkin set them with the points uppermost and tucked the flattened grass around them so they could not be seen. He put a dead animal on top and attached to it a cord which he led to a nearby bush.

In the morning Wyju gathered up his hunting weapons.

"You don't hunt walliow with weapons," Kirkin laughed. "We'll look for the nests together. When we find one you can kill it. All you have to do is to jump on the nest."

They fossicked about in the long grass. Presently Kirkin whispered, "Here, Wyju! Quietly! Lie down and peep through the grass. Tell me if you see anything move."

"Yes, I see a nest," Wyju exclaimed. He went down full length in the grass. While his attention was directed to the nest, Kirkin crept to the bush and pulled the string, causing the dead animal to move.

"He's there! He's there!" Wyju whispered.

"Jump on it now," Kirkin said. "Be sure you jump right in the middle of the nest."

Wyju drew himself up to a sitting position with his legs under him. He sprang into the air and stamped both feet on the nest.

As the sharp spikes penetrated his feet he threw himself forward with a shriek of agony.

"Kirkin! Kirkin! Help! Something dreadful has happened."

The man with the golden hair laughed aloud.

"You are an easy victim, my friend Wyju," he gloated, "That will teach you to come to me another time – if ever there is another time. See if the girls want to marry you now! I have plenty to do, so I am afraid I must leave you."

He strode away laughing, while Wyju rolled in agony in the grass. He could not put his feet to the ground, nor could he bear to touch them to pull out the splinters. His blood kept on flowing until it filled the hollow where he was lying.

Long days and nights followed. The imprisoned Wyju kept struggling to free himself. Where his body threshed to and fro the earth became saturated with his blood and dyed a vivid red. In after years men made long journeys to that place to gather the red ochre that resulted from the mixing of Wyju's blood with the soil.

Sometimes he cried for help, and at last he was heard by the Great Spirit.

"It is the voice of Wyju who has helped so many of my children," Baiame said to two famous hunters, the Winjarning brothers. "Go quickly to his aid."

Faster than the wind the brothers ran until they came to the bloodstained hollow where Wyju lay. Quickly and painlessly they removed the spikes that pierced his feet, and touched them with soothing fingers that relieved the pain. They lifted him to his feet and watched him as he took a few steps; then they disappeared.

"Tomorrow will be the last day this man with the golden hair will ever see," Wyju muttered to himself. He waited till the first heralds of dawn sang their song, then he crept through the grass till he came to a place where he could see Kirkin clearly.

As the sun rose Kirkin glanced round to make sure that he

could be seen by the men and animals who had gathered together to see his golden hair in the sunshine. Then he threw his hair up and forwards like a golden fan. At that moment Wyju stepped out of his hiding place and with one swift stroke of his boomerang severed Kirkin's neck. The head rolled down the rock and into the grass in a tangled net of golden hair.

Wyju picked up the body and put it on the fire, and that was the last of the man with the golden hair, except for a little bird that flew from his body looking for grubs and insects to keep alive.

WINJARNING BROTHERS AND THE EVIL ONE

ALONE in an enchanted valley lived a man who was prematurely old. When he passed from boyhood to manhood and had completed his initiation tests, he had wandered off by himself and had discovered this lonely valley. It was known to the elders of the tribe, who feared it and never went near it. The rocks were twisted into fearsome shapes, and the valley was believed to be the abode of spirits. Knowing nothing of its reputation, the young man found it an idyllic place. A clear stream splashed and tumbled from pool to pool in a setting of grass terraces; trees and caves made cool shelters from the burning sun, and the valley teemed with life. Fish swam in every pool and animals provided an endless abundance of food.

"This is a good place for a man to live," he thought.

Months passed like days and he could not bring himself to abandon a place which seemed so perfect. The only thing he needed was a wife to cook food and hold in his arms through the scented hours of the night. He remembered the young girl to whom he had been betrothed after the manhood rites.

"I will wait for her," he reflected. "She has been chosen for me. When the fulness of womanhood comes on her I will seek her out and bring her here to live with me."

But when that time came the old desires had passed.

"I still want her, but it may well be that she has now seen other young men who are more attractive to her. I would not wish to spoil her life: I shall wait here and seek the will of the Great Spirit."

*   *   *   *

Meanwhile the girl had grown up to desirable womanhood, and there were many young men who would gladly have taken her in marriage. Her tests had been conducted alone. From them she had emerged with even greater beauty. She had been told of the bridegroom who had been selected for her, and how he had disappeared into the enchanted valley where none dared follow him.

"He is old and we have no doubt he has become peculiar from

living by himself for so long; but he is still your husband," she was told.

The young woman was bewildered. At one time she thought of him as a man in the full strength of life, with whom she would find unimaginable delights; at other times she shuddered as she thought of him as a repulsive hermit who would feed on her beauty and drive her to work for him night and day.

"You have passed all the tests, Palpinkalare, but there is yet another ordeal. You are to go on a long journey, during which you will skirt the enchanted valley. This time you will not be alone. Your mother and I will go with you, but we shall not speak to you, nor you to us. And you will have eight companions to be your protectors. Four will be young men, and four will be elders who will give advice when you are in doubt."

Her father turned away, and Palpinkalare's heart beat faster. Would she see her chosen husband? And if she did, what sort of man would he be?

The hunting party set off in high spirits. It was a further training period for Palpinkalare. During the day the young men taught her where to find edible plants and roots, how grubs and insects could be found by various signs, and how to follow the tracks of animals. At night the elders spoke to her, instructing her in the traditions and inner mysteries of her tribe. She had little time to think of the man who might soon be her husband, for sleep came quickly when she lay down late at night, and the young men roused her early in the morning.

One night she had a dream. She was overcome by a desire to find an enormous grub. In her dream she went to a tree and lifted a piece of bark. Underneath there was a round hole, almost large enough to accommodate her hand. She found a stick shaped like a hook and put it into the hole. Inside was something soft which moved when she prodded it. She drew it out and raised it to her mouth . . . and then she woke.

In the morning she said, "I must find a certain grub soon. A big one, larger than anyone has ever seen before. I dreamed about it last night, and now I am filled with longing for it."

All day she kept referring to the wonderful grub of her dream. The elders looked at each other uneasily, and at night they sat apart from the others and conferred together.

"There is something wrong with Palpinkalare," said one venerable old man. "The dream and the craving for the grub are not natural. Something or someone has put the thought into her mind by taking possession of her spirit."

"It must be Marmoo the Evil One," said another, looking furtively over his shoulder into the darkness. "We must sleep close together tonight and keep the fires replenished. Also we must take it in turn to watch."

The others agreed, but the night hours passed uneventfully.

In the morning Palpinkalare rose before the others were awake and made her way to a certain tree which she recognised as the one she had seen in her dream. The bark hung loosely in exactly the same place. She lifted it and looked at the hole without surprise. There was the hooked stick, on the ground at the foot of the tree, waiting to be used. She caught the grub with the hook, pulled it out, raised it to her mouth, and turned round. And there, almost touching her, was the Evil One.

Half spirit, half man, and wholly evil, he had come across the track of eleven people some days before. After examining them, he came to the conclusion that there were five young people, one of them a girl; a man and his wife who walked apart from the others; and four old men. The Evil One had sat for a long time studying the tracks, and knew that the most important person was the young woman who was being guarded and educated by her companions.

He had followed the trail tirelessly for three days. When he came closer to the travellers he sent part of his mind ahead and probed the brain of the young woman. He discovered that, deep down, she was a prey to conflicting emotions, but that most of her thoughts were centred on her training. That night he had put the dream of the huge grub inside her subconscious mind; and now, on the fourth day, she was at his mercy.

Palpinkalare opened her mouth to scream, but no sound came. The Evil One entered into her mind, which was filled with such a sense of horror that she fell down in a faint. The Evil One picked her up, threw her across his shoulders, and ran off with her. He climbed a hill and dropped down into a valley. It was the valley of enchantment where her betrothed husband lived. Reaching a grassy space, the Evil One laid the body of the young woman among the flowers and sat down to gloat over her beauty. His mind had lost contact with hers while she was unconscious.

Slowly Palpinkalare regained her senses. At first her mind was blank. Then she opened her eyes and saw blue sky above her, the

There, almost touching her, was the Evil One.

graceful, drooping branches of the trees, and a riot of bright blossoms. She heard the song of a stream, smelled the perfume of the flowers: and then her eyes rested on the Evil One.

Now terrible sounds came from her throat. Scream after scream rang through the sunny valley, while the Evil One grinned as he listened. Slowly and deliberately he raised his spear and held it poised over the young woman.

The hermit of the valley was startled by the noise. It was the first time for years that he had heard the sound of a woman's voice. Picking up his waddy, he raced towards her. As he broke through the bushes a single glance showed the young woman sitting up, and the figure of the Evil One in the act of thrusting his spear into her body. Before he could move, or even shout, the spear point entered her heart. The Evil One looked up and saw a man bounding across the grass towards him. He shrunk back and vanished under the trees, while the hermit's waddy glanced harmlessly off the trunk of a tree.

The man stooped over Palpinkalare's lifeless body. In some mysterious way he knew that this was the girl who had been betrothed to him. She looked innocent and defenceless. Before he could even touch her living flesh, she had been snatched away from him. The tears rolled down his cheeks and beard and dropped on her face as he vowed he would dedicate his life to avenging her death.

*　　　*　　　*　　　*

There was consternation in the camp of the elders and the young men. They had called many times, but Palpinkalare had not answered. The young men had followed her footprints to a tree, where they found an enormous white grub lying on the ground. It took only a moment to find the footprints of a stranger, and to know that he had carried the girl away with him. The young warriors reported their discovery to the elders. The old one who had spoken the previous night was the first to speak again.

"I said the Evil One was not far away. We took what precautions we could, but he has outwitted us. We are no match for evil such as this. One of you young men must go to Palpinkalare's mother and father and tell them what has happened. The others must go to look for the Winjarning brothers. They are the only ones who can help us now."

The others agreed. The young hunters ran quickly, and the

following day they returned, bringing the famous wirinuns with them.

"Your daughter has been stolen by the Evil One," the brothers told her parents. "You must leave everything in our hands now. We shall take the young men with us; the rest of you will remain here until we come back."

The Winjarning brothers were not frightened of the enchanted valley. When they saw that the trail led into it, they followed without hesitation, while the young men followed closely behind. They came to the sheltered glade, and their hearts sank. The body of Palpinkalare was wrapped in bark, and by its side knelt the hermit of the valley. There was no need for him to tell them what had happened. The events of the morning were written clearly on the earth and the grass, and their trained eyes could read every word of it.

"Help me to avenge her," pleaded the lonely man, and the brothers agreed to do so.

"We cannot bring this lovely woman back to life," they said. "Her spirit has gone to the keeping of the Great Spirit, who must surely love her so much that he will not let her go. All we can do is to exact revenge, and to kill the Evil Spirit, body and soul, so that never again will he be able to harm mankind."

The seven men followed the trail left by the Evil Spirit. It was not easy because he had run so swiftly and lightly that only the faintest impression of his feet remained, even on patches of sand. But the trackers were experienced men, and as darkness fell they saw the gleam of a distant camp fire.

"Let us go on through the darkness," said the elder Winjarning. "We can catch him unawares while he is sleeping."

The words were scarcely out of his mouth when the fire began to spread, leaping from crest to crest of the hills, spreading like a living curtain along the mountain range. They knew now that their task would not be an easy one: the Evil One possessed powers that were denied to the wisest wirinuns.

They prepared their evening meal and waited for the morning. At first light they were on the trail again, and the sun had barely risen when they reached the deserted camping place.

"Look!" a young warrior exclaimed. "He must have left as soon as we did this morning. He has passed us on the way."

They retraced their footsteps hastily and reached the site of their own camp, which had been made on the edge of a steep valley. There was no sign of life except an emu which was cautiously picking its way down the slope. The Evil One's trail had stopped abruptly by a bare rock, and beyond it were the unmistakeable prints of the emu's feet.

The younger Winjarning gave a shout.

"I have it!" he cried. "The emu prints begin where the Evil One's left off. He has changed from a man to a bird."

The hermit poked round among the bushes.

"Come here quickly," he called to the others. They ran to him and he showed them the dead body of an emu. The legs and body were there, but the head and neck had gone, and no feathers were left on it.

"It is easy to see what has happened," said the hermit. "The Evil One has not changed into a bird. He has killed the emu and taken its feathers, its head and its neck, and covered himself with them. And he has made emu shoes for himself. We have not been looking at an emu at all, but at the Evil One himself, who has been walking with his back bent to make us think he was a bird. Let us go down into the valley and kill him."

"No, not like that," one of the Winjarnings warned him. "Remember the camp fire that seemed to blaze for miles last night? He has many ways of deceiving us. We will spread out and approach the valley from different directions. When we are ready I will light a fire and send up a smoke signal. As soon as you see it, move in on him."

They did as the Winjarning told them, and presently they were within a hundred yards of the emu. He was standing with his back to a rock ready to defend a narrow path which ended in a steep rock climb facing the open plain.

"We will never overcome him unless we use subtlety," thought the elder Winjarning. He stepped behind a rock, where he was hidden from the Evil One, but whence he could see his younger brother. He made signs that the enemy should be attacked. Then, breaking off a long, straight branch from a tree, he tied a bundle of grass on the end, and held it up so that the Evil One could see it above the rock.

The sudden movement caught the Evil One's eye. He fitted a spear to his woomera, waiting to see what would happen. The grass tuft rose again, looking like a man's head. The Evil One stepped forward and threw his spear. At the same moment two spears flew towards him from the east and the north, entered his chest, and pierced his heart. The young Winjarning and the hermit had ended the Evil One's life.

*   *   *   *

Sad at the thought of the girl whose life had been taken, the men dragged the body of the Evil One down to the plain, made a pyre of twigs and branches, and threw the body on top with its head to the north and its feet to the south as a sign of derision.

"Now begins the most important part of our task," the elder Winjarning warned them. "The body of the Evil One is dead but his spirit is still alive. It will try to escape, and it will take many forms. As soon as the fire is lit we must kill every living thing that crawls out of it."

The flames roared up and consumed the ugly body. Without warning a full-grown kangaroo jumped out of the flames, and fell to the waddies of the young men. They threw it back into the fire; at once an eagle-hawk flew up with strongly-beating wings. A spear transfixed it, and it fell back. There followed in succession a dingo, a goanna, a snake, a frilled lizard, a crow, a magpie, and a wombat, each of which was killed and burnt.

At last the body of the Evil One collapsed into ashes amongst the embers.

"That is the end of the Evil One," said the hermit.

"Wait!" the elder Winjarning warned. "It may not be the end."

They waited until the glow of the red embers faded and grey ashes lay on the ground. There was a slight movement. A caterpillar humped itself up and crawled across the sand. Winjarning stamped on it and threw it back. It sizzled and curled up in the heat. A centipede darted out, and met the same fate. A moth fluttered upwards and was caught with difficulty.

"The end?" asked the hermit when many hours had passed, and the last of the embers was barely visible in the darkness.

"Wait!"

Winjarning held a torch close to the ground and examined it carefully.

An ant was slowly threading its way between the stones and scattered blades of grass. Winjarning picked it up and placed it on the embers. Its body crackled and snapped, and dissolved, and the last ember winked out.

"The end!" Winjarning said with a sigh. "The end of the Evil One!"

197

No longer can he take the form of any animal, or bird, or insect, or reptile, but alas! Winjarning overlooked Man. It is in the form of Man, and Man alone, that Marmoo the Evil One still appears, making trouble everywhere, and perpetuating evil in the world.

THE KEEN KEENGS AND THE FLAME GOD

In the middle of the cave was a smooth, round hole, bleached white by fire. Beneath it slept the Flame God. A red light shone through the hole, staining the rocky walls with pink and lighting up the pallid features of a Keen Keeng, who tossed restlessly in sleep.

Another Keen Keeng, who had been out on reconnaissance, folded his wings and alighted at the entrance. He was a typical specimen of the strange race descended from the giants. He had to bend his head to enter the cave. When he straightened up, his wings were folded back in grooves that ran the length of his arms, and he had the appearance of a tall man, the only difference being that he had only two fingers and a thumb on each hand. The sleepers in the cave woke up and asked for news.

"There are two men on a bare plain many miles from here," he said.

"Why didn't you bring them back with you?" they asked. "We need men and women to offer to the Flame God when he wakes up. He is bound to be hungry, and if we have no sacrifice to offer, we will be seared by his anger."

"There is a reason," the scout replied. "You are too impatient. They are no ordinary men: they are the Winjarning brothers!"

This statement silenced the Keen Keengs for several minutes. They well knew that the Winjarning brothers were the two most powerful wirinuns in all the land. Special gifts had been conferred on them by the Great Spirit, which enabled them to protect ordinary men and women from attacks by the non-human creatures who haunted desert and mountain. No one had ever appealed to the Winjarnings in vain. They had often saved their fellow men from Keen Keengs who tried to snatch them up as offerings to the Flame God. In consequence the descendants of the giants had suffered from the Flame God's anger.

"Did these men see you?" one of the older creatures asked, shuffling forward to warm his hands at the glowing hole in the floor.

"No; I flew at a great height, and only went low enough to see who they were. They did not lift their heads."

"Then this may be the opportunity we have been waiting for. It is our chance to put an end to them, and to please the Flame God with a sacrifice that is worthy of him."

"But they are too powerful for us to overcome," someone objected.

The old Keen Keeng drew himself up and spoke more vigorously.

"Wisdom comes only to the aged," he said. "Listen to me. The Winjarning brothers have never seen us. They may have heard the beating of our wings in the darkness, but they have been too intent on saving others to notice us. Let us invite them to visit us. If we speak gentle words and show them we are friendly, their curiosity may be roused."

Far across the plain the Winjarning wirinuns looked at each other and smiled. Their spirits had heard every word that had been spoken in the cave.

Presently they heard the beating of wings. A man-like figure appeared in the sky, grew larger, and landed on its feet in front of them.

"Who are you?" asked the older brother.

"Greetings! I am one of the Keen Keengs, who are the friends of everyone. I saw you from a great way off and have come to invite you to our home."

The brothers appeared to consult together.

"Why should we go?" asked the younger one. "We have heard strange tales about you. You are trying to trap us."

"No, no," the Keen Keeng replied earnestly. "The sun is hot and there is no shade, no water to drink, no food here. Come with me and we will give you all these things and show you the mysteries and delights of the Keen Keengs."

"Why should you do this for us? We are perfectly happy where we are."

"We have heard about you. I know that your name is Winjarning, and that everyone respects you. Perhaps we will need your help some day."

"Perhaps! How far is it to your home?"

"Many, many miles, but my wings are strong. I can carry you both on my back."

"I should like to see the world as it looks to a bird," said the younger brother. "Let us go."

They climbed on to the Keen Keeng's back. He spread his

A man-like figure appeared in the sky and landed in front of them.

wings and ran along the ground until he was airborne. His wings flapped and he rose swiftly from the ground with his heavy burden. Currents of warm air caused him to dip and sway as the wirinuns clung to his shoulders.

The Keen Keeng mounted higher. Fleecy clouds sailed by. Looking down, the wirinuns saw, as if from a mountain top, a flat plain with little dots and elongated shadows that were bushes. They saw the darker depressions of water holes, and far away a glint of silver at the foot of the mountain which, the Keen Keeng told them, was a lake close to his home.

Presently they were surrounded by other flying forms. These were the young Keen Keengs who had come to escort them. The distant mountain drew nearer, the lake passed under them, and they came to the mountain side and the black hole which was the entrance to the cave.

The brothers alighted and went inside. When their eyes grew accustomed to the dim light, they could see the older Keen Keengs ranged round the walls, and a very old man who advanced towards them and gave them a formal welcome. Then the younger Keen Keengs came jostling in, shouting and laughing. Food and water were put in front of the visitors, who were seated in the place of honour.

"Is this not a good place?" the oldest Keen Keeng asked. "Here is shelter from the sun, protection from our enemies, and food and warmth."

"We thought you were friends of everybody. How is it then that you have enemies?"

"There are wild beasts and creatures of the night," the old one replied. "But let us not think of unpleasant things. Sleep for a little while and then our young people will dance for you."

For three days the Winjarning brothers were entertained by the Keen Keengs. They observed the dances of the young people closely, for they had never seen such rhythmic movement before. They memorised them, and in later years taught them to mankind, bequeathing to them the ritual of the dances that are used at the initiation rites of the young men and women who are verging on manhood and womanhood.

Each day the glow from the pit grew stronger. No one said anything and the brothers were careful to make no remark about it. The Keen Keengs knew that the Flame God was waking, and rejoiced that they had such a splendid offering to make to him.

"We must return to our camp now," said one of the brothers. "You have been hospitable to us, and we shall never forget your kindness, but now it is time for us to return and live our own lives."

"Wait one more day," the old Keen Keeng said. "We have saved the best till last. Tonight the young women will perform the emu dance for you. You must not leave until you have seen it."

A tongue of flame danced up out of the pit as though to emphasise his words.

"Very well, then. But tomorrow we must leave. That is our word."

"You will not be sorry. After the emu dance there will be something you have never experienced before, nor will you ever see it again."

The brother wirinuns went to the furthest corner of the cave and lay down as if they would sleep.

"This is the night," whispered the elder brother. "The last words were a warning that the old one thought we would not understand. Tonight we shall put an end to the wicked ways of the Keen Keengs, but we must be careful. When I whisper '*Now!*' you must leap to your feet and run out of the cave as swiftly as a hunting spear leaving the woomera."

"Why?" protested the younger brother. "I always take the lead in battle. Why should I run away?"

"Don't you remember what was said when we listened with our spirits? 'Wisdom comes to the aged', were the words. I am not an old man, but I am older than you. It is your vigour and my wisdom working together that bring success. Alone they could accomplish nothing."

"Very well," the young brother replied, "but I still don't know why you chose me for this part."

They pretended to sleep, until they were roused by the old one.

"It is time now. The girls have assembled. You must not look at them, for it is a sacred dance that men are not allowed to see. Turn your backs and watch the wall of the cave."

The brothers were fascinated by the dance that followed. Flames darted out of the pit, painting the walls blood-red. Silhouetted against the glowing panel were the black shadows of emus, who stretched their necks and leaped in the air, and made graceful movements with their wings.

Out of the corner of his eye the elder Winjarning saw other stealthy movements. The Keen Keengs were sidling round the walls below the shadows. There was a hiss and a roar that drowned the chant and the drums which accompanied the dance. Red and yellow flames shot up to the roof and flowered like waratah blossoms.

"*Now!*" shouted the elder brother.

The younger man darted forward and vanished through the entrance with the Keen Keeng men running after him. They lost him in the darkness and returned to the cave, to discover a strange sight. The elder Winjarning was dancing round the pit, with the appearance of blood and fire, and was followed by all the girls and the older women. He went so quickly that the females became dizzy; one after another they fell sideways and dropped into the fiery pit of the Flame God.

Brandishing their weapons, the men ran to the attack, but they too were caught up in the furious dance that gyrated round the pit of death. It did not stop until the last Keen Keeng sacrificed himself involuntarily to his Flame God.

The young wirinun put his head round the entrance to see what was happening.

"Let us leave this place quickly," said the older brother. "The god is fed, but he has no worshippers. The place is accursed."

They felt their way down the mountain side, skirted the lake, and walked across the plain. Sunlight was gilding the peak of the mountain when they looked back. It was like a tongue of living fire on the rocks. As they watched, the stones tumbled down and a long shaft of flame touched the sky. It sank, and was followed by a cloud of sparks which spun upwards until they were lost to sight. The mountain folded in on itself and settled down until there was nothing but bare flat plain as far as the eye could see. The brothers returned cautiously, but all they could find were swarms of ants scuttling in and out of crevices in the ground.

That night they made their camp far away. The starry mantle of night was spread across the heavens.

"Look!" one of them exclaimed. "The Keen Keengs! The sparks are still there, in the sky; they are telling us that the Flame God and his followers are dead."

THE DOG-FACED MAN

CHEEROONEAR and his six hunting dogs were the scourge of the Nullarbor plain, but no one had ever seen them. It was only at the time of his death that the full horror of the Dog-man was realised. Up to the time of his capture, the man and wife and their evil dogs were but a story to frighten naughty children, or to cause backward glances when the shadows of the trees sprang frighteningly into the circle of firelight. Hunters who came across their tracks were puzzled by deep indentations made by human feet and marks that trailed beside them like the fingers of a hand. What had been most frightening of all was that no one had seen these grim monsters who snatched children, women, and men away, leaving only gnawed bones to bear witness that they had been living people.

There came a summer of intense drought. Leaves drooped limply from the trees, and the land was scorched to cinders and dry earth. Water holes steamed in the sun, and soon dried up. Nothing moved under that burning sky. Human beings had taken shelter near the top of a hill above the last water hole, which was shaded by rocks and bushes; snakes, birds, and animals huddled close to them on the steep hillside.

"What is that?" an old woman croaked, trying in vain to moisten her lips.

The people feebly lifted their heads; with bloodshot eyes they gazed out across the plain. They were too weary to show interest. But one, more active than the others, kept watch. Suddenly he gave a cry of horror. A solitary figure had reached the bottom of the hill and was climbing up towards the water hole. The hair rose on every scalp, for as he came closer men saw such a sight as they had never seen before. The figure was tall and heavily built, with the arms and legs of a man, but his head and ears were those of a dog. From his mouth and chin hung a loose bag like that of a pelican. It was deflated, and the loose folds swung in a hollow in his chest. His arms were unnaturally long, and as he walked they swung to and fro, trailing along the ground. By this the hunters who had sometimes seen his tracks in the sandy soil knew that he must be Cheeroonear.

The Dog-man walked past them to the water hole. As he drank, the bag in his chest began to swell out like a ball, the skin became swollen and distended. He was so thirsty that he gulped the water, careless of the consequences of over-indulgence. Hardly had he taken more than a dozen steps down the hill than he was sick, vomiting water and food which contained human bones and skulls. He turned savagely towards the petrified onlookers and said in a deep, distorted voice, "Now you have seen Cheeroonear; but you shall not live to tell the tale. Long ago it was foretold that if ever I were seen by men and women my death would follow quickly. You have seen me; but I shall wipe out your memories before another sun rises, I, and my wife, and my dogs."

Before the men could reach for their weapons, he plunged off down the hillside, running with great strides which soon carried him across the plain and out of sight.

"Alas, what shall we do?" wailed the old woman who had first seen him.

"Lie in wait for him and kill him when he returns," suggested one of the younger men, and his companions agreed.

"Wait a moment," a wise old hunter counselled. "This is no matter for hasty decision. You think you can kill him; but what of his dogs?"

"We shall kill them too."

"And his wife?"

"Kill, kill!"

"It needs more skill than you seem to think. Remember, Cheeroonear has never been seen until today. It was not carelessness that revealed him to us, but the urgent need for water – a need that has brought animals and reptiles and men together. This is a strange day that will be remembered long after our spirits have left our bodies. Do you think that Cheeroonear has lost the skill to snatch us one by one in the dark? Can you tell where he will come from, he, and his wife, and his dogs? How will you protect your women and children? And where will you be when death melts like a shadow under the trees, darker than night itself?"

"What else can we do?" they asked sulkily. "We must defend ourselves."

"You can try to do that; but if you are as sensible as you appear to be brave, you will seek for help."

"Who will help us?"

"The Winjarning brothers, who respond to every appeal that is made to them. The time has come for you to bury your pride."

The young men consulted among themselves and agreed that the old hunter had counselled wisely. They made a swift journey to the sea, in spite of the heat, and told the Winjarnings of the plight of their tribe.

"We shall come," was the answer. "Take the word back to your people, and tell them not to be afraid. The ancient prophesy that when Cheeroonear is seen by men he will meet his death will come true. Expect us when the moon is at its zenith."

*   *   *   *

At midnight on the night of full moon the bushes parted and the wirinuns walked into the camp.

"Wake up, friends," they said. "There is work to be done."

The people gathered round them eagerly.

"Let the young men stand over here."

The brothers looked at them and counted them, and said, "There are enough of you to do what we want. And you have the moon to help you. Go down the hill and gather as much brushwood as you can. Bring it back here and we shall show you where to put it."

The young men brought piles of brushwood so large that they looked like ants walking underneath them.

The light wood was laid in two long rows hundreds of yards in length, making a path that led to the water hole, and converging to a narrow exit.

"It will be like a kangaroo hunt," the Winjarnings explained.

As the sky began to grow light in the east, the warriors were given their orders.

"Take your weapons and stand behind the barricades. If any of the dogs break through, you know what to do; but if they keep to the path we have made for them, leave them to us."

The women and children were sent off to hiding places among the rocks. Everybody was now in position. A silence hung over the hill and the plain; birds and animals were mute as the light grew stronger. A little breeze lifted over the hill, stirred the leaves, and died away again. From far away came the barking of a pack of dogs.

207

The light was strong enough for the waiting men to see them as they ran up the hill. The dogs were running silently. They stood nearly as high as a man at the shoulder, and there was something blood-chilling as they ran with loping strides, their paws padding softly on the hard ground. Sharp white teeth glistened in their open mouths. One after the other they passed through the bushes and on to the long path bordered by masses of brushwood, between the motionless warriors whose spears and clubs were lifted in the air.

The first dog reached the end of the path and stopped, his muzzle lifted high, his eyes blazing. One of the Winjarning brothers brought his boomerang down and severed the head from its body. He kicked the head to one side and dragged the body clear of the track. The next dog bounded through, and the second Winjarning struck off its head and tossed the body back to one of the warriors. Unsuspectingly the dogs rushed to their doom, and a few moments later the bloodied boomerangs were lowered; six heads and six bodies lay severed on the ground.

The brothers took flint knives from their belts and cut off the dogs' tails, handing them to one of the warriors who had been given special instructions. The silence fell once more. No one moved or spoke. Time stood still while man and beast, bird and reptile and insect waited for what was yet to come. The sun leaped over the hill and mounted into the sky.

Now a hoarse panting broke the silence. Cheeroonear was tired of waiting for his dogs to return and had come up to see what had happened to them. He pulled himself over the rocks with his long arms. The Winjarnings prayed to the Great Spirit, and the hilltop was wreathed in mist. Women and girls wailed as though in mortal fear, and amongst the low bushes six warriors danced and whisked the tails of the dogs so that Cheeroonear believed his dogs were hunting human quarry.

The Dog-man chuckled deep in his throat and raced along the track to help them.

"It is Cheeroonear who has come to kill you," he shouted. "Tremble, you little people, and look your last on the red sun."

His pouch at his throat throbbed and distended in anticipation of the coming feast. He reached the end of the trail. Out of the mist the waddies of the brothers crashed on to his head and struck him spinning to the ground, his arms flailing, his long claw-like hands clutching for the prey he could not find. Again and again the clubs descended until his body lay lifeless on the rocks, with one hand grasping a stone at the edge of the water hole.

The warriors relaxed and women began to emerge from their hiding places; but the brothers whispered a warning.

"Back! The danger is not over yet. Back to your places, warriors and women!"

The men stiffened and returned to their places, the women scrambled back into hiding. The silent vigil began again. Without warning another figure loomed through the mist: it was Cheeroonear's wife. She stood still and listened, but there was no sound to break the silence. She crept stealthily along the path. When the men had seen Cheeroonear they had tightened the grip on their weapons; but at the sight of this woman they shut their eyes for they dared not look at her. Slowly she advanced, step by step, peering into the fog, her ears pricked to catch the smallest sound. Her swollen sides brushed against the bushes. At the end of the path she saw the body of her husband.

The nearest warriors fell on her and hacked her body in two. Then from every tree and from behind every bush rushed the exultant men and women of the tribe.

The two halves of the body twitched. From the upper part emerged a boy. The men recovered quickly from their astonishment and ran towards him, but he changed into a reptile that escaped from under their feet.

Cheeroonear was dead; the six dogs were dead; the woman was dead; but the devil that came from her body is alive in the bush – today!

THE JEALOUS TWINS

THE twins Perindi and Harrimiah were renowned as an example of brotherly love. No quarrels ever marred their affection: they played together as boys, went through their initiation test together and, as young warriors and hunters, worked together as a team. Each esteemed the other more than himself and was proud of his brother's prowess.

Scheming uncles sought them as husbands for their nieces, but Perindi and Harrimiah were satisfied with their own company. They took no notice of the girls who tried to attract their attention, and it seemed as though they might never marry lest their friendship should be broken by women.

Much as they admired the twins, the elders of the tribe were concerned about this.

"It is not natural that two men should live together and not take wives for themselves," grumbled an elder in the council meeting. "It is only what you would expect of twins."

"Don't worry," laughed another. "The girls will soon plan something."

"Then it will be a good thing, as long as they do not offend against our customs."

"The twins will never know what has happened to them," replied the second speaker. "The wiles of women are beyond the understanding of men. The tribal games will soon begin, and we shall see what will happen."

Perindi and Harrimiah took part in the contests. They made their encampment at a little distance from the others, but mingled with the excited young men and women during the day. Sometimes they were separated, and on one of these occasions Perindi met a young woman who had many interesting things to tell him about himself. She said little or nothing about Harrimiah, but she spoke in glowing words of Perindi's physique and appearance, of his prowess as a hunter, and his wisdom.

"All we girls admire you," she said before they parted, "but some of them keep talking about your brother. He has been boasting that he is braver and more skilful than you, and better-looking too. So don't let him overshadow you in the games. Some of the girls expect that he will make you take second place to him tomorrow."

Perindi went home in thoughtful mood. He could not think of anything that Harrimiah had done to belittle him in any way, but dark suspicions flitted batlike through his mind. They did not disappear during the night, but grew darker and stronger than ever.

"I must teach my brother a lesson he will not quickly forget," he thought.

"Come, Harrimiah, we must prepare ourselves for the corroboree," he said in a loud and cheerful voice. "Let me paint your body."

"No, I will do yours first," said Harrimiah, for he dearly wished to see how handsome his brother would look when he was painted.

He took white clay and yellow ochre, and carefully drew circles and spirals, broad bands and wavy lines on his brother's dark body. Standing back to admire his work, he felt that he had done justice to his greatly loved brother.

Perindi felt a moment of remorse. His brother seemed so genuinely interested in seeing that he made a brave show at the games. Then he remembered what the girl had told him and his heart hardened.

"Now I will adorn you, brother," he said. "I will put charcoal on you first to make a background for the pattern."

He smeared Harrimiah with charcoal from head to foot, and painted the patterns, but he made them smudged and indistinct, and they did not stand out clearly.

As they walked towards the main encampment, they were greeted by the young women who came out to meet them. Most of them ran up to Perindi. They surrounded him and bore him away, exclaiming with admiration at the beautiful colours and designs with which he was decorated. A few remained with Harrimiah, but they giggled, as young women often do, and spoke to each other in whispers. Harrimiah was puzzled. He looked across and saw his brother in the centre of a large and admiring throng of girls.

"Is there something the matter with me?" he asked. "What are you laughing at?"

"Nothing, nothing," they assured him, and ran off to join the others.

Harrimiah shook his head in a puzzled manner and sat down by the edge of a pool, wondering why he had been deserted. He was glad that his brother was so popular, and he had no envy in his heart; yet it was strange that the girls should take no notice of him, because it was usual for them to divide their favours equally.

He bent over the pool to drink. When he saw his reflection in the water his eyes narrowed. No wonder the girls had laughed at him! He looked as drab as a crow in his dowdy plumage.

"Perindi is no good at painting," he said aloud. "I did the best I could and everyone is admiring him. I wonder what has happened."

He rose and made his way across to his brother.

"Come on, Perindi," he said. "The girls are in a foolish mood this morning. Leave them and we will take our part in the games together."

"The girls have been admiring the designs on my body, Harrimiah. Now let us see how we can perform in the dances."

"Why did you paint me so badly, Perindi?"

"There's nothing wrong with my painting, brother. Perhaps it is because I have a better body than you that everyone is attracted to me today. But let's see what happens in the dances. I'm certainly a better dancer than you."

Harrimiah was downcast as they walked together. It was the first time there had been any suggestion of competition between them.

In spite of Perindi's boastful words, it was difficult to tell which was the better dancer of the two; that they were both more skilful than all the other young men was never in doubt.

In the wurley that night the brothers had little to say to each other; Perindi was sulky and quarrelsome.

The following morning they were called on to perform the frog dance. Perindi was again admired for his skilful ornamentation, but when the performance was over a number of the girls flocked round Harrimiah and flattered him, loudly praising the energy and grace of his dancing. Perindi frowned. Something seemed to break inside him, and he was consumed with anger as though a fire had been lit in his bowels.

He shouted at his brother.

"I am through with you. From now on you can go your own way and do what you like; but if ever I see you again I will put my spear through your heart!"

He strode off and made a new camp for himself far away from the hunting grounds he had shared with his brother. In the course of time young women became attractive to him, and he married a girl of the Blue-tongued Lizard totem. Harrimiah grieved for a long time. The love he had felt for his brother was not something that could be wiped out in a single day. He suspected that it was the flattery of the women that had turned Perindi against him.

It was lonely living alone. When he heard of Perindi's marriage he realised that there was no hope of reconciliation. He chose an attractive young woman of the Frilled Lizard totem and settled down to married life, discovering that the devotion of a woman who needed protection was even better than affection shared with a brother.

"Perhaps it has all turned out for the best," he was thinking one day when he was out hunting for wallabies. He saw a movement behind a bush and crept round it warily, to find himself looking into his brother's eyes.

"Perindi!" he cried.

Perindi's eyes blazed like flaming coals. He leaped on Harrimiah and fastened his teeth in his throat, tearing the skin from his neck.

Unseen by either of the brothers, their families had drawn near to the scene of the fight. They pulled them apart and led Harrimiah away. His wife bathed his lacerated neck and applied a poultice of ashes of mulga wood. The wound healed, but it left an ugly scar which can still be seen on the neck of the Lace Lizard.

Perindi's vicious treatment of his brother antagonised his own wife and her relatives. They even drove him out of their camp; he took to the bush and developed peculiar habits.

Harrimah's life was changed, too. He had never ceased to love his brother in spite of all that Perindi had done to him. He spent much of his time away from his camp, sleeping alone under the stars. Birds and reptiles, trees and bushes, sorrowed with him in his grief, and their anger against Perindi grew deeper. For Harrimiah the trees lowered their branches to shield him from the burning sun, and the birds sang their sweetest; but to Perindi the trees denied their shade and the birds sang no song. Perindi's heart was like a stone; but his twin felt that his would melt in sorrow.

The birds urged him to take revenge, and promised their support. The trees offered their wood for spears, and snakes their

He shouted and threatened his brother.

poison fangs, but Harrimiah kept on repeating that the only help he needed was in winning back the love of Perindi.

The hopes that he had cherished began at length to fade. Wearily he dug a pit underneath a wattle and a wild apple tree, and lay down in it. The night wind blew the sand over him and he slept. His tears were swallowed by the thirsty earth, which in return gave him peace and rest.

Harrimiah's wife was heart-broken at his long absence. She gathered her friends together and they followed his trail. It wound through the bush and across the empty sands, coming to an end by the shallow grave, which was guarded by a solitary crow.

"Harrimiah is sleeping," the crow told them. "It is the end of his grief. He loves you all – wife, relatives, and brother; but life was not big enough to contain his sorrow. Let him rest. In sleep he forgets."

"He will forget," said his wife. "Peace will come to him in sleep, and when he wakes it will be to the joy of another life."

She begged the apple and wattle trees to receive her spirit and to take the spirits of all her people. The trees embraced them, and continued to stand patiently beside the grave of Harrimiah.

When they bloom he will rise from his grave to new life, and the spirits of his wife and her people will emerge from the sheltering trees and join him in a new world where jealousy and grief are never to be found.

THE DOG OWNERS

OF Newal and his wife and dog it was hard to say which was the most heartless. They lived together in a hollow tree with only one entrance, several feet from the ground. Their access was by means of a log which leaned against the trunk. All three were flesh-eaters, and they enjoyed all kinds of meat except birds.

Their favourite food was human flesh. They had such a craving for it that a great deal of their time was spent lying in ambush trying to capture unwary hunters. At this they became so successful that tribes for many miles round began to grow anxious. Many of their finest warriors and hunters disappeared and were never seen again; no one could tell what had happened to them.

Newal and his dog grew over-confident, and so suffered a shock that taught them a lesson. They were hiding in thick scrub one day when they saw two hunters coming towards them. A kangaroo was feeding close by. The hunters saw it and began to stalk the animal, crawling from bush to bush, getting closer to Newal all the time. He whispered in the dog's ear.

"They will pass between us and the bush over there. Be ready!"

Before long the men were crouching under the very bush which Newal had chosen to hide behind. Both man and dog leaped at them, one with uplifted spear and the other with bared teeth; but these hunters were quick-witted and agile – they snatched their nullanullas and belaboured man and dog until they fled. As one man, the hunters picked up their boomerangs and threw them. The first inflicted a gash in Newal's arm, the second severed the dog's tail at the root.

It was an unhappy man and dog who climbed up the sloping log to the tree house that night. Their wounds took a long time to heal and kept them from hunting. Newal's wife did what she could, but she was only a woman and unskilled in hunting. The only provisions she could gather were roots and grubs. It was many weeks before the man and dog recovered.

"We are weak from lack of good red meat," said Newal to his wife. "Today the dog and I go hunting. Wallaby meat, kangaroo meat, wombat meat will not satisfy me. I need the flesh of man."

He set off with his dog. In the distance they espied a band of young men hunting emus.

"Let us cut one of them off," said the dog.

They advanced stealthily under cover of the scrub, but the sharp-eyed hunters saw the bushes moving and came over to investigate.

"It is Newal and his dog," they shouted, because the news of the man and his dog had become widely known while they were recovering from their wounds. They set off after them and pursued them so hotly that they barely escaped with their lives.

A solemn discussion was held in the hollow tree that night. Newal had been badly scared.

"The whole trouble is that we were seen by the men who wounded us," he said. "Everyone is on the lookout for us now, and we are too easily recognised. From now on we will have to satisfy ourselves with animal meat. When we can't get that we may even have to eat the flesh of birds."

The other two set up a howl of protest.

"You give up far too easily," the dog told his master. "If you can't get what you want by force, you must use guile. We must not be seen together, but you can get what we want by yourself."

"By myself!" Newal exclaimed. "Why should I have all the work to do?"

"Don't be upset. I will play my part. You must go out and walk through the bush until you meet a solitary hunter. Choose one who has walked a long way and is tired and thirsty. Tell him to come to your home where he may rest and refresh himself."

"That is right," the woman said. "We cannot live without human food, and that is how you can get it."

So the following morning Newal set out by himself, grumbling as he went. In the late afternoon he met a hunter and spoke to him ingratiatingly.

"You look tired. Have you come a long way?"

"You can see that for yourself," the hunter answered shortly. "A man does not catch kangaroos easily or quickly."

"You have a long walk before you reach your camp?"

"Yes."

"Then come with me to my home. It is only a little way off. You can rest there and enjoy the coldest water you ever drank. It bubbles from an underground spring inside a hollow tree, and there I live with my family."

The hunter was curious, never having heard of such a thing before, and accompanied Newal to the tree.

"Stay a moment," Newal ordered. He ran up the log and put his head through the entrance.

"Here is our supper," he whispered excitedly. "Are you ready?"

"Ready," growled the dog.

"Ready," grinned the wife.

Newal returned to the hunter.

"All is well. Leave your burden here. Go up the sloping log and put your head through the hole in the tree and look down. There you will see something you will never forget."

The hunger climbed the log, put his hands on the tree trunk, and thrust his head through the hole. The dog sprang at him and sank his teeth in the man's neck, while Newal's wife struck him heavily on the head with her club. His body slid down and fell lifeless at the foot of the tree.

"See how simple it is," the dog barked as he bounded out of the tree and scampered down the log.

"Hurry, woman. Light the fire. It is two moons since I tasted human flesh."

The experiment had been so successful that it was repeated many times. Once more word went from tribe to tribe that some hidden danger lurked in the bush; but no one was able to discover what form it took until one day two strangers arrived in that part of the country. They were tall men and walked with dignity. Everyone made them welcome, and they talked to their hosts until far into the night, telling of the wonderful sights they had seen in their travels. No one dared to ask their names, though there were some who whispered to each other that they might be the Winjarning brothers who had come to do justice.

It was an old man nodding over the fire who discovered the truth. He was dreaming of sights he had seen many years before when a memory rose out of the past. He stood up and in a quavering voice said, "This is Buda Gooda, and this is his brother."

Other men sprang to their feet looking expectantly at the strangers.

"Yes," said the older brother, "you have guessed aright. We

Buda Gooda went slowly up the log ramp.

have heard of your troubles and have come to see whether we can help you."

Tongues were loosened. The visitors were told of the many hunters who had been lost, and how no man knew what had happened to them.

"We will go out tomorrow and will see what will befall," Buda Gooda and his brother promised.

*　　　*　　　*　　　*

Newal met them some miles from the encampment.

"You look hot and tired," he said.

"Yes," Buda Gooda replied, not knowing that this was the man he was seeking. "We did not bring water bags with us and we are thirsty. Do you know where we can find a water hole?"

"I can do better than that," Newal replied. "My home is not far away. It is in a hollow tree in which there is a spring of pure water that bubbles up from the depths of the earth. You are welcome to come and satisfy your thirst."

The brothers went with him.

"Wait here," Newal said to the younger brother. "My wife is a little nervous and will be afraid if two strangers enter her home at once."

Buda Gooda accompanied Newal. In his bones he felt that there was something curious and a little sinister about the man.

"Wait by this tree," Newal said to his guest. "My home is in the hollow tree over there. I will tell my wife that you are coming."

He walked over to the tree, climbed the log, and went inside to prepare his wife and the dog to receive two separate meals. As soon as he was out of sight Buda Gooda tiptoed forward and looked round the camp fire. The ground was covered with skulls and human bones. His brother followed him and hid behind a tree.

Newal returned.

"All is ready," he announced. "Come, climb up the log, and put your head inside the opening. You will see something you will never forget as long as you live."

Buda Gooda went slowly up the log ramp. Before he put his head through the hole he held his parrying shield in front of him. Inside the tree the dog saw the man's head appear. He sprang at his throat, but his teeth sank into the wood of the shield, and he could not let go. Newal's wife struck at Buda Gooda's head, but he caught the club, wrenched it from her hand, and brought it down with such force that her skull was crushed. The dog was still hanging on to the shield. Buda Gooda dashed it against the side of the tree, but as he was doing this, Newal sprang on to the log and swung his nullanulla in a terrific blow directed at the base of Buda's skull.

The nullanulla was poised high above Newal's head when a searing flash of light seemed to pass through him and he fell lifeless from the log. Buda Gooda's brother had fitted a spear to his woomera and sent it whistling through the air to lodge in the heart of the last of the eaters of human flesh.

MUMMULBERY AND THARDID JIMBO

THERE were few giants in Australia. The greatest of all was the mother of the dwarf Woo, whose tear-channelled sides are seen in Mount Gambier. Thardid Jimbo was only seven feet tall . . . but a man of this height is surely a giant among other men. It was a sad day for Mummulbery when he met Thardid Jimbo.

Mummulbery was the gentlest of men. He went his own way and preferred to make his camp far from the rest of his tribe. He had two wives. Being young women, it might be thought that they would have preferred the company of girls of their own age, but they took delight in looking after their man. They were sisters.

The tiny encampment often rang with happy laughter. It was only when all three were together that they felt that their lives were complete; but as they depended on the strong arm of Mummulbery for meat and the industry of the girls for vegetable foods, it was necessary for them to separate during the day. The loneliness of the daylight hours was always compensated by the reunion round the fire in the evenings, and the long hours of darkness were enlivened by the comforting glow of the fires and the sleepy talk in which the day's adventures were gaily related.

One day Mummulbery came upon the fresh trail of a kangaroo. It was a powerful beast and by the time he caught up with it, he had strayed far from his usual hunting grounds. Mummulbery thrust the butt of a long pole into the ground. To the other end he had fastened the wings of an eagle-hawk. He shook the pole vigorously until the wings flapped like those of a bird in flight. The kangaroo stopped to investigate. While its attention was occupied, the hunter crept close to it and clubbed the animal to death before it was even aware of his presence.

Mummulbery picked up his weapons, slung the animal across his shoulders, and turned, to find himself face to face with Thardid Jimbo. The giant, who liked human flesh as a change in his diet, had picked up the hunter's trail and had been following him. Mummulbery was startled, but he spoke words of cordial greeting. A broad grin spread over Thardid Jimbo's face.

"Greetings to you, hunter. I followed you to see whether you

Mummulbery turned to find himself face to face with Thardid Jimbo.

were a man of skill, and I see you are. That is a fine kangaroo."

"Yes," agreed Mummulbery. "It will be better still when its flesh is roasted. I have plenty of meat now. Would you like some?"

"I am rather particular about my food. Come closer so that I can examine it. Now turn round. I can only see the head and legs, the way you are holding it."

Mummulbery turned round for the giant to inspect the body. As swift as lightning Thardid Jimbo severed the hunter's head from his body with a single snap of his strong teeth. He kindled a fire, cooked Mummulbery's limbs, and sat down to eat. It was a huge meal, as befitted a giant: flesh, skin, and bones, all went into his capacious belly. The body was left. He tucked it under his arm and followed Mummulbery's trail back to his camp. His long legs carried him quickly over the ground, and he arrived just as the young women were returning with the day's supply of yams.

They looked up, ready to greet their husband. It was a fearful shock to see the bushes part and Thardid Jimbo's body looming over them. He threw his burden on the ground before them and said, "I am hungry. Hurry up and cook the meat for me."

Their hands flew to their mouths to suppress a scream, for they had recognised the body of their dearly loved husband. But they stood their ground, for Mummulbery had trained them to be resourceful and self-reliant.

"If anything ever happens to me, I want you to be able to look after yourselves," he had often told them. "My brothers would doubtless be ready to marry you if I died, but remember that you see little of your families. You would have to support yourselves during the year of mourning, and I would not like you to be frightened or to go hungry."

They looked at the poor, helpless body and remembered what he had told them.

"We are hungry too," they said. "We will cook a meal for you, but we cannot eat human flesh. You can save the body for another time."

"Very well," Thardid Jimbo replied. "I don't mind what it is so long as it's meat. But hurry up. I am going to take you for my wives because you are fine girls. We will be leaving the camp soon, and we have a long way to go."

"We would be proud to be the wives of such a man as you," said the elder sister. "For the first meal to celebrate our new life we would like you to kill something specially for us."

224

The giant was much flattered by the interest the girls showed in him. "What do you want?" he asked.

"In the cave you can see from here there lives a dingo. It is a long time since we had a meal of dingo meat."

Taking his nullanulla with him, Thardid Jimbo strode off and entered the cave. It was some little time before he returned, carrying an armful of puppies.

"Are these what you want?"

"Oh no. Pups are no good. It's the mother dingo we want."

"I didn't see one there."

"You will have to go right to the far end of the cave."

"A foolish woman's whim," he grumbled, but he went back again.

It was a deep cave. The women knew it would take Thardid Jimbo a long time to go to the end and come back. They gathered armfuls of scrub, piled it up at the entrance till it touched the roof, and set fire to it. The wind carried the smoke into the cave, while the branches crackled and burned furiously. Before long the girls heard the giant coughing and spluttering. The scrub had settled down and was burning fiercely by this time. Thardid Jimbo appeared out of the smoke, begrimed, with red eyes and singed hair, and very furiously angry. He flung his nullanulla at them, but missed. Taking a short run he attempted to jump over the fire; but he had forgotton his height. His head met the rock roof of the cave with a sickening thud, and he dropped unconscious into the fire. There he lay still, and the spirit left his charred flesh.

The danger was over now, but the girls had time to remember their grief. They sat with their arms round each other while the tears rolled down their cheeks. Night and day passed unheeded, for they neither ate nor slept.

Eventually the sharpness of sorrow was blunted, and they were ready to face the future.

"We must ask our father to come and help us," they decided.

So they lit a fire and sent up a smoke signal. Before long an answering column rose from their parents' home. The next day their father arrived, and they showed him the pathetic remnant of Mummulbery's body, laid reverently on a pile of green leaves and branches.

"That is all that is left of our dear husband," they wailed. "He

225

was killed by the wicked Thardid Jimbo. Oh father, can you not bring him back to us?"

"As a wirinun I have great power," their father said gently, "and there is much that I can do for you, my daughters; but to bring the spirit back into the mutilated body of a man is more than anyone could or should attempt. Of what use would a headless, limbless husband be to you? His spirit is happy, clothed in radiant flesh. Is your love for Mummulbery so great that you are willing to throw your earthly bodies away and join him?"

The hope that shone in their eyes was sufficient answer.

"Then let me embrace you for the last time," he said.

The wirinun spoke mystic words and pleaded with the Great Spirit who rules the destinies of his children, begging him to restore his daughters to their husband.

Silence fell, a silence unbroken by the song of bird or insect, or even by the rustling of a leaf, as though the world were waiting for another day to begin. Then before them stood the spirit of Mummulbery, clothed in the flesh that had been so warm and satisfying in days gone by. He embraced his wives, reached out a hand to their father as though in blessing, and mounted up with them into the sky. Their bodies dwindled and were lost to sight in the infinite hunting grounds of the sky while they also remained standing by the cast-off flesh of their husband.

The sorrowful father buried their earthly bodies, and said to himself, "Their light will never stop shining!" and he went off to tell his wife all that had happened.

ABORIGINAL WORDS

INTRODUCTION

READERS of this book will no doubt realise that only a small proportion of the words used by the aborigines of Australia can be included in a book of this size. There were hundreds of languages in use among the tribes. The most that can be said for such a compilation is that it gives a fairly representative selection of aboriginal words from all parts of the continent, arranged both in English and aboriginal alphabetical order, with a short selection of phrases and sentences, and an indication of the origin of the words. The curious, and those who are in search for names of houses, children, boats, and for other purposes, will find a rich treasury of words native to their own land.

There were two main divisions in the languages of the aborigines, northern and southern. The northern region comprised the Northern Territory, the north-western region, part of central Australia, and the Cape York Peninsula. In this large area there was little affinity between the various languages.

The main division of the southern tribes also consisted of many different languages, quite dissimilar from the northern tongues, but having some affinity in structure, and with a number of words which were used by separate tribes whose vocabulary was in other respects quite distinct.

Unfortunately there has never been any uniformity in recording the spelling of aboriginal words. The *Australian Encyclopaedia* quoted an early example of seventeen vocabularies of the Wiradhuri language collected by one research student in which the word for "water" was rendered as kaling, kul'en, karlee, kalleen, galling, kalling, kalli, kullung, kaleen, kalun, karlin, karlee and gulli, and by others as guleen, gulleen, culleen, cully, callein, colleen, collin, cullie and calle. Obviously it would be impracticable to show all the variants of the words in the present volume. On the other hand, well-known variants are quoted after the spelling accepted (often arbitrarily), and also indexed in alphabetical sequence and referred back to the main entry.

Some linguists substitute "k" for "c" in spelling aboriginal words but this has not been followed here, because the change in many well-known words (korroboree for corroboree, koolabah for collabah) would be confusing to the general reader. The spellings given, whether using "k" or "c", are those in common usage.

In earlier comprehensive lists there has seldom been any indication of the area of use of the words quoted. In the present work some attempt has been made to show the location of the words. The superior figures shown in the Aboriginal-English section refer to the following areas:

1.	Western Australia	5.	New South Wales
2.	South Australia	6.	Queensland
3.	Northern Territory	7.	Tasmania
4.	Victoria	8.	Central Australia

The use of a superior figure does not however preclude the use of the word in another area. On the other hand it may have been used only in a single small district, and therefore unknown in the wider territory. The omission of a figure implies either that the exact source of the word has not been located, or that it was in fairly widespread use.

The Aboriginal-English is more comprehensive than the English-Aboriginal section. The words relating to natural phenomena, parts of the body, simple pronouns, numerals up to four (after this number a word meaning "many" was usually employed), and other important subjects, have been recorded by many students, and little would have been gained by providing a large number of variants in the English-Aboriginal section.

Listing of animals, birds, fish and crustaceans, insects, plants, reptiles, shellfish, snakes, trees, and weapons and tools, are given under these general headings in the English—Aboriginal section. For convenience, these listings follow the alphabetical sequence of the aboriginal words and their meanings, rather than the reverse. At the same time the English and Aboriginal words, and their meanings, appear alphabetically and individually in the appropriate sections of the book.

Many books and periodicals have been consulted in the preparation of the lists. The most valuable were those that were published early in the history of European exploration and settlement, when missionaries, amateur anthropologists and philologists, and others rescued some of the vocabularies before the tribes became extinct. It is impossible to acknowledge all the sources, for an odd word or two has sometimes been taken from a single book. Grateful acknowledgment is made to the following publications:

Edward E. Morris: *Austral English* (Macmillan and Co. Ltd); K. Langloh Parker: *Australian Legendary Tales* (Angus and Robertson Ltd); W. Ramsay Smith: *Myths and Legends of the Australian Aboriginals* (George G. Harrap & Co. Ltd); K. C. McKeown: *The Land of Byamee* (Angus and Robertson Ltd); Ursula McConnel: *Myths of the Munkan* (Melbourne University Press); and the following works long out of print: A. M. Duncan Kemp: *Where Strange Paths Go Down*; E. I. Watkin: *Australian Native Words and their Meanings;* G. Taplin: *Folklore, Manners and Customs;* W. H. Willshire: *The Aborigines of Central Australia* and *The Aborigines of South Australia*, and early issues of *The Science of Man*.

Mention must also be made of the Australian Institute of Aboriginal Studies (Box 553, Canberra) which as one of many activities, concerns itself with the study of Aboriginal linguistics, including the standardisation of spelling and pronunciation.

With its many shortcomings, some of which no doubt are attributable to the compiler, and others due to a study which can never become an exact science, the publishers hope that the little book will be useful as well as interesting. To those who wish to pursue the subject further we commend the advice of Sidney J. Baker in his excellent work *The Australian Language* (Angus and Robertson) pp. 218-9: "The most extensive work . . . is probably *The Australian Aboriginal Dictionary* by W. Bishop (1929) which is in MS. form in the Mitchell Library, Sydney. This contains many thousands of terms, but is rather a catalogue than a dictionary. No effort is made to indicate the dialects or districts to which the words belong. An incomplete although interesting *vocabulary of Aboriginal Words and Names* was published in 1916 by James J. Baylis, but contains some patent inaccuracies. Another work—again incomplete and misleading—in MS. form is a *vocabulary of New South Wales Aboriginal Dialects*, compiled by members of the staff of the Mitchell Library, Sydney (1908)."

To these, and the books mentioned above, we would add the collection by Sydney J. Endacott entitled *Australian Aboriginal Words and Place Names*, now published by Georgian House, which is currently in print in an enlarged edition.

A.W.R.

WORD LIST

ENGLISH-ABORIGINAL

A

abduct: pettin
aborigine: arrilla; daen
above: booloot; kerau kiath
abundance (abundant): kembla, ngruwar
abuse (verb): ngaiyuwun
acacia: boobyalla; coobah; mulga; sallee
accompany: wallin
ache (verb): wirin
adolescent girl: wirreebeeun
adultery: moruldun
affection: woorinyin
afraid: blukkun; gerringong; gnoyalanna; jirrand; wai-i
after: ung

ABORIGINES

afternoon: kulkawura
again: kangulandai; munganye
against: nerambo
agreement: monomeeth
ah!: yakkai
alarm: blukkun
alas!: eeo eeo
albatross: pookanah
alive: tumbe
all: ngruwar; parehana
almost: ngak
alone: konkinyeri; naityi
along: illpun
also: inye
altogether: ipminger
always: kaldowamp
amateur: myall
ambush: gerringong
ancestor, totemic: pulwaiya
ancient: ranwul
anger: ngraye
angry: cooler; ngrakkuwallin

ANIMALS:

alait: dog
alli: dog
aloota: kangaroo rat
alpugi: kangaroo
arinya: kangaroo
arrurrer: kangaroo
arutchie: native ferret
baan: dog
baarlijan: platypus
bailaquar: bullock
bamburr: kangaroo
banjora: koala

banya: black-tailed possum
beereek: native cat
berontha: flying squirrel
biggoon: water rat
bilba: bandicoot; bandicoot rat
billeang: bat
bindar: kangaroo
bohra: kangaroo
bokkar: dog
bonelya: bat
boolgana: kangaroo
boondar: kangaroo
boorbee: native bear
buggoo: flying squirrel
bukkandi: native cat
bullula: kangaroo
bunderra: black wallaby
burra burra: sheep
burrendong: native bear
butterga: flying squirrel
carbora: native bear
coolabun: native bear
cowirrie: rat
durda: dog
erawar: rock wallaby
ertargwar: rat
gaya-dari: platypus
goomai: water rat
goonur: kangaroo rat
inger-godill: horse
innar-linger: echidna
jirrah: kangaroo
joatgba: kangaroo
kaddely: dog
kangaroo: kangaroo
kekuyan: spiny ant-eater
keli: dog
kinie-ger: native cat
koala: native bear
koob-bor: koala
kooim: kangaroo
koola: kangaroo
koonappoo: mouse
koongarra: kangaroo

kooraltha: spotted ferret
kroman: kangaroo
kulai: echidna
kulan: possum
kulla: koala
kundal: dog
kur-bo-roo: koala
kur-rook-ar-rook: koala with young
kwimpy: kangaroo
kyema: kangaroo
leena: possum
longootpar: kangaroo
lottheggi: bat
madba: kangaroo
madhi: dog
maikurri: bandicoot rat
mammerool: dog
mangaroo: phalanger
mari: wallaby
marloo: kangaroo
miga: dog
minyun: kangaroo
mongan: a mammal
moochambilla: kangaroo
moodai: possum
mooroo: bitch
motthari: seal
munthu: kangaroo
murra-wunda: climbing rat
murri: kangaroo
myorli: small red kangaroo
naggi: dog
narahdarn: bat
nargoon: koala
ng'rui moch: native cat
nilee: bush rat
nurrumpi: koala
omalwin: kangaroo
pademelon: scrub wallaby
pargi: wallaby
piggi-billa: echidna
pongo: flying squirrel
porlta: possum

potoroo: kangaroo rat
pulyara: long-snouted rat
pundeol: mouse
pundi: dog
punkunduli: bandicoot rat
puppa: dog
purnung: dingo
purtia: kangaroo rat
qualpar: large rat
rekaldi: water rat
taranna: wallaby
tarmaroo: possum
theen-who-ween: platypus
thirlta: kangaroo
tjukaro: kangaroo
tuan: flying squirrel
umorra: rat
uwurta: bush wallaby
wallaby: small kangaroo
wallaroo: large kangaroo
warreen: wombat
warregal: dog
warrew: wallaby
warrie: dog
warrigal: dog
waroo: kangaroo
warta: wallaby
wenjoitj: kangaroo
werunnunn: dog
windawitycri: bullock
wirlpa: hare
wirngill: native bear
wombat: a marsupial
wongguri: ring-tailed possum
wuka: flying fox
wurgulin: short-legged kangaroo
wutta: dog
wyehoota: possum
yallara: long-eared bandicoot
yangatan: native cat
yangor: kangaroo
yarraman: horse
yarraringy: possum

yarri: native bear
yarunmundule: bat
yelka: dog
yukunder: kangaroo

ankle: tunge
anoint: tyetin
another: kangulun; kaso; kultha; kutsha; yammine
answer (verb): werentun
ant: prilde; teeta; wirpa; yerra
ant, bulldog: carltooka; kotbityerowe; nalgarmyeri; tokiejonburnba
ant, small black: minga
ant, sugar: yeramba
ant, white: mirta; odunepa
ant-eater: kekuyan; piggiebilla
anxious: pairpin mewe
any: hii hii
apart: konkinyeri
appear: pappora; terpulun
apple, kangaroo: gunyang
arm: erricha
arm, lower: puthawing
arm, upper: tyele
armpit: elunba; ngiakkai
arrange: yuppun
arrive: puntin; tainbarilin
arrowroot: wiinki
as: luk
ascend: loru; wangkin
ash, Moreton Bay: ilumba
ash, mountain: warreeah
ashamed: kulyulaikin; palthawangalnappa
ashes: narcoola; quinja
ask: kurrin; reytyunggun; wankin
asleep: oongarra

assemble: torarin; yuntuwar-rin
at: noondha
athletic: carrangall
attack one man: throttun
aunt: barno; konkea
aunt, maternal: num-ba-di
Aurora Australis: Pillie thillcha
autumn: marangani
awake: kinma
away: konk
axe, stone: mogo
axe, wooden battle: woggara

B

baby: birra-li; milla milla; puka; umbacoora; wangoo-ra
baby girl: quei-marla-goobita
back: artippa; moorapoo
backbone: ngiampi; polgumpi
bad: ngontha; thulga; wadleena
bag: dilly; wanka; yergutta
bag, food: koorngoo
bag, kangaroo skin: kumbi; punauwe
bag, skin water-: attower
bag, string: goolay; mera; wullanti
bag, water-: gulli-mayah
bait: berley
bald: dooliba
ball: pulyugge
ball game: pulyugge
bamboo: omil-dadgee
banana bird: nutam
band, forehead: garbai
bandicoot: bilba; punkundu-leol

BANDICOOT

bandicoot, long-eared: yallara
bandicoot rat: bilba; punkunduli; maikurri
bandicoot, spotted: mikurri
bank: engorra; thacka
banksia: werite
banter: borak
bare: merate
bark (verb): ronggummun; kunakunakasno
bark, tree: bingarra; opera-yenpa; pulthar; yulthi
bark hut or **shelter:** dardur; gunyah; humpy; wurley; mai-mai
barking lizard: wallu-barl
bark of kurrajong tree: mooroomin

bark vessel for holding water: wirree

barracoota: kyena

barramundi fish: anka

barter: munmunde

barter shell: arama; wela

basket: beenak; tareema

bat: billeang; bonelya; lottheggi; narahdarn; yarunmundule

bathe: boge; pullun; yakake

battle axe; wooden: woggara

bay: thalme

beach: booner; minna

beach, sandy: koynaratingana

bean tree: enunta; irtalie

bear native: see koala

bear, native, with young: kur-rook-ar-rook

beard: ngernka; yaran

beardless: tolai

beat (verb): began, marnin, mempin

beat time: winamin

beautiful: dandloo; endota; nunkeri; wambalano

beauty: eleebana; elleenanaleah; lowanna

because: marnditye

bed: tudhuki; yoyangi

bee: warra-nunna

bee, brown: ollo

bee, honey: kuyan

bee, small black: cooba

beech tree, white: binburra

beefwood tree: illginga; mubbo

bees' nest: calimpa

bees, sign of: coorigil

beetle, black: ouratta

beetle, orange and blue: noora-gogo

beetle, water: boongurr

before (in front of): ngunggurank

before (of time): ungunai

beg: raraityungun; wankin

behind: karlowan; mangka; nananook

believe: wurruwallin

bellbird: jumjum

belly: atnitta; bingy; kurunto; mankuri

below: moru

belt, man's: wakoola; waywa; bor (the "belt of manhood", invested during initiation ceremonies)

beneath: maremuntunt

bend (verb): kertun; leewun

BELT

bend (trans. verb): menaikundun

bend, river: ngarte; thuckara

bent: pipa

beside: thinana

between: tarangk

bewitch: millin; ngadhungi

beyond: moondah

bidyan ruffe (fish): kooberry

big: booral; buntor; ecmurra; grantali; murna; proi

billy: wolbitta

bird: otayba

BIRDS:

aroo: cygnet

arunta: white cockatoo

atyimba: emu

baiamul: black swan

barook: teal

bartill: parrot

beela: black cockatoo

beereegan: quail

beerwon: swift

benalla: musk duck

berallah: musk duck

berigdra: orange-speckled hawk

berontha: crow

berrimilla: kingfisher

betcherrygah: budgerigar

biaga: hawk

bibbi: tree-runner

bilbungra: pelican

billai: crimson-wing parrot

bilyana: wedge-tailed eagle

bilyarra: eagle

bingami: mopoke

boobook: mopoke

boogoo-doo-ga-da: rain bird

boolongena: emu

boolungal: pelican

boondoon: kingfisher

booran: pelican

bootoolga: blue-grey crane

brolga: native companion

bullai bullai: green parrot

bulln-bulln: lyre bird

buln buln: green parrot

bulooral: night owl

burrandool: quail

burrengeen: peewit

carnka: crow

chipala: whistling duck

chippia: duck

cockalella: white cockatoo

currawong: bell or black magpie, donkey bird, or crow-shrike

curriequinquin: butcher bird

curringa: black duck

deereeree: willy wagtail

degeen-boya: soldier bird

dinewan: emu

dulloora: small grey bird

du-mer: brown pigeon

durroon: night heron

eerin: small grey owl

galah: rose-breasted cockatoo

ga-ra-ga: crane

garaweh: white cockatoo

garganj: chicken hawk

gidgerigar: small parrot (budgerigar)

gooboothoo: dove

goola-willeel: topknot pigeon

goolay-yali: pelican

gooloo: magpie

goomble-gubbon: bustard turkey

goonaroo: whistling duck

goonarook: wood duck

goonawarra: swan

goroke: magpie

gowi-nee-bu: robin redbreast

gumalkoolin: willy wagtail

hungappa: crow
iyebana: peewit
jabiru: stork
jenning-gherrie: willy wagtail
jumjum: bellbird
kaar: white cockatoo
kakalan: chicken hawk
kalperri: shoveller duck
kaltee: emu
kaneky: yellow-crested cockatoo
kauert: swan
kearka: bower bird
kelunji: galah
kibulyo: whistler duck
kilkie: water hen
kirli: coot
kirrkie: whistling hawk
kirrpiyirrka: seagull
koa: crow
koiranah: eagle
kolet: dove
konkon: white fish hawk
koodnapina: brown duck
kookaburra: laughing jackass
koolootaroo: magpie lark
koolyn: black swan
koorowera: black diver
koortgang: speckled teal
kora: native companion
korneok: whistling duck
korrorook: stork
koruldambi: white owl
krowalle: blue crane
kuboin: scrub pigeon
kultown: duck
kumalie: small duck
kuracca: crestless white cockatoo
kurrowera: shag
kur-ur-rook: native companion

kuyulpi: parrot
lidjet: finch
lirralirra: wren
lowan: mallee fowl
mantaba: bustard
marbangye: black diver
menmenengkuri: martin
millemurro: pelican
miowera: emu
moatah: pigeon
monti: stork
mooaloonyah: pigeon
moogana: white-breasted shag
moogra-ba: black-backed
magpie
mooregoo: mopoke
mooroocoochin: black swan
mooyi: white cockatoo with
yellow crest
mugana: willy wagtail
mulduri: magpie
mullian: wedge-tailed eagle
mulundar: swallow
munggi-wurray-mul: seagull
munkᴄr: small hawk
murranudda: bustard
murrara: duck
nakkare: musk duck
nangkero: pelican
ndruila: native companion
neenca: sparrow
neeyangarra: eagle
ngerake: teal
ngutam: banana bird
nierrina: hawk
nompie: wedge-tailed eagle
nutam: banana bird
nyungu: Torres strait pigeon
oorooninannee: grey owl
ooya: quarrion parrot
ooyan: curlew
orra curra: large owl
orrapoora: magpie

padilpa: parrot
paipan: black ibis
panje: black-eared cuckoo
pelde: musk duck
pengana: hawk
pewingi: swamp hawk
pillambi: black cockatoo
pinpi: parrot
pinyali: emu
pipipa: sandpiper
piralko: native companion
pookanah: albatross
poorparta: sparrow hawk
powenyenna: magpie
prolggi: crane (brolga)
punkerri: brown duck
punnamoonta: emu
pupperrimbul: spotted-side finch
puratte: black and white shag
puyulle: emu wren
ragaralti: egret
tallarook: wattle bird
tallawong: bell magpie
tamba: ibis
tappak: bronze-wing pigeon
tarkoori: bittern
tarlarang: red-billed plover
tatea: whistling duck
tchaceroo: magpie
teepookana: kingfisher
tempi: swamp duck
tete: kingfisher
thanpathanpa: snipe
tharalkoo: duck
thowla: spoonbill duck
tiltili: magpie
tityarokan: willy wagtail
tloppere: ibis
toolka: Cape Barren goose
tumakowaller: swan
tuta: parrot
tyepi: quail

tyit: fish hawk
unchurunquar: painted finch
ungjeeburra: crane
urra quarra: grey goose
wahn: crow
wainkan: curlew
wakaje: emu
wakerdi: crow
wanye: mountain duck
warritsha: emu
wata: crow
waukatte: small hawk
wauk-wauk-wa: pigeon
wauwakkeri: grey hawk
waylehmina: swallow
weedah: bower bird
weeloo: curlew
weelya: parakeet
weringerong: lyre bird
wili: pelican
windtha: grey owl
wi-oombeen: robin redbreast
wiwieringgere: native pheasant
woggoon: brush turkey
wollowra: eagle
woltsha: eagle
wonga: pigeon
wonga-wonga: pigeon
woorail: lyre bird
woorawa: wedge-tailed eagle
worippa: storm bird
wornkara: crow
wulde: wedge-tailed eagle
wullaki: black cockatoo
wungghee: owl
wurchiewurchie: white owl
wyralla: black and red cockatoo
yara: seagull
yeranda: black cockatoo
yoldi: black shag
yolla: mutton bird

birth, spirits of: Walla-gudjai-wan; Walla-guroon-bu-an
bitch: mooroo
bite: ngolkun; nullgoonie
bittern: tarkoori
black: kineman; kokereka; marroo; ourapilla
black-backed magpie: moogra-ba
blackberry, native: munda-wora
blackfish: weerap
black snake: ooyu-bu-lui
bladder: kaintyamande; towa
blanket: ititika
blaze (verb): kuntun; towulun
bleat: wirakulun
bleek (fish): mado
bless: kaukau
blind: alknarar-killja; boko; milbung; tonde
blood: atnalure; burrabee; gerra; kandora; kruwe; kula; midgee; yeildo; yerricknar
bloody: kruwalde
blow (verb): kumpun; kurunkun; pooney; popa
blowfly: korrumburra; mulgamurra
blue: woorkarrim
blue-gum: eurabbie
blue-tongued lizard: ooboon
blunt: menarte
boat: meralte; warriuka; yuke
boil (noun): engoordna
bone: engwarnar; mulali; neelong; pehah; turika
bone, pointing: gooweera; neilyeri**

B

BOOMERANGS

boomerang: kiley; paketye; wadna; warroo; yerrawar
boomerang, hunting: maki
boomerang, returning: bargan; bubbera
boot: terninyeri; tinabulka
bough: kaki; muldi
bow (verb): meningkundun
bow down: pallarang
bowels: mewe
bower bird: kearka; weedah
box, dwarf: goborro
box tree: angorra; kunakuna
box tree, broad-leaved: bibbil
box tree, flooded: coolabah
box tree, grey-leaved: goolabah
box tree, narrow-leaved: bilkurra
box tree, poplar-leaved: bimbil

boy: apmurika; mutto; ronumdo; weehi; wilyango;
worlba; yerlieyeega

brain: ngurangpar

branch: kandeer

branch, small: ngarlengarl

brand: mah

bread: krepauwe; myhee;
nurong; wikky

break: luwun; yakalya

breakers: lyeltya

breakfast: peggerambe

break in pieces: tipundun

bream: kooberry; tinuwarre;
tukkie

bream, bony: gandjari; wolkolan

breast; ibi; mundi; namma;
ngumpura

breath: injerima; moldar

breath, offensive: injerima
unditta

breathe: narrinyee; winkundun

breathless: piruwallin

bride: carina

bright: ngorkulle; ooliekirra

bring: burreman; morokkun

bring in: yappundun

broke: oltarkim

broken: lulur; yilin

broom wattle: wallowa

brother: binghi; gelar;
uckillya

brother, elder: gelane

brother-in-law: ronggi

brother, younger: tarte

bruise (verb): ngultun

brush myrtle: barranduna

brushwood: looranah

buckbush: unmerta

bucket: yirtuggi

budgerigar: betcherrygah;
gidgerigar

build: ngarrin

bull oak: belah

bullock: bailaquar; windawityeri

bull roarer: churinga; moiya;
pakapaka; gayandi (man's
word); gurraymi (woman's
word)

bulrush: birwain; wonga

bundle: batturi

burn (verb): kulkun; nyrangkin

bury: grauwun; kralin

bush: see scrub

bush fire: kimba

bush rat: nilee

bustard: goomble-gubbon;
mantaba; talkinyeri

busy: burra burra

butcher bird: curriequinquin

butterfish: kundgulde:prand-
yi

butterfly: bulla bulla; undee-
lablab

buttock: lewurmi; piningi

by: il

by and by: palli; yun

C

cabbage tree: konda

cake (made of grass seed flour):
durri

calf (of leg): kur; pordenpar

call (verb): kaikundun; mearann

camp: baanya; ballarat; koonje; koornkoo; oorla; thulloo-munal; upmurra; uralla

camp (verb): wilpy

camp, deserted: oompi bong

cane grass: appunga

cannibal: bunna

canoe: booltaroo; koorong; likoo; mallana

canoe, bark: goombeelga

Canopus: Womba

cape (point of land): pitye; thrumari

Cape Barren goose: toolka

carp: morwong

carpet shark: goonnear; wobbegong

carpet snake: guridjadu; nurawordubununa

carpet snake, small: dayaminya

carry: thuppun

carry in the arms: pandin

carry off: pintamin

carry on the back: lammin

carry on the shoulder: yityumbarrin

castor oil plant: kudgee

casuarina: see she-oak

cat native: beereek; bukkandi; kinie-ger; ng'rui-moch

cat fish: tandan

cat's cradle (to play): yambalin

catch (verb): argoonie; enamalla; kongwak; nanbundun

caterpillar: kelgelli

caught: loorapa; nanbundelin

cause: nungana

cave: narkindie

cave dwelling: gibber-gunyar

caw (verb): wakulun

celebration: yackic

centipede: uaburika

ceremony, initiation: bora

chalk: boolpooli

champion: yoyangamalde

chant: ringbalin

charcoal: yalta

charm (verb): millin; ngadhungi

cheek: make; pertill-lerra

cheerful: narbethong

cherry tree, native: ballat; panpande

chest: munde; omenderry; tuldengk

chew: yayin

CARPET SNAKE

chicken hawk: garganj; kakalan

chief: rupulle

child: motepa; porle; tyinyeri; warooga; umbacoora

childbirth: punden

children: koolyangarra

chin: nootoo; numbe; orodina; wacka

chip (verb): drekin; tultun

chisel: binyana

choke: tummun

choose: tambelin

chop (verb): balgoungo

chough (bird): waybung

cinders: keni

circle: arrinyenin; riawunna

circular: larelar

claw: beri; ulbra-cullima

clay: maitlia; tyelde

clay, yellow: wilgee

claypan: alteripa; marloorie

clean: balpewallin; ooliekirra

clean (verb): nyrippin

clematis: minamberang

clever: munkumbole; wi

clever man: koradji; wirinun

clever stick: wimouyan

climb (verb): anjee-malla; caloola; pinera

climbing-rat: murra-wunda

cloak: maiyinggar

close (verb): muriltpun

close (adj): ngake

closely woven: kuranye

clothes: see garments

cloud: hotooworry; makoo; moorang; okolyer

cloud, white: jombock

cloudy: moki

clover: kuloomba

clover fern: nardoo

club: kanake; kutha; marpanye; plongge

club (with head bent at an angle): leawill

club (with heavy head): nullanulla

club, double-pointed: mattina

club, fighting: kalduke

club, long: boogoo

club, short: nunkardeol

club, war: waddy

club-headed weapon: boondi

Coalsack, The: Gowa-gay

cobweb: ngilde

cockatiel: ooya; ouyarh

cockatoo: yongana

cockatoo, black: beela, pillambi; yeranda; wullaki

cockatoo, black and red: wyralla

cockatoo, crestless white: kuracca

cockatoo parrot: ouyarh

cockatoo, rose-breasted: galah

cockatoo, white: arunta; cockalella; garaweh; kaar; mooyi

cockatoo, yellow-crested: kaneky

cockle: kuti; tagera

codfish: goodoo

cod, Murray: ponde

cold: appointa; boolea; kilpalie; mia; munyertoo; paiala, yake; warr-ringa

cold (adj): nruwi

collect: torauwun

come: arndu; burremah; go-oh

come back: yaldeeme; yawoma

come down: yorlun

come here: alleari; kowia; purni ngomerna; warrawee

come on: nallak; pichi-malla

command: taiyin

companion: mullaya; nara; waminoa

company of people: meli; milpara

compassionate: ooyella

conceal: nampulun

conch shell: pundira

conference: yarnirumi

content: noojee

continually: kaldowamp

contrary: ngrelggi

CROCODILE

convolvulus: tharook

cook (verb): nammin; prempun

cooked: imbunga

cooking place: myrniong

cool: kilpa; murunkun

coot: kirli

corner: nanowie; ngarti

corpse: utem

cotton bush: mootcha

cough: attong-givilina; cullgenborn; memerangi; ngingeranggi

cough (verb): ngrengkulun

count (verb): tumpun; yelpia

country: mirrow; pimble

cousin: nguyanowi; nonedia; runde

cover (verb): poltha

cover up: turelin

coward: turi kalkir

crab: karlye; krangalang; ugundyi

cramp: plowallin

crane: ga-ra-ga; prolggi; ungjeeburra

crane, blue-grey: bootoolga; krowalle

crane, white: ragaralti

crayfish: kuniekoondie; meauke

crayfish, small: yabbie

creek: billungah; carroo

creek, small: kurrnung

creek which dries up in summer: koorrnong

creep: malkin

crocodile: kambara; kurria

crocodile, freshwater: kena

crocodile, saltwater: pikuwa

crooked: kutkuti; nukuldi; quear; ungiverta

cross (bad-tempered): kunewallin mewe; nyenunkun; talkiwallin

crow (bird): carnka; hungappa; koa; wahn; wakerdi; wata; wornkara

crow shrike: currawang; tallawong

crows, dance of: kwa

crowd: yunt

crowd (verb): marangane; tokkun; yuntuwallin

crush: tipuldun; wurruntun

cry (verb): holanyee; nyerin; parpin; yandarlana

cry out: ngangaranden; taikundun

crystals, magic: gubbera

cuckoo, black-eared: panje

cure (verb): ngrallin; nguldun; patyuwarrin

curl (noun): lamaldar

curlew: moolyera; ooyan; wainkan; weeloo

currant, native: karoom; palberry; ungolar

curse (verb): naiyuwun

cut (verb): ampan; coondanie; karrabai; katan; illdo-malla; merippin

cygnet: aroo

cypress pine: jinchilla

D

dance: corroboree

dance (verb): korobra; ngrilkulun

dance of the crows: kwa

danger: birrie

dark: boolool; ingwa; markrah; moabu; moonga

darkness: ngende; yonguldye

daughter: ngarra

daughter, eldest: pangalarke

dawn: kyeema; trelin ngreye

day: bertana; booroowal; ellhimalla; koora; nunga; pirria; wooremolleen; woorun

day after: kinankurnunk

day before yesterday: kangulun nungge

day, fine: naweenda

daylight: arrah-cardie; awring-gamalla; chintu-ruigin; minkie; woodgera

dead: bong; ill-loong; piruwallin

DANCES

deaf: irita; plombatye; womba
death: pornurumi
death (spirit that warns of coming): Yowi
death adder: tityowe
death, place of: gunmarl
death wail: goonai
decayed: mirramirildin; pentin
deceit: merrina; wininaru
deceive: winin; yelpulun
decision of the elders in council: tendi
deep: gauware; kummun; quorna; yepperta
delay: garalin; tortuwallin
demon spirit: coocoo-loora; marmoo
deny: nanampundun; tyirpin
depart: nainkulun
depend on: nyerin
depression (forming a natural water hole): gilguy
descend: yorlun
desert: pindan
desert oak: orra-curra; yerracoppa
desire (verb): duwatyin; parpin mewe
destroy: jindivik; kilkilrarin; ngoweyin
devil: arrunja; brupe; melape
devil, bora: gayandi (man's word); gurraymi (woman's word)
devil-devil: muldarpe; wulgaru
devil, mountain: minn-narie
devil, water: mulloka

DIGGING STICKS

devil, whirlwind: wurrawilberoo
devil's bread (fungus): wayway
devils, white: wunda
dew: bananee; ildmurra; pilepi; warroong
diamond-leaved laurel: burrawingie
diarrhoea: prangpin
die: barloona; kukabuka
died: porn il
different: malde
dig: kaltin; towarnie; wyera
digging stick: gunni; wanna
dingo: kua; purnung
dirt: pilbe
dirty: pilbiwallin
disappear: ngokkun
disappeared: tottung

DINGO

discard: wanta
discussion: yarnirumi;
(yarny rumour)
disease: yerrakincha
disobedient: plombatye
dissatisfied: nyenkulun
distance, long: beer; bunora
distance, short: kielpa
distant: kummaiyem; kuarun
distinct: narr
district: pimble
dive: tirkundun
diver, black: koorowera; marbangye
divide: threttin
divide amongst: peranbim;
trandararin
doctor: koonkie; kulduke;
makga; wiwirremalde
dog: irinka; kaddely; madhi;
pundi; puppa; ucnullya;
warrigal; warri-kundall;
yelga
donkey bird: currawang; tallawong
don't: bael
dove: gooboothoo; kolet
down: moru; thanga
down (feathers): ngupe; yunde
down in: loldu
drag: yultun
draw (depict): macooloma
drawing: coolbyngga; wolka
draw towards: yultun
dray: thettherre
dream: aljerer; chooka-
chooka; pekeri
dream circle: droonoodoo
dream spirit: doowi
dream spirit (of wirinun):
mullee mullee
dreaming: peggeralin
Dreamland: Alcheringa
dress (verb): yuppundelin
dried: meraldi
drink (verb): alguna; merendamin; muttun; quasha-
unjewma; tenjumar
drip (verb): trippin; yanmulun
drive: pildin; waiyin
drive away: trangkin
drop: bartungaran
drop (verb): trippin; yanmulun
drought spirit: Yalkara
drowned: nunbalo
drum: plangge
dry: errurraga; kakuri;
tyiwi
duck: chippia; kultown; murrara; tharalkoo

duck, black: curringa; nakkare; punkerri

duck, brown: koodnapina

duck, mountain: wanye

duck, musk: benalla; berallah; pelde

duck, shoveller: kalperri

duck, small: kumalie

duck, spoonbill: thowla

duck, swamp: tempi

duck, whistling: chipala; goonaroo; kibulyo; korneok; tatea

duck, wood: goonarook

dugong: warama

dusk: kaoota; milyaroo

dust: holemunda; mure; oldburra; poi

dwarf box tree: goborro

dying: pornun; pulhiner

E

each: yammiam

each other: mulluna

eagle: bilyarra; koiranah; neeyangarra; wollowra; woltsha

eagle, wedge-tailed: bilyana; mullian; nompie; woorawa; wulde

ear: banarra; beekbeek; thina; thultie; yuri

earth: bimble; munda; pompindho; teangi; tya

earth, red: mooroolbark

east: cocararra; gurra; kumbooran

east wind: gun-ya-mu

eat: mungi; nucka; patter

eating: algooma; nullgoonie; takkin; yayin

echidna: innar-linger; kulai; piggi-billa

echo: iyoura

edge: dilkera

eel: noyang

egg: ambo; booyanga; pateenah; pipi; pompo

egret: ragaralti

eh!: ke

elbow: kuke; neecoo

elder: inkata

elf: nungheenah

ember: kene

embrace (verb): moondani; plunden

emerge: terpulun

empty: maratulde; pek

empty (verb): pekin

emu: boolongena; dinewan;

ECHIDNA

kaltee; miowera; pinyali; punnamoonta; warritsha

emu shoes: kurdaitcha

emu, solitary: gundooi

emu spear: mooroon

emu tail feathers: boobootella; kunarle

emu wren: puyulle

emus, flock of: yallart

end: dalthing; puttheri

enemy: yenamalde

enjoyment: monomeeth

enough: kunye; yikkowun

enter: yappulun

entangle: yenempin

epileptic fit: kungenyeriwallin

equal: mani

escape: tekin

eucalypt: bibbil; coolabah; karri (used only for the W.A. species)

eucalypt, timber of: bangalay (used only for mahogany gum)

evening: kaoota; kongka; pangarinda; tong; wattangger

evening star: marbeangrook

ever: kaldowamp

evergreen: tumbeelluwa

evil: kadaitcha; mungunni

excellent: budgeree; nunkeri

excrement: kunarl kurta

expect: nyerin

expert: munkumbole

extract: yunkundun

exult: nangurwallin

eye: alkingar; cooroo; mea; midna; mil; moonoroo

eyebrow: mague; nanbimba

eyelash: illpilla; nanbean

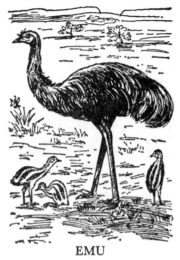

EMU

F

face: petye

fainted: piruwallin

fairy: nungheenah

faith: nglelurumi

fall (verb): ignum; nangalla; ningana

fall backwards: nenengkin

falling: pingkin; wonenie

familiar spirit: yunbeai

fan of emu tail feathers: aroo

far: ku-utyun

far away: katya

farewell: ngoiyun

farm: kulde

fast (speedy): tiwiwarrin

fat: bilpuli; goori: menbi; mooroon; neetee; womma

father: beeyung, cartoo; igeelu; mamma; ngaiyeri; parpinga; uc-neer; yakkoeela

father and child: retulengk
father who has lost a child:
  randli; waltye
fear: jirrand; wai-i; wauwauwi
feather: entoo; yunde
feathers (down): untita
feathers, band of emu:
  wurdwurda
feathers, bunch of: kalduke
feathers, emu tail: booboo-
  tella; kunarle
feed (verb): munguwun
feel: pleppin
female: booyangan
fern: geewan
fern, clover: nardu
fern tree: kakowera
ferret, native: arutchie
ferret, spotted: kooraltha
fertility, spirit of: Mundook
fester: lanyalin
fetch: kldeimindin
feud: dullay-mullay-lunna
few: lakebi; maltaiar
fiercely: murri-cooler
fig: hill-lee; ngarningi
fig, blue: callangun
fig tree: natan; taree
fig tree, rough-leaved:
  balemo
fight: yoyangi
fight (verb): durellie; goon-
  der-rah; mendin; yarrak
fighting stick: worraworra
fill (a hole): thungana
fin: lidjet; manar; wunba
finch, painted: unchurunqua
finch, spotted-sided: pupperrimbul
find: pingyin

finger: illcha; kerlpra; murra;
  punjil
fingernail: geppmorra; melinya; perar
finish: chenka; dalthing; moodunna; nguldin; pekin
fire: booreah; kudla; nandalie;
  warroo; wi; wi-buloo; wur
fire, bush: kimba
fire, large: orucknurra
fire, small: maka
fireplace: goorung
firestick: kene; tauwangi
fire-walking: weeriga
firewood: wiena
firework: poolooloomee
firm: pritye
first: kangulandai
fish: errabunga; kooya; mame;
  wunta
fish (verb): werguttulun; werkin

FISH and CRUSTACEANS:

akama: whale
anka: barramundi
bangnalla: golden perch
barramundi: giant perch
culma: a spiny fish
dyintan: nail fish
gandjari: bony bream
goodoo: codfish
ita: swamp fish
kaandha: whale
karlye: crab
kondarle: whale
kongoola: river fish
kooberry: bidyan ruffe or silver
  perch
koo-ee-lung: porpoise
kringyang: sand mullet

kunara: tiger shark
kundgulde: butterfish
kyena: baracoota
lerunna: flounder
luderick: black fish
mado: bleek or trumpeter fish
mallowe: Murray mouth salmon
maray: pilchard
meauke: crayfish
miitinta: sea turtle
morwong: jackass fish
nannygai: redfish
ngarakkani: shark
noyang: eel
otama: porpoise
pomeri: mud-fish
ponde: Murray cod
prandyi: butterfish
puntyaiya: swamp turtle
tandan: cat-fish
tarki: perch
tealedyan: shark
tinuwarre: bream
trata: knight-fish
tukkeri: flat, silvery fish
tukkie: bream
tupong: marble-fish
tyeli: swamp fish
ugundyi: crab
umpara: stingray
warama: dugong
weerap: blackfish
welappe: mullet
wi: a small fish
wirralee: gin-fish
wobbegong: carpet shark; snapper
wolkolan: bony bream
wollomai: snapper
yabbie: small crayfish
yauoanggi: porpoise

fish hawk: tyit

fish hawk, white: konkon
fishing line: nunggi; perlka
fishing net: kulkulook
fish trap: barameda
fist-fighting: nguldunguldelin
five: kuk kuk ki; ngerla; yeyakki
flame: aloripma; color; leripma; ngorkulli
flap (verb): mapa
flat: nanarlin; wurrook
flathead, freshwater: tupong
flea: tittadi
flee: nginbundim
flesh: kooka; manba; ngulde
flick: pernmin
flock: malyar
flood: koorpa
flood water on polygonum flats: warrambool
flounder: lerunna
flour: nunungki
flow (verb): adnamira; pombulun; raiaralin
flower: patya; thiewie
flowers, place of: girraween
flute: ulpirra
fly (insect): bun-yal; mongana; tyilye; yumbera
fly (verb): koomeela; ngarntin
fly, march: ill-lulta
flying fox: wuka
flying squirrel: berring; buggoo; butterga; mangaroo; pongo; tuan
fog: ubeeterra
foliage: muldi
follow: warreyin
fondle: tunkun
food: diale; mai; myrna

food (fruit and vegetable): mai; maiye; ngune

food, animal: kooka; mam; ngulde

food bag: koorngoo

food, bush: rarkee; undarnga

food for a journey: potyanambe

foolish: bailpulun

foot: chinna; jenoong; mintchie; mundooie; thina

footprint: geenong; tshina

for: ambe; arami

ford: penghanah

forehead: bruye; nullar; rogoona

forehead band: garbai

foreign: malde

foreigner: yammin uwar korn

forequarter: tuldi

GALAH

forest, dense: kiambram

forget: bailpulun; tainpulun

four: koorunga; wima

friend: mullaya; ngaitye; runde; waminda; wirake

frighten: nganden

frightened: hatarear-amalla; turlin

frightening: thrunkun; turlemindin

frog: bun-yun bun-yun; menperre; tata; tiddalick; yuaia

frog, bull: tuki

frog, climbing: tendu

frog, green: withinka

from: anyir

frost: parattah; peti

froth: kulde

frown: indarnie; pilkundun

fruit: nunungki

fuel: ooeena

full: yalkin

fun: borak

fungus (devil's bread): wayway

fur: inntoo; yunde

future: paldi; yun

G

galah: kelunji

galaxy: warring

game, wild: kembla

games: riawena

gap: undia

garment: kambie

garment (cloak): maiyinggar

garment (woman's skirt): goomilla

garment, skin: poltha

garments: mundarra

gently: mant
geranium: iperta
get: morokkun
get inside: thopramolla
get on: thopramolla
get up: akamarei
ghost: moma; onya; wunda
ghost, female: pino
gin fish: wirralee
girdle: see belt
girl: bami; birra-li; cue-on-buntor; lowana; unkeegeega; whitkitha
girl, adolescent: aragoodgea-wonga; quei-marla; wirree-beeun
girl, big: quei-marla; yar-tuwe
girl, little: cue-on-mema; quei
give: antye; gnoka; pempin; ungooroo; warrina; youhi
glad: carbethon; kunthun
gladness: kunthuld
go: loru; ngomerna; ngowalle; padewer; yan
go!: ngowalour
go away: brimhillah; yinbai-kulun
go away!: taiyin; thrunkkun
go back: colba; collumbum
go before: ngunkurawallin
go down: birrama; loldu; moru
go on: albye; byenie
go up: gulle
goanna: adjunepa; awadabir; beewee; googarh; hurra-mira; mungoon-gali; tatya; weenduga

goanna, short-tailed: klare; munnari
goanna, yellow and brown striped: perindi
goblin: wullundigong
gold: karakara
golden perch: bangnalla
good: boorala; budgeree; goo-runna; gubba; kandelka; nunkeri; yetto
good, being: nunkowallin
goose, Cape Barren: toolka
gooseberry, native: booka-booda
goose, grey: urra-quarra
gorge: undia
grand-child (on father's side): maiyarare
grand-child (on mother's side): bakkare

GOANNA

grandfather: nerbungeron; ngaityapalle; pola; tipi; ulwai

grandmother: bargi

grandmother (paternal): maiyanowe

grandmother (maternal): bakkano

grass: kindyerra; korra; narmar; putta; wongoonoo

grass, good: tour-ur-rong

grasshopper: chintillga; ungee-gungee

grass, rat-tail: jil-crow-aberry

grass seed: doonbur

grass for thatching: illpellpa

grass shelter: nunnoo

grass tree: karwin; nglaiye

grass, wire: elilger

grassy: kilto

gravel: lilla

gravel, brown: coorang

great: battur; cabon; matong; murna

greedy: pele; pulkeri

green: iterika; ngthummulun; norabeetya; thumelin; worooa

grey: kenkulun

grey-haired: kenkank

grind: ngenempin

grindstone (for grinding grass seed): dayoorl; doori

ground: aka; tuni; yerilla

ground, level: wirrelyerna

ground, parched: klallin ruwe

ground, soft: ditta

ground, stony: mrangalli

grow: kringgun

growl: ngrakkuwallin

grub: nuttoo; poontee; yulumara

grub, edible: witchetty

grub, edible (found in banksia): pellati

guard: tupun; turuwun

guilty: ngommi

guilty of murder: malpuri

gully: dheran

gum, edible: tangari

gum of pine or gumtree: pitchingga

gum leaf: ghera

gum; river red: yarrah

gum, slaty-: arangnulla

gum, tuart: tooart

gum, wandoo: wandoo

gumtree: bael-bael; bernaroo; choota; heeterra

gumtree, blue: ballook

gumtree, large: waranyukbeal

gumtree, red: wuri

gumtree, white: tooart; wandoo

gun: pandappure; popogina

H

hailstones: moogaray; paldharar

hair: alta; arkoola; burlkie; dhilla; hooray; kagailya; nguroo; yaran

hair, grey: kuna

half: mirimp; ngalluk; oticha

hand: atnitta; ilchar; mah; murra; turni

hand, left: warrame

hand, right: nunkeri-mari; purrinunggi

handsome: nunkeri
hang: wallin
happy: yackatoon
hard: piltengi
hare: wirlpa
hat: morquita
hatchet: drekurmi
hate: paiyin
have: annin; watyin
hawk: biaga; nierrina; pen-gana
hawk, chicken: garganj; kakalan
hawk, grey: wauwakkeri
hawk, orange-speckled: berigora
hawk, small: munker, waukatte
hawk, swamp: pewingi
hawk, whistling: kirrkie
he: atye; ba; kitye; yato; yetni
head: cobbra; cutta; kokora; konkaer kukaa; kurle; therto
headband (painted white): nulu-gail
head-dress: oogee
heal: tumbetin
healthy: nguldun
heap: batturi
heap up: pokkoremin
hear: coleenie; kungun; ung-roo; yuri
heart: gootagoodo; ngele; otorkweta; panda
heat: goornan; kiata; pukara; woolta
heaven: booloot; bullima
heavens: see sky
heavy: bunckanee; enborra; poonta; thackory

heel: moocoo; retyinne
help carry a load: kalparrin
here: alye; kalyan; nia
heron, night: durroon
hiccough: tummun
hidden: nammuldi
hide: nampulun
hide-and-seek: wahgoo
high: booral; neerim; warre
hill: banool; deetoo; poyma-langta; purri
hill, wooded: moliagulk
hillside: warraroong
hills, many: callemondah
him: ityan; kin; noonga
hip: alknarlee; cullebee; pil-pati
his: kinauwe; yato
hit: balka; battana; poongan-yee
hold: mama; morokkun; tal-dumbarrin; wettinnie
hold on: wonnewarra
hole: auwa; chookola; gnam-ma; iperta; merke; pinah; yeppa
hole, deep: mooroopna
hole in the ground: minga; nerntulya
hole in the side: namero pinah
hole, large: perki
hole, small: merki
holiday: pink-hi
honey: kurmoonah; pinya-towe
honey-ant: yarumpah
honeysuckle: warrah; woorak
honeysuckle tree: lakkari
hoof: inger

hope (verb): wruwallin
horn, bullock's: yourula
horse: inger-godill; yarraman
horse, wild: brumby
hot: comebunyee; kaloola; ottinna; wappilka
house (see also hut): taldumande
how: mengye; yarild
howl (of wind-verb); tullun
howl (dog—verb): lokulun
hunger: ringmail
hungry: hungiaquar; unmaturra; ycyauwe
hunt (noun): konkonbah
hunt (verb): thumpun
hunter: mundurra
hunting ground: noorumba
hurry (verb): murrunmil; tyiwewar; wutherama
hurt (verb): partin; wirin
husband: coorie; lielu; murta; napalle
hut: hillta; mia-mia; ngura; oorla; wiltja; wurley
hut, bark: dardur; gunyah; humpy
hut, grass: nunnoo

I

I: nappa; ngai-i; niu
ibis: paipan; tamba; tloppere
ice: ellulger; plomare; wolka
if: ungun
iguana: see goanna
ill (illness): minga; wirin
immediately: hikkai; karlo
infant: kelgalli; malagenna; milyali; partumbe
inform: rammin; tingowun

c

initiation ceremony: bora; engwura
insect: bulga-nunnoo; mongana; teeta

INSECTS etc.:

arrama: louse
atnaterta: scorpion
bogong: edible grey moth
boongurr: water beetle
brupe: spider
bun-yal: fly
carltooka: bulldog ant
chintillga: grasshopper
chumbee: torpedo bug
cooba: black stingless bee
ill-lulta: march fly
kelgelli: caterpillar
koongun: scorpion
korrumburra: blowfly
kotbityerowe: bull ant
kunabinjelu: mosquito
kundy: mosquito
kuyan: honey bee
mako: edible wood grub
minga: small black ant
mirta: white ant
mongana: fly
mulgamurra: blowfly
murga muggai: trapdoor spider
murule: mosquito
nalgarmyeri: bull ant
nanarinyeri: sandfly
neanye: fly
nokarugge: locust
noora-gogo: orange and blue beetle
nuttoo: grub
odunepa: white ant
ollo: brown bee
oomborra: maggot
ouratita: black beetle

pellati: edible grub
petachall-lily: scorpion
pintapinta: moth
poontee: grub
prilde: ant
teeta: ant
tittadi: flea
tokiejonburnba: bulldog ant
tunkeri: louse
tyilye: fly, maggot
uaburika: centipede
undee-lablab: butterfly
undeneya: wasp
ungee-gungee: grasshopper
unya: louse
uwinnia: mosquito
uwoppa: spider
warra-nunna: bee
warroo-culla: moth
wirpa: ant
witchetty: edible grub
wonka: spider
yarumpah: honey-ant
yeramba: sugar-ant
yerra: ant
yulu-mara: grub
yumbera: fly

inside: maremuntunt
intelligible: narr
intestines: tipi
into: angk
ironbark, narrow-leaved: parragilga
ironbark tree: odenpa
is: el
island: kallakkure; karte; thankomalara
it: ba; kitye; yetni
itch (noun): wirrullummi
itch (verb): kirkuwe; kuwulun

J

jackass fish: morwong

jackass, laughing: goo-goor-gaga; kookaburra
jealous: kraiyelin; toorange
jealousy: biminya
jew lizard: armoolya; kunnie
joint: tunggar
joke (verb): rumalduwallin
joy: kunthuld
joyful: kindilan
jump (verb): taitpullun; walla
jump quickly: walla-walla

K

kangaroo: arinya; arrurra; bamburr; bohra; boolgana; boondar; koola; koongarra; marloo; munthu; woora
kangaroo apple: gunyang
kangaroo, large: wallaroo
kangaroo rat: aloota; goonur; millia; potoroo; purtia

KANGAROO

kangaroo, short-legged: wurgulin

kangaroo skin: cudgewong

kangaroo skin bag: kumbi

kangaroo, small: wallaby

keep: daiyuwun

kelp: koonthooi

kick (verb): atninebeemalla; cundoonie; illgulldenem; ngultun

kidney: purri; therna-perty

kidney fat: yuntheyunthe

kill: mempin; poonganyee; pornumindin

kindle: ngungyen

kingfisher: berrimilla; boon-doon; teepookana; tete

kiss: kunden; moinpunden; neenjeweny; ol-dorry-e-way; tshuppana

KNIVES

knee: jirriman; murtee; tur-tangi

kneel: luwun-turtangk; umbee-leedin-gorra; wakkin-turtangk

knife: drekurmi

knife, stone: muggil; womba

knight-fish: trata

knock: ngurunguldun

knot: kerlpa; tirkeri

know: nglelin

koala: banjora; boorbee; bur-rendong; carbora; coolabun; koala; koob-bor; kulla; kur-bo-roo; nargoon; nurrumpi; wirngill; yarri

kurrajong tree: nonga

kurrajong tree bark: moor-oomi

kurrajong trees, many: too-langatta

KOALA

L

lagoon: beeree
lagoon, freshwater: kolora
lake: boloke; marloorie-buntor; mungkule
lake, brackish: keilambete
lament (verb): plowallin
lame: muntye; turokkul
land: pelepe; ruwe; thockyar; yerta
land, area of: panitya
land beyond the sky: Ungant: Barachi
landing place: krambruk
language: kalde; tunggarar
languid: munainpulun
large: cabon; grauwe
larger: grauwe ru
lark, magpie: koolootaroo
last (final): karlowan atye; ngurukuwarrin
laugh (verb): incarnie; kangkin; kinedana; kinka; kinkuna
laugh at: kanggen
laughing jackass: goo-goorgaga; kookaburra
laughter: karbeethong
laurel, diamond-leaved: burrawingie
lay eggs: pindattulun
lazy: etrakee; hetrala; putta
lead (verb): wrendu; yultun
leaf: baibaiye; illperipa; kirra; palpera
leaf, gum: ghera
leaf, palm: tuta
leak: pombulun
lean on: tauwin
leave (verb): imbye; jeetho; nemmin

leave off: nemmin
leaves: muldi
leech: manninkki; uwa
leg: karaka; mundooie; tarrukengk; wittha
legends: woggheeguy
let out: adaka-palai
lick: arntuney; timpin
lie (falsehood): purragia
lie down: ngar-binya; tantin; woonah; yuppun
life: tumpinyeri
lift: meya; plunden; preppin; walpa
light (adj): dalyo; kaikai
light (noun): baringa; burra; nunkalowe; pitura
light (verb): ngungyen
light, rays of: tyelyerar
lightning: doon-gara; nalin; nalurmi; pinpan
lightning man: Mamaragan
like (similar): luk; nglalin
like (verb): pornun
lime: bulpuli
limestone: drik-drik; marti
limpet: banawara
line: pitti
linger: ngaralin
lip: arrie-enpa; munengk
liquid: pan
listen: nurrungar
listen!: kung our
little: mije; muralappi; narang
live (verb): numberleya; tumbe
live at a place: yallambee
lively: narbeethong
liver: allue; kalkerri; yerhillga

lizard: kendi; lurki
lizard, barking: coorabin; wallu-barl
lizard, blue-tongued: ooboon; wala
lizard, jew: armoolya; kunnie
lizard, large: elloi-jerra; punka
lizard, prickly: kami
lizard, red: gudda
lizard, red prickly: oola
lizard, sand: goolee
lizard, small prickly: beereeun
lizard, wood: bu-maya-mul
locust: nokarugge
log: ngarari
long: gora; mahn; neerim; wattora
long ago: ngulli
long time: arr-reedy
long way: ill-lamanoo; wernma
look: nokuna; tumaquoi
look for: tuyulawarrin
look out: nak our; nunghungee
look round: nanauwun; willkilla
loose: yankulun
lose: jindivik
loud: tyiwewar
louse: arrama; tunkeri; unya
love: wombalano; yooralla
love (verb): kungkungullun; pornun; woorinyan; yoorami; yoorana
love, will: yooralanni
loved: kungkungundun
low (verb): morallie
lungs: pelberrimunt

lying: winin; yelpulun
lying on the back: korowalkin
lyre bird: bulln-bulln; weringerong; woorail

M

mad: pilyaulun; womba
Magellan Clouds: prolggi; wurrawilberoo
maggot: oomborra; tyilye
magic, black: ungwilla
magic stones: gubbera
magpie: gooloo; goroke; mulduri; orrapoora; powenyenna; tchaceroo
magpie, bell or **black:** currawang; tallawong
magpie, black-backed: moogra-ba
magpie lark: koolootaroo
mahogany, swamp or **bastard:** jarrah

LYRE BIRD

mahogany tree: coo-in-new

make: ngarrin; pinjaroo; winmin

mallee fowl: lowan; woggoon

man: atwa; bartoo; korne;
kurda; malie; naroa-mine;
yerdlee

man and wife: nandroya

man, married: napowatyeri

man, old: bartoo-gilbee; pinaroo; wherto

man, unmarried: yan yean

man, white: amerjig

man, young: kaingani; oolyarra; taldree

mangrove: egaie; korpie

mangrove, red: kowinka

manhood: thalera

manhood, girdle of: bor

manna (exudation from tree):
buumbuul; wahler

manna (secretion of insect):
lerp

many: multuwallin; murna;
murri; ngruwar

many times: ngurintand

marble-fish: tupong

march fly: ill-lulta

mark: minar

married man: napowatyeri

married woman: hokarra

marrow: bailpuli

marry: napwallin

Mars: gwai-billah

martin: menmenengkuri

mat: punde; tullingapperi;
yallane

mate: kuldi; mullaya; wiraki

mating fever: unja

me: an; guana; natoah; ngan;
ngottha; nihooloo

mean: thirti

meat: barru; minna

meat, raw: tumbe an ngulde

medicine: ungwarlyer

medicine man: boyla; corad-
ji; kobi; wirinun

meet: thuldun; uwan

melt: yalkundun

mesh: mea

messenger: brigge

messmate tree: kampa

midday: gauwel; kalkree; kardingoola; warridanga

midden, shell: mirnyong

middle: tunte

middle one: tarrinyeri

midnight: odneler

milk: ngumperi; woolladge-
ilkna

Milky Way: warrambool

mine: atchina; guie; mirambeek; ngaitshi

mirage: eer-dher; hipmilta

miserable: talkiwallin

mist: boorrang; injeer-mayjeer; jombok; pouraller

mistletoe: bahn

mix: yultuwarrin

mock: kabbulun; kappin

monster: bunyip; eer-moonan; nulu-yoon-du

monster with two toes:
eleanba wunda

moon: bahloo; bigha; etninja;
merrican-kein; peer; pitoa

moon god: Bahloo

moon, new: ingitja

moonlight: goolara; nulgerong

mopoke: bingami; boobook;
mooregoo

more: kutsha; nerntoma; owademma

more, much: ngruinyerar

Moreton Bay ash: ilumba

morning: barperipna; nooroobunda

morning, early: tong kongka

morning star: mullian-ga; nunkumbil

mosquito: kunabinjelu; kundy; murule; uwinnia

moth: pintapinta; warrooculla

moth, edible grey: bogong

mother: babaneek; gunee; igera; meer; namarra; numba-di; wia; yackhoo; yanga

mother and child: rattulengk

mother-in-law: karinye; nielongan

motherless: kulgutye

mother who has lost child: wirratye

mountain: barree; ngurle

mountain ash: warreah

mountain devil (a spiny lizard): ming-ari; min-jin; minn-narie; nai-ari

mountain, high: wollumbin

mountain range: pullybuntor

mouse: koonappoo; pundeol

moustache: muninyeri

mouth: arrakata; mumnunah; nimi; tar; thunbira; tore; yelka

move: ellin; ngoppun

much: murna; ngruwar; waycoot

much, too: multuwarrin

mud: ditter; menengi

mud-fish: pomeri

mud-shell: kumala

mullet: welappe

mullet, sand: kringyang

murder, guilty of: malpuri

Murray cod: ponde

muscle: ngulde

mushroom: bambra; parrumbal; wanappe

musical instrument: didjeridoo

musk duck: benalla; berallah; pelde

mussel: lokure; munggi; tyelokuri; yea

mutton bird: yolla

my: nganauwe

myall, weeping: boree

myrtle bush: barranduna

myself: kooronya**

NATIVE COMPANION

N

nail: milltee

nail-fish: dyintan

naked: merate; palthawangalana

name: arrainya; mitye; nakame

name (verb): krunkun

narrow: tokorauwe

native or **native born:** myee

native companion: brolga; kora; kur-ur-rook; ndruila

nautilus: wietatenana

navel: bullyee; inyeppa

near: munggai; tapàngk

near me: alyenik: hik alye

near you: tapangk

neck: arruleta; erringer; hontee; kure

necklace: intinne

necklace, reed: tarrgoorn

needlebush: binga-wingul

neighbour: tauel

nest: malunna; ngauandi; oorla; worda

nest, bees': calimpa

net (verb): ngerin; tuldin

net, fishing: kulkulook; ngeri; puntaman

nettle, giant: irtaie

never: tarnalo

new: mokari; ooliekirra

"new chum": munjong; myall

night: biangri; bolool; maltthi; mundil; nuta; wiltcha

night heron: durroon

night owl: bulooral

nipple: ngumperi:

no: baal; bael; illa-illa; jitcha; mopa; mukka; wahl; weumpa

no!: tauo

no good: arcoona; quear

noise, to make a: turrammelin

noisy, to be: panelgorana

none: nowaly; wee-ar

noon: kardingoola

north: alinjarra; gurburra; walkandi

north-west wind: mundewudda

north wind: douran douran

nose: allar; ammoula; mendolo; mudla

nostril: allang-goola; olltoo

not: bael; illa-illa; nowaiy; tarno; tauo

nothing: nowaiy ellin; thundarta

now: au

nurse (verb): plunden; tunkun

nut tree: burrawang

NET

O

oak, desert: orra-curra; yerra-coppa
obtain: morokkun
ocean: panamuna
ochre, red: korralo; olba; werrup
offended: nyenunkun
offspring: milyali tinyeri
often: ngurintand
oh!: yakkai
old: coolbaroo; kaldowinyeri; ranwul; yande
old man: bartoo-gilbee; pinaroo; wherto
old woman: koon-ja-gilbee; meetawarri
one: cooma; goochagoora; tarlina; yammalaitye
open: pintannie
open (verb): ngiralin; ngramin
open!: ngramal
opening: tari
opossum: see possum
orange (colour): milkurli
orange-speckled hawk: berigora
orange tree, native: bingelima; bumble; umbellditta
Orion's belt: amayworra
ornament, string: munda-munda
orphan: kukathe
other: kangulun; yam
our: ngurnauwe
ours: nindethana
ourselves: moonthalie
outside: itye; ngurukwar
oven: goorung; krugapupe; purni
oven, prepare an: prumpun
overcome: wityungyin
overflow: raiaralin
over there: warra
overthrow: pinggen
overturned: ngerakowen
owl (see also mopoke): wung-ghee
owl, grey: ooroowinannee
owl, large: orra curra
owl, night: bulooral
owl, small grey: eerin; windtha
owl, white: koruldambi; wurchiewurchie
oyster: koonwarra; wara; yerlata

P

paddle (verb): ngibalin
paddymelon: mai-ra
pain: minga; wiwirri
paint (verb): macooloma
painted finch: unchurunqua
painting: coolbyngga; wolka
pair: ninkaiengk
palm, feathery-leaved: bangalow
palm leaf: tuta
pandanus: kuntyan
pant: ngrengkulun; nyerpulun; wankin mewe
paper-bark: see tea-tree
parakeet: weelya
parrot: bartill; kuyulpi; padilpa; pinpi; tuta
parrot, crimson-wing: billai
parrot, green: bullai bullai
parrot, quarrion: ooya

parrot, small (budgerigar):
gidgerigar
part (verb): threttin
passion: ngrakkuwallin
pass (verb): ngauwun
path: yarluke
pause (verb): cooragook
pea, Sturt's desert: meekyluka
peace: gwandalan; thoomee
yant
peace-maker: mereki
peach tree, native: quandong
pear tree, native: thoopara
pearl shell: namaga
pebble: moomowroong
peel (verb): wurtun
peewit: burrengeen; iyebana
pelican: booran; goolay-yali;
millemurro; nangkero; wili

PELICAN

pendant: wallin
penis: carloo; menane
people: narrinyeri
pepper, native: mao-warang
perch (fish): tarki
perch, giant: barramundi
perch, golden: bangnalla
perch, silver: kooberry
perch, trumpeter: mado
periwinkle: moondara
permanent: killara
persuade: nanampundun
pheasant, native: lowan;
wiwieringgere
pick up: makkin; mama;
mungeenie; pintyin
pick out: pindyin
piece, small: narteol
pieces: pruwuttar
pied crow shrike: tchaceroo
pierce: tappin
pigeon: moatah; mooaloonyah; wauk-wauk-wa; wonga;
wonga-wonga
pigeon, bronze-wing: tappak
pigeon, brown: du-mer
pigeon, scrub: kuboin
pigeon, topknot: goola-willeel
pigeon, Torres strait: nyungu
pigface (plant): canajong;
karkalla
pigweed root: kunnan-beili
pilchard: maray
pillow: kalbe
pinch (verb): minntin; puttun; tokkun
pine, cypress: jinchilla
pines, place of: carawatha
pine tree: bunya-bunya;

maroo; maroong; mowantyi;
pimpala; pyingerra
pipeclay: bulpuli; durdaak;
marloo
pity (verb): wanbin
place (noun): wal
place (verb): throttun; yuppun
plain: arcurrata; kaikai; maneroo; woorak
plain, sandy: koolena
plain surrounded by forest:
koyuga
plant (verb): nompulun; rata

PLANTS:

appung: cane grass
aquaie: pink water-lily
arika: small blue water-lily
arnurna: blue water-lily
bahlaka: saltbush
bambra: mushroom
binga-wingul: needlebush
birwain: bulrush
bookabooda: native gooseberry
boringkoot: native raspberry
canajong: pigface
chilla: poison bush
chucky-chucky: wax cluster
berry
elilger: wire grass
erladgeer: yam
evrah: a drooping shrub
geewan: common fern
goberta: plum bush
goborro: dwarf box
gunyang: kangaroo apple
gweebet: creeper with edible
fruit
honggar: reed
iperta: geranium
irriakura: edible tuber

irtaie: giant nettle
ita: scrub
iyouta: spinifex
jil-crow-a-berry: rat-tail grass
kanpuka: white water-lily
kaooroo: water-lily
karagata: umbrella bush
karoom: native currant
kindyerra: grass
kineyah: rice
kodala: reed
koonthooi: kelp
korpi: mangrove
korra: grass
kudgee: castor oil plant
kuloomba: native clover
kuntyari: plant with edible
leaves
kurrajong: kurrajong tree
kurrawan: reed
loombrak: water grass
looranah: brushwood
mai-ra: paddy-melon
mallee: scrub of dwarf eucalypts
meekyluka: Sturt's desert pea
minamberang: clematis
mirria: polygonum shrub
mootcha: native cotton bush
mulwala: possum grass
mundawora: native blackberry
murr-nong: plant with edible
tuber; yam
nardoo: clover fern
naretha: salt bush
narmar: grass
omil-dadgee: bamboo; large
reed
palberry: native currant
parrumbal: mushroom
pitchery: plant with narcotic
leaves
putta: grass
talga: sow thistle

tallerk: thistle
thalaak: sow thistle
tharook: convolvulus
uc-aliera: reed
ungarunya: rush
ungolar: native currant
unmerta: buckbush
wanappe: mushroom
warrah: honeysuckle
watye: polygonum shrub
wayway: devil's bread fungus
wididna: truffle
wiinki: arrowroot
wonga: bulrush
wongoonoo: grass
woorak: honeysuckle
wotiya: yam
yallaban: native raspberry
yerrear: saltbush

PLATYPUS

platypus: baarlijan; gaya-dari; theen-who-ween
play (verb): era cunalerme; nanyima; tunkuwallin
pleasant: murrumbung
pleasant place: elouera
Pleiades, The: maya-mayi
plentiful: woowookarung
plenty: curbarra; kowa; marandoo; moona
plenty, place of: bullarrto
plover, red-billed: tarlarang
pluck: thrintin
pluck feathers: teriltin
plucked: takkure
plum bush: goberta
plum tree, native: boomarrah; goberta
point (noun): padmuri
pointed: padmurwallin
pointing bone: gooweera; neilyeri

poison bush: chilla
poison stick: toorli
poke: tolkun
polygonum shrub: mirria; watye
pool: billabong; mianameena
pool with reeds: mallanbool
poor: woomelang
porcupine: see echidna
porpoise: koo-ee-lung; otama; ya uoanggi
portion, small: minti
possessions: maiyinggar
possum: kulan; leena; moodai; porlta; tarmaroo; wyehoota; yarraringy
possum, black-tailed: banya
possum grass: mulwala
possum, ring-tailed: wongguri
pour: raiaramin; yaramin

pour water into a vessel:
thickathickana
prayer: marmingatha
prepare: anangkwarrin
press (verb): poroany
press heavily: wityungyin
pretence: merrina
pretty: nunkeri
prickle: chillkalla; licka
prickly lizard, red: oola
prickly lizard, small: beer-
eeum
promise (verb): ngoiyir
protect: koolkuna
proud: plaityinggin
pull (verb): hetarracadin;
werendun; wonthaggi
puppy: wunbi
pursue: prildin
pus: thuldi

push (verb): pinbittulun; pinpin
put: pinpin
put down: throttun
put together: tanpundun; tulgeen

Q

quail: beereegan; burrandool;
tyepi
quarrel (verb): yabm-irriti
quarrion parrot: ooya
quartz: allirra
quick: burra burra, mickie;
murinmelin; nooroo; tiewiwar
quiet: gwandalan; tortuwallin;
weeronga; wepe

R

rage: ngraldi
rain: allabuckinee; chillberto;
eehu; mangnoo; mincarlie;
wainbaru
rain (verb): cobbycoononyee;
cobbyworrall; quasha-
undema
rain, much: trawalla
rain-bird: boogoo-doo-ga-da
rainbow: koninderie; ooranye; wee-y-teena; yulu-wirree
rainbow snake: Yurlunggur
rain-making, stone for: oodoolay
raise: preppin
raspberry, native: boringkoot; yallaban
rat: cowirrie; ertargwar;
umorra

POSSUM

rat, bandicoot: bilba
rat, bush: nilee
rat, climbing: murra-wunda
rat, kangaroo: aloota; goon-ur; millia; potoroo; purtia
rat, large: qualpar
rat, long-snouted: pulyara
rat, water: biggoon; goomai; rekaldi
rat-tail grass: jil-crow-a-berry
raw: erlicha; tumbi
receive: pultin
recline: allambee
red: beebeething; gwai; itichika; prolin
redbreast, robin: gwai-nee-bu
red pigment: kuging-cudgen
reed: hong-gar; kodala; kurra-wan; uc-aliebra
reed, large: omildadgee
refuse (verb): petin; wenkin
rejoice: tunthun
relative: kurnkuni; morannie
remain: allambee; aumin-thina
remains: nemmuran; yertau-wullar
remember: ngullun
repose: eumina

REPTILES (see also snakes):
  adjunepa: goanna
  armoolya: jew lizard
  awadabir: goanna
  beereeun: small prickly lizard
  beewee: goanna
  binking: turtle
  bu-maya-mul: wood lizard
  bun-yun bun-yun: frog

coorabin: barking lizard
elloi-jerra: large lizard
garbarli: shingleback
googarh: goanna
goolee: sand lizard
guddha: red lizard
hurramira: goanna
kambara: crocodile
kami: prickly lizard
kena: freshwater crocodile
kendi: lizard
kinkindele: tortoise; turtle
klare: short-tailed goanna
kunnie: jew lizard
kurria: crocodile
lurki: lizard
menperre: frog
ming-ari: mountain devil
minjin: mountain devil
minn-narie: mountain devil
mungoon-garli: goanna
munnarie: short-tailed goanna
nai-ari: mountain devil
ooboon: blue-tongued lizard
oola: red prickly lizard
perindi: yellow and brown striped goanna
pikuwa: saltwater crocodile
punka: large lizard
tata: frog
tatya: goanna
tendu: climbing frog
thidnamura: toad
tiddalick: frog
tuki: bull-frog
wala: blue-tongued lizard
wallu-barl: barking lizard
wangarang: tortoise
warka: tortoise
wayamba: turtle
wayembeh: tortoise
weenduga: goanna
withinka: green frog
yuaia: frog

resemble: nglalin
resin: giddie
rest (verb): gwandalan; kunden
resting place: weeroona
return: ngaiambin
rib: prewarrar; wolter
rice: kineyah; tyilyi
ridge, sand: urdera
ridge, stony: morilla
right: nunkeri
right hand: nunkeri-mari
ring: illyer-manda
ringlet: poenghana
rise (verb): doonkami; prakkin; prakour
river: balun; billa; bindaree; kur; lerra; milloo
river bend: nerreman
river red gum tree: yarrah
river, rocky: corowa
river, winding: nambucca
road: uworra; yutthero
robin redbreast: gwai-nee-bu
rock: gibber; gnamma; marti
rock shelter: gibber-gunyah
roll (verb): menamenakarin
root: itickera; tipi; werrook
root, pigweed: kunnan-beili
root, tree: kahar; meralki
root, young (of reeds): lintyeri
rope: kandari; nunggi
rose-breasted cockatoo: galah
rosewood tree: boodha
rot (verb): pultuwarrin
rotten: mirramerildin; rorari
rough: wirritin
round: larelar
round about: laldilald

rub: kilkilyalin; partin
rug, possum skin: pirriwee
run: klein; mana; moa; unti
run about: likkaldin
run away: nginbundun
rush: ungarunya

S

saliva: kulde
salmon, Murray mouth: mallowe
salt: boodha; bunto; ill-luka; tainki
salt bush: bahlaka; naretha; yerrear
salt water: ill-luaquasha
sand: karkarook; miyer; munta
sandfly: nanarinyeri
sandhill: alba; tally; wanda
sandpiper: pipipa
sand ridge: urdera
sassafras: caalang
save: daiyuwun; tumbetin
save life: yultun
saviour: tumbutilamaldi
saying: yarnin
scald (verb): klallin
scare (verb): nganden
scatter: kilkilyarin
scold: naiyuwun
scorpion: atnaterta; koongun; petachall-lily
scorch: kulkun
scrape: tullun
scratch (verb): wirrannie
screech: tyinkulun
scrub: ita; mallee; ngeragge; punthari
sea: lyaleetea; thadelete; warringa; warna; woorree; woor-oonga

sea, rough: kurrawa
seagull: kirrpiyirrka; munggi-
   wurray-mul; yara
seal: motthari
seashore: thammi
seaweed: bomberry; pinggi;
   wunggi
second: karlowan; wyang
secretly: numald
see: mina; nagooroo; nangana; wingaro
see!: nacooma
seed: kulu
seed, edible: kuldoo
seed, grass: doonbur
seed, small black edible:
   munyeru
seek: tuyulawarrin
seize: muranpun; plunden
selfish: thirti
send: konkuwarrin; taiyin
shade: boongala; liliiri; pangari
shade (verb): melkin
shade of trees: carramar
shade tree: kurragong
shadow: minnta; pangari; undoolya
shady place: moola
shag: kurrowera
shag, black: yolde
shag, white: puratte
shag, white-breasted: moogana
shake: roralgarin; uc-nun-
   alemem
shake the head: pilyau-undun
shallow: inberra; thame
shame: inyerra-alcrim; oloorinann

share (verb): peranbin; pinpuna
shark: ngrakkani
shark, carpet: wobbegong
shark, tiger: kunara; tealedyan
sharp: padmuri
sharpen: padmurwarrin
she: ba; kitye; yetni
sheep: burra burra; jumbuck
shell: ngipi; niley; wa-ah
shell midden: mirnyong

SHELLFISH:
   arama: bailer shell
   banawara: limpet
   koonwarra: oyster
   kumala: mud shell
   lokure: mussel
   moondara: periwinkle
   munggi: mussel
   namaga: pearl shell
   pundira: conch shell
   tagera: cockle
   tyelokuri: mussel
   wara: oyster
   wela: bailer shell
   wietatenana: nautilus
   yea: mussel
   yerlata: oyster
shelter: mia-mia; nangare;
   wiltja; wurley
shelter, grass: nunoo
shelter, bark: dardur; gunyah; humpy
shelter, rock or cave: gibber-
   gunyah
she-oak: kolge; kurtli
shield: alquirta; goolmarry;
   hillimung; pirramurra; wakkalde; woonda
shield, oval: bamarook

SHIELDS

shield, wooden: boreen
shin: cherarra: jorrer
shine: beelarong; klartin
shingleback: garbarli
ship: ngarraraipari; warriuka
shirt: mundarra
shiver: ngionkun
shoal: partyi
shoe: unterlina; turninyeri; urtathurta
shoes, emu: kurdaitcha
shoot (verb): icherramal; popa
shore: dilkera
short: katoa; menurte; tluiye
shortest: tluyeol
shoulder: alliebree; markulde; ungunyer-pollipa
shoulder blade: markulde
shout: kaidundun
show: reyin

D

shrike, pied crow: tchaceroo; tiltili
shrubs, place of: terrara
shut: muritpun
shut in: muriltpun
sick: halcoppatunein; mendic; minga
sickness: budgel; minga; wiwirri
side: prewirri
sieve (verb): morokkun
sign language: kumaloro
signal, smoke: kowandi
silence: kapo; thoomee
silent: tortuwallin
silver perch: kooberry
silver wattle: currong
sing (verb): beria; boroyah; bundah; poonja; ringbalin; warrannie; wonkana
singe: nyringgen
sink (verb): mirpin
sister: kongaroo; marauwe; nowantareena
sister, elder: koongoora; maranowe
sister, younger: tarti
sister-in-law: mambo
sit: barribunda; nangalla; ningana; nyang; nyinna; tergoonee
sit down: allambee; ninnann; yangalla
sit on: thopramolla
skin (noun): bungkee; imba; pultha; yenpar
skin (verb): wertun
skin, kangaroo: cudgewong
skirt: goomilla
skull: cobbra

sky: goonagulla; illcarrie; morang;waiirri;warratinnah
sky, blue: loaranneleah; wullun
sky camp: Bullima
sky, rainy: quasha-ul-kurre
sky, ruler of the: Nepelle
slaty-gum: arangnulla
sleep: bomburra; dora; mia; miala; muwe; uncoo; ungwyndei; weeronga
sleeping place: woongarra
sleeping place in the bush: noonameena
sleepy: muwe watyeri
slow: mant
small: gidju; goobita; kateewailwo; kutyo; minya; toogaadya; weema
smell (verb): pendin
smile (verb): kunthamawerana
smoke: boorana; kare; muldi; poyyou; pumdo
smoke signal: kowandi
smoke tobacco: muttun; timbelin
smooth: kilkulun
snake: endracoon; koorang; upmoa; wobma; wommee

SNAKES: (see also reptiles)
  biggarroo: wombat snake
  bubbur: large brown and yellow snake
  daya-minya: small carpet snake
  goonnear: carpet snake
  gununo: black snake
  guridjadu: carpet snake
  kikinummi: black snake
  ngumundi: black snake
  nurawordubununa: carpet snake
  oiyangopan: carpet snake
  ooyu-bu-lui: black snake
  pranggiwatyeri: tiger snake
  taipan: giant brown snake
  tintauwa: black snake
  tityowe: death adder
  uka: white sand snake
  waiye: light brown snake
  wititurar: small snake
  yalakki: carpet snake
  yuwam: black snake

snapper: nannygai; wobbegong; wollomai
sneeze: injaracna; newchin; tyrintyin
snipe: thanpathanpa
snore: normananyee
snow: goonama
so: lun
soak: yalgin
soft: munangpallan; noinpalin
soil: kooruck
soldier-bird: degeen-boya
some: maltaiar
somewhere: winthunga
son: brauwarate; ngauwire
son, eldest: pamgali
song: ringbalin
song, sacred: quabara
sorcerer: boyla; koradji; wirinun; wiwirimalde
sorcery: millin
sore: marma; picca
sorry: ngarpin; parpin
soul: pangari; urrie urrie; yowi
sour: lukun

south: mirreen; nuru-buan; olebyra; rikkara

south-east: bulli-medi-mundi

south-east wind: yarrageh

south-west: gurra

south-west wind: gurra malye

south wind: gooroondoodil-baydilbay; merringannee; nuru-nuru-bin

Southern Cross: Birubi; Chucullba; Koodyoorinad-yal; Yaraandoo

sow: wingamin

sow thistle: talga; thalaak

spark: orinjetta; tundi

sparkling: tilpulun

sparrow: neenca

sparrow-hawk: poorparta

speak: kulpana; panelgorana; piyaller; wenkana; yaman; yarnin; yarra

spear: cadgee; gummy; kia; winta; yarnde; yerracharta

spear (verb); pandana; wakkin

spear, acacia wood: gidya

spear, bamboo: pinta

spear, bamboo, with four points: pita

spear, emu: mooroon

spear, fish: gowdalie; punkulde

spear head: borral

spear, jagged: kalkro

spear, large: orumbera

spear, long heavy black: wunde

spear of medicine man: thingairipari

spear, reed: kaike

spear shaft: marrongie

spear tree: etnurra

spear with several barbs: kaiya

spear with stingray barb: wolka

spear with two barbs: pillara

speech: wika

speed: mitamit

spider: brupe; uwoppa; wonka

spider, trapdoor: murga muggai

spill: yaramin

spin: ngembelin

spinifex: iyouta

spirit: mooroop; purkabidni; thambaroo

spirit, bora: gayandi (man's

SPEARS

word); gurraymi (woman's word)

spirit, demon: coocoo-loora; marmoo

spirit, dream: Doowi

spirit, drought: Yalkara

spirit, drought (of wirinun): mullee mullee

spirit, evil: brupe; melape; muldarpe; wunda

spirit, familiar: yunbeai

spirit, grand-mother: Puck-owe

spirit, great: Baiame

spirit-haunted tree: mingga

spirit land: Bullima

spirits of birth: walla-gud-jail-wan; walla-guroon-bu-an

spirits, old: nurrumbunguttia

spit: doleboin; pill-ler

splinter: indenima

split: threllin

spoonbill duck: thowla

sprat, Murray mouth: kun-gulde

spread: nenartin; wiltun

spring (season): nartee, re-wuri

spring of water: brim-brim; narmare; prilpulun

spring, spirit of: Yarrageh

spring wind: mayra; yarraga

sprinkle: thrippin

squeeze (verb): moondak; pantin

squirrel, flying: berontha; buggoo; butterga; manga-roo; pongo; tuan

stab: tolkundun

stake: tappan

stamp: grokumbalin; tolkun

stand: tangulun; yuka; yum-mun

stand up: buckali; tana

star: burley, kulka; pinterry; quarallia; tuldar

stare: ngenyarin

stare at: pilkundun; wildin

start (jump with fright): pran-tin

starve: onengarkwa

stay (verb): yallambee

steady: moranjee; murungar

steal: pettin

steep: perke; rengbari

step (verb): kowundun; ngop-pun

stick: holta; kooroorook; wonna; yapar

stick, barbed (for catching grubs): midjeer

stick, digging: gunni; wanna

stick, fighting: waddy; worraworra

stick, man-killing: birra-ga; konnung

stick, message: mungi, thrig-gi

stick, painted (with feathers on top): wilgu-wilgu

stick, pointed: dindi

stick, poison: toorli

stick, striking: waddy

stick, talk: tulpi

stick, throwing: bellata; bir-rana; rarramba; taralye; witwit; woomera

sticks for beating time: tartengk

stiff: paipe
stiffness; milterree
sting (verb): wiitii
stingray: umpara
stink: bucka, pentin; unditter
stir: wuralparin
stomach: bingy; mankuri; weelar
stone: apurta; burnta; eeerilya; gibber; marte; mayama; merri
stone for grinding grass seed: dayoorl; doori
stone for rain-making: oodoolay
stone knife: muggil
stone, large: burra
stone, magic: gubbera
stone, pounding: wallong
stone tomahawk: karragan; kumbu
stony place: mrangalli
stony ridge: morilla
stoop: tingin
stop (verb): balyarta; burra; kalyan; nemmin
stop a while: warma
stork: korrorook; monti
storm: kokipijira; willy-willy; yarrawah
storm bird: worippa
straight: chucowra; thure
strait: thurar
strange: malde
stranger: merkani; myall; yunkara
stream (small tributary): mubboon; pani-millie
strength: prityururmi; thalera

STONE FOR
GRINDING SEED

strike: balka; mempin; poonganyee
string: mintambe; oleara; pertorrue; undooeata
string of wombat or wallaby hair: wariya
stringybark tree: goondool; yangoora
strong: matong; piltengi; thilhya
stubborn: intulka; willawallin
stump: ernar; thulye
stump, burnt: wallangar
stupid: arcoona; plombewallin; wanbana
Sturt's desert pea: meekyluka
suck: cooan-dunning
suffer: relbulun
sugar: marngowie; pinyatowe

sugar ant: yeramba
sugar bag: maiyatta
sulky: konegerana
summer: booragul; kiata; lowalde; welya
summit: barina
sun: allunga; chintoo; deentoo; thummyerloo; tonahleah; tshinta; uuna; yindi; yhuko
sunbeam: tyelyerar
sun goddess: Yhi
sunlight: nunkalowe
sunrise: baapanannia; wunu-wa-tirring; yhuko pappora
sunset: berringar; wirruna; yhuko hippy
sunshine: woornack
superior: oomoomurla
surround: tuldin
suspect: nunde
swallow (bird): menmenengkuri; mulundar; waylehmina
swallow (verb): kunkun
swamp: bullook; tainke
swamp duck: tempi
swamp fish: ita; tyeli
swamp oak: billambang
swan: goonawarra; kauerti; tumakowaller; youngoloy
swan, black: baiamul; koolyn; mooroocoochin
swear: naiyuwun; olumbera
sweat: kanguama; kantarlie
sweat (verb): arcoorie; kangnarra; wertuwallin
sweet: bunyarra; kinpin; lerp; moruga
sweetness: kumbelin

sweet water: beal
swell: tinkelin
swift: loongana
swift (bird): beerwon
swim: cheropin; pullun; quasha-yerra-pichica; thurakami; woka
swing: uc-nulla-mull

T

taboo: gunmarl
tadpole: ngikunde
tail: kaldare; kotla; poora; whippoo; yanka
take: mummjeeli; plunden; pultin; tean
take away: pintamin
take care of: moerpun
take hold: wato
talisman made of quartz crystal: murramai
talk: tauwa; yabber; yarnimindin
talk stick: tulpi
talk together: jumbunna
tall: albungec-nurra; yulde
tame: nare
tasty: nunkeri; timpin
tattoo: mungaiyuwun; parlcoon
tattoo mark: munggar
tea: nguni; pelberri
teal: barook; ngerake
teal, speckled: koortgang
tear (verb): daraimin; trelin
teat: ippeeculca; papa
tea-tree: kimmuli; nama; wirreecoo
tea-tree, broad-leaved: unoyie

teeth: carteta; nerndoa; teeya; tuyalie-dusali; undie; yeera

tell: paialla; rammin; tingowun; whytalla

thank: kaukau

that: kakie

that here: anaialye

that there: naiyuwe

their: kandauwe

them: kan

then: wanye

there: karthro; munggow; nowieya

these: harnakar

they: kar; unengoo

they (two): kenggun

thicket: mallee; yerang

thief: petamalde

thigh: chewenta

thin: kutyeri; yrottulun

think: kungullun

thirst: mungara

thirsty: klallin; moorelli; mungara; nantoo

this: hikkai; nia

thistle: tallerk

three: booroora; kabu; munkurippa; neppaldar

throat: kalde; kunga-gnarra

throw: wonninny; wunmun; youamalla

throw a spear: lakkin

throw away: throkkun

throw down: pinggen

throwing stick: mirla; mullamunale; taralye; witwit; woomera; yarramba

thumb: maigamaigawa; narkale

thunder: dooloomai; mundara; munte; toney

tickle: gidgee; tittimbalin; tuckatuck

tide, advancing: moilong

tide, flood: baragoola

tie: premin; pringgarimmin

tiger shark: kunara

timber, large: wyelangta

timber, small: wyelangta

timid: blukkun

tin: poomong

tire: nguldamul-mindin

tired: nguldammulun; pandeanen; tarntunnerrin; umbeeramalla

to: angk; ungai

toad: thidnamura

tobacco: cudgel

today: hikkai nungge; karinga; yingoorna

TOMAHAWKS

toe: pulca; turnar
together: karobran; mul-launa; yunt
tomahawk: by-a-duk; gwee-on; karragain; kumbu; taree; willara
tomorrow: kanawinkie; min-yaka; ngrekkald
tongue: kaiaking; tallangge; therlinya
TOOLS: see under weapons
tooth: lea; leongatha
top: nglulun
topknot: walla-boondi
topknot pigeon: goola-willeel
torpedo bug: chumbee
tortoise: kinkindele; wangar-ang; warka; wayembeh
tortuous: gunbower
toss: throkkun
totem: mah; murdu
totem centre: auwa
totem, hereditary: dhe
totem, individual: yunbeai
track: barreng; pukkan; tshina; turnar; yarluke
track (verb): wartin
track (of foot): darri
trapdoor spider: murga muggai
trap, fish: barameda
tread: towun
tree: ernar; wadelang; yape; yuka
tree fern: lapoinya; pooeet
tree, growing: warwanbool
tree, hollow: winani
tree-runner: bibbi
tree, spirit haunted: min-gga

tree struck by lightning: binganah
tree, water-holding: goola-gool

TREES:

    angorra: box
    amulla: edible fruit
    arangnulla: slaty-gum
    bael-bael: gum
    balemo: rough-leaved fig
    ballat: native cherry
    ballook: blue-gum
    bangalay: mahogany gum
    bangalow: palm
    barranduna: brush myrtle
    belah: bull-oak
    bibbil: broad-leafed box; myrtle
    bilkurra: narrow-leaved box
    billambang: swamp oak
    bimbil: poplar-leaved box
    binburra: white beech

TOTEMS

bingelima: orange
bira: whitewood
boelgi: willow
boobyalla: acacia; native willow
boodha: rosewood
boomarrah: native plum
booreea: turpentine
boree: weeping myall
bumbel: native orange
bunya-bunya: large tree with edible fruit; pine tree
buriagalah: acacia
burrawang: nut
burrawingie: diamond-leaved laurel
callangun: blue fig
choota: gum
coobah: acacia
coo-in-new: mahogany
coolabah: eucalypt; flooded box
coranderrk: Christmas bush
currong: silver wattle
deenyi: iron-bark
dheal: sacred tree of the Noongaburra tribe
egaie: mangrove
enunta: bean
etnurra: spear
geebung: persoonia
gidya: acacia
goolabah: grey-leaved box
goon-dool: stringybark
gruee: tree with bitter fruit
heeterra: gum
illginga: beefwood
ilumba: Moreton bay ash
irtalie: bean
jarrah (jerrhyl): eucalypt species
jinchilla: cypress pine
kakower: fern
kampa: messmate

karri: eucalypt, W.A.
karwin: grass-tree
kimmuli: teatree
kirrang: wattle
kolge: she-oak
konda: cabbage-tree
kowinka: red mangrove
kula: bloodwood
kunakuna: box
kuntyan: pandanus
kurrajong: *Brachychiton populneum*
lakkari: honeysuckle; banksia
lapoinya: fern
mao-warang: native pepper
maroo: pine
maroong: pine
midjee: acacia
mowantyi: pine
mubbu: beefwood
mulga: acacia
myimbarr: black wattle
myndee: sycamore
nama: tea-tree
natan: fig
ngarningi: fig
nglaiye: grass-tree
nonga and **noonga**: kurrajong
odenpa: ironbark
orra-curra: desert oak
panpande: cherry
parragilga: narrow-leaved ironbark
pimpala: pine
pooeet: fern
pootikkatikka: wattle
pyingerra: pine
quandong: native peach
taree: wild fig
thoopara: native pear
tooart: tuart
toolain: brown wattle
umbellditta: orange
unoyie: broad-leaved tea-tree

wallowa: broom wattle
wandoo: wandoo gum
waratah: flowering tree
warreeah: mountain ash
wilga: dogwood; willow
wirreecoo: tea-tree
wirildar: an acacia
witjuti: acacia
wuri: red gum
wyterrica: wattle
yangoora: stringy-bark
yaraan: white gum
yarrah: river red gum
yarran: an acacia
yerra-coppa: desert oak

trees, clump of: bundara
trees, place of: googoorewon
tremble: ngoinkun
tributary, small: mubboon
trousers: kurrinyerengk
truffle: widdidna
trumpet: didgerido
trumpeter perch: mado
truth: thur
tuber, edible: irriakura
turkey: goomble-gubbon; talkinyeri
turn (verb): wandelana
turn inside out: menaikulun
turn over: mackunya; ngera-kowun
turn round: karlowun
turpentine tree: booreea
turtle: binking; kinkindele; turtauwatyeri; wayamba
turtle, sea: miintinta
turtle, swamp: puntyaiya
twenty: boolarra
twilight: pangarinda; wattar
twist: ngempin; yenempun

two: barkool; boola; godarra; pullatye
two, only: mundroola

U

umbilical cord: kalduke
umbrella bush: karagata
uncle: kamaroo, kaya; wimmera
uncle (father's side): wanowe
uncle (mother's side): ngoppano
uncooked: erlicha
understanding: kungun
understanding, lack of: wanbana
unfasten: yanedana
unknown: nammuldi
unpleasant: arilperill
untamed: myall
up: karranga; loru; war
upside down: laremuntunt
urine: kumpa; umboa
us: alie; nam
useless: yande; yuntuwarrin

V

vain: plaityingyin
valley: plurampe
vegetable: rata
vein: pillcoo; yarngge
vendetta: dullay-mullay-lunna
Venus: warte
vermin: tittadi
very: murri; pek
vessel, bark (for holding water): wirree
vessel, wooden (for holding water): bingui; cardeenie;

coolamon; kanakie; mimbo; pitchie; yerra-colya
view, extensive: yurnga
visitor: alkoo
voice: tunggare
vomit: bulkun; holcoppa-tunein

W

waddy (weapon or club): kanake; puri; mooroola
wade: yondun
wail, death: goonai
wait (verb): balyarta; burra; ngaralin
wait awhile: ouraka
wakeful: muwityiwallin
walk (verb): koorala; ngopuld; tampin; yannathan; yanning
wallaby: mari; pargi; taran-na; warrew; warta

WALLABY

WADDY

wallaby, black: bunderra
wallaby, bush: uwurta
wallaby, rock: erawar
wallaby, small: mai-ra
want (verb): mewultun
warm: boorook; molbangen; wurtun
warrior: wundurra
wash (verb): gnolo; nyrippin
wasp: undeneya
watch: moerpun
water: apanie; cobbie; gulli; napanopa; nucko; quasha
water bag: gulli-mayah
water-bag, skin: attower
water beetle: boongurr
water, big: warde yallock
water, clear: wyuna
water, deep: binda; parnggi
water devil: Mulloka

water, dirty: ulluricna
water flowing over rocks: goondnomda
water grass: loombrak
water hen: kilkie
water hole: dungel; gilguy; kaga; mandurama
water hole, deep: quasha-iperta quorna
water-lily: kaooroo; umpiya
water-lily, blue: arnurna; kanpuka
water-lily, pink: aquaie
water-lily, white: kanpuka
water, little: pirron-yallock
water, muddy: burrumbeet
water rat: biggoon; goomai
water, running: adnamira; burmpa; nunkuluthen
water, salt: ill-luaquasha; yilgi
water, small: quasha-booga
water, spring: narrawa
water, sweet: kiewa
water, sweetened: beal
water, twisting: warriwillah
water vessel: see vessel, water
water, wild: trawalla
waterfall: murrumbooee
watering-place: baringup
waters, meeting of the: wollombi
wattle: kirrang; pootikkatik-ka; wyterrica
wattle bird: tallarook
wattle, black: myimbarr
wattle, broom: toolain; wal-lowa
wattle flower: ngolika

wattle, silver: currong; un-durra
wave (noun): murdiella; ule
wax cluster berry: chucky-chucky
we: adloo; allena; gnawela; ngodli
we (all of us): yangennanock
we (two): nam; nullegai
weak: pultue

WEAPONS and TOOLS:
alquirta: shield
ammeara: throwing stick
antyan: spear with four points
bamarook: oval shield
barakadan: boomerang
bargan: returning boomerang (not a fighting weapon)
belettah: throwing stick
binyana: chisel
birrana: throwing stick
birra-ga: man-killing stick
boogoo: long club
boondi: club-headed weapon
boreen: wooden shield
bubbera: returning boomerang
bulgoon: stone tomahawk
burgoin: stone tomahawk
by-a-duk: stone tomahawk
dabberi: club
dowak: club
drekurmi: hatchet; knife
gidji: spear
gidya: long spear of acacia wood
goolmarry: shield
gowdalie: hardwood fishing spear
gummy: spear
gweeon: stone tomahawk
hillimung: shield
jerambitty yarka: spear
jimari: stone knife

kaiher: spear
kaike: reed spear
kaiya: stingray barbed spear
kalduke: fighting club
kalkkalk: club
kalti: spear
kama: spear
kana: spear
karkaro: spear
karnick: throwing stick
karragain: stone tomahawk
karu: spear with stone head
keda: boomerang
kertum: boomerang
kia: spear
kiley: boomerang
kondu: club
konnung: man-killing stick
kullack: club
kullin: throwing stick
kunnai: spear
kutha: club
leawill: club with bent head
lianwill: club
likoorler: spear
maki: hunting boomerang
maller: throwing stick
manyeekerrik: spear
marriwirra: club
marpanye: club
mattina: double-pointed club
meralde: quartz-headed spear
metpadinga: club
mirla: throwing stick
miro: throwing stick
mooroola: waddy
mooroon: emu spear
muggil: stone knife
mulla-munale: throwing stick
mulla-murrale: boomerang
naripal: spear
nullanulla: club with heavy head
nunkardeol: short club

nurula pundi: club
orumbera: large spear
panketye: boomerang
pera: club
pilar: spear
pillara: spear with two barbs
pinta: bamboo spear
pirramurra: shield
pita: four-pointed spear
plongg: knobbed weapon for inflicting punishment
punkulde: fish spear
quunder: club
taralye: throwing stick
taree: tomahawk
thingairipari: spear of medicine man
tunta: spear
tura: spear
tuu: three-pointed spear
waaljerrumbuddy kewat: spear
waddy: war club
wadna: boomerang
wakkalde: shield
wangin: boomerang
wantyandyindn: three-pointed spear
wanya: boomerang
warroo: boomerang
watnah: boomerang
wenbener: throwing stick
winta: spear
woggara: wooden battle-axe
wolka: stingray-barbed spear
womah: boomerang
wommurer: throwing stick
woomera: throwing stick
worraworra: fighting stick
wunde: long spear
yandala: spear with one long point
yarnde: spear
yarramba: throwing stick

yarrum: throwing stick
yarrumba: boomerang
yerracharta: spear
yerrawar: boomerang
youa: throwing stick
wear (verb): ngolun
weather, fine: woorookool
weeping myall: boree; yarran
well (noun): minga; nerntulya; ulla; wunjugur
west: dinjerra; rumaiy; weloorarra
west wind: gheeger gheeger; werderh
wet: tallbee; undunga; wurte; yalkin
whale: akama; kaandha; kondarle
what: minna; ngongi
what?: yari
when: ungunuk
when?: yaral
where: tang
where?: windarra; whinya
while: pallai
whirlwind: boolee; onbellera; willy-willy; wurrawilberoo
whistle (verb): obernilimer; winberongen; winkulun
whistling duck: chipala; goonaroo; kibulyo; tatea
white: balpi; lill-lill; pitereka
white ant: mirta; odunepa
white cockatoo: garaweh; kaar; mooy
white man: Amerjig; kupa
white woman: amerjig-orok
whites (ghosts, devils, also applied to white people): thambaroo; wunda

whitewood tree: bira
who: ngongi; unnee
whole: ngruwar
whose: nauwe
why: mengye; mind
widow: mambamya; pumo; yakea
widower: randi
wife: berguna; coorie; kurtoo; murtamoo; yungara
wild (of animals and men): myall; warrigal
wild: merkani; myall
wild man: myall, purinyeriol
willow, native: boelgi; boobyalla; wilga
willy wagtail: deereeree; gumalkoolin; jenning-gherrie; mugana; tityarokan
wind: barega; boomori; burramarona; lillkar; malbooma; may; rawlinna; wolpa; yarto
wind, contrary: ngrelggimaiyi
wind, hot: kulgarnie
wind, east: gun-ya-mu
wind, north: douran douran
wind, north-west: mundewudda
wind, south: gooroondoodilbaydilbay; nuru-nuru-bin; merringannee
wind, south-east: yarrageh
wind, south-west: gurra malye
wind, west: gheeger gheeger; wederh
windpipe: kalde; untoo
windy: burando

wing: tyele
wink: kalpulun
winter: kilpanie; kolya; yorte
wiregrass: elilger
wise man: inkata
wish: ellin
withered: meraldi; mirramirildin; pentin; tyiwiwallin
with: al, ungai
woman: gin; kore; loa; lubra;
  nongo; toora; willawatta-
  thuyin; unkee
woman, childless: plotye
woman, married: aragudgeha; hokarra
woman, old: kombona; koon-
  ja-gilbee; meetawarri
woman, tabooed: goorewon
woman, white: amerjig-orok
woman, young: kamballa;
  wirreebeeun; yartuwe
woman, young, married:
  wanty pian
womb: atnar; manyee
wombat: warreen
wombat snake: biggarroo
women, a number of: kumbumbana
women, two: cooroonya
wommera: see throwing stick
wonder: prantin
wonderful: ngranyeri
wood: kurla; mootta; oura;
  worrue; karrara
wood, dry: erlinya; ernar-
  injerika

wood duck: goonarook
wood lizard: bu-maya-mul
wool: yingge
word: tunggare
work: wimmin; yakka
worm: miningkar; tyilye
wound (verb): wakkin
wren: lirralirra
wren, emu: puyulle
wrestle: partambelin; yenembelin
wrist: minna; molta; tungge
write: mungaiyin
wrong: wirrangi

Y

yam: erladger; murr-nong;
  wotiya; yelka
yam stick: adnumma; gunni
yawn: tappenitin; tarloorin
yearn: duwatyin; parpin mewe
yes: katyill; na-wo; ya-yowi
yesterday: ellow; goolawa;
  watangrow
you: ngune; neena; nindoah;
  waimba; yentoo
you (two): lom; ngurle
young: muralappi
young man: kaingani; oolyarra; taldree
young woman: kamballa;
  wirreebeeun; yartowe
yours: gnoma; nomauwe; un-
  gwynyer

PHRASES AND SENTENCES

ENGLISH—ABORIGINAL

Many Aboriginal languages have been drawn on for the phrases that follow; therefore they must not be considered as coming from a single language, but rather as offering interest and amusement to those who want to add the occasional Aboriginal phrase to their vocabulary.

All right: Cull-la.
Jaba.
Be quick: Iterra.
Bring plenty of money: Mani bumanai nasendag.
Close the door: Muriltp.
Come back: Yaldeenie.
Yawoma.
Come here: Alleari.
Kowia.
Ngai ouri.
Purni ngomerna.
Warrawee.
Come here, boy: Umba-coora.
Come on: Nallak.
Pichi-malla.
Come on, get up!: Hetra akamarei.
Come quickly: Alidgea-guy-pichi.
Come up: Pichi-malla.
Do not have (no got): Arrun-gwa.
Do not look: Illa winjaw-tana
Do not let it go: Illa thor-kaninde.
Do not talk so much: Illa Panelgorinba.

Do you hear?: Barrdarr-gindo?
Farewell! (said by those who are leaving): Kalyan ungune lewin.
(The reply is: Nginte, or Ngune ngoppun.)
Follow him: War i atyan.
Follow me: War i an.
Get up: Akamarie.
Give me: Gnoka.
Kernaumer.
Unyook.
Give me some water: Koppi unga.
Go!: Ngowalour.
Go away: Brimhillah.
Go away!: Thrunkkun.
Go back: Colba.
Collumbum.
Go on: Albye.
Byeni.
Go to the scrub and bring me some firewood: Pun-thari ngomerna ngaitshi kurla murrana.
Have you any food?: Hii hii onom takuramb.
He is laughing: Yato kande-dana.

He is not there: Nilee.
Hit it: Balka.
How many?: Minyai.
Minyandai.
Munyarai.
Naltra.
How often?: Minyai.
Minyandai.
I am going on a journey: Jilalan.
Nagugari.
I am sending a message: Nawargbun djanbin.
I am sulky: Konegrannappa.
I am very hungry: Ngai-i murnna.
I did not hear: Illa bana noto.
I did not touch it: Illa uatena.
I do not know: Indeato.
I hear: Bana nato.
Barra.
I laugh: Karreda nappa.
I see the dog: Ngai-i yelka mina.
I shall send him: Maduldul janama.
I sleep: Ngai-i mia.
I speak to you: Kulperna-toma.
I will: El ap.
I will not let it go: Illa thor-kanyerato.
I will not talk so much: Illa panelgorippa.
Is that your husband?: Kakee murtanna.
Is that your wife? Kakee nongoma.
It is mine: Ninamanima.

It looks like rain: Quasha illdeegood-munda.
It must be here: Kalyan en el our.
Let me think: Nangy.
Let us dance: Gar wunala-minju.
Let us eat food: Majin nanarnun.
Listen!: Kungour.
My dear: Gnernpa.
No good: Arcoona.
Quear.
No I'm not: Arrun-derique.
Now I go: Wija narani.
Peace be with you: Yant el our ou.
Put it here: Hik ahk in oura.
Put it there beside you: Yup our ityan tapangk.
Run!: Iterra.
Speak to me: Kulperaguana.
Stop crying: Thapolo.
Stop talking: Merild our.
Thank you: An ungune.
(while saying this the clasped hands are thrown away from the stomach).
There it is: Yate.
The soul will not die: Illa booker mer ley urrie urrie.
The sun is setting: Allinger yerra-bamalla.
This place is called . . .: Wuna wunaia wuniingu . . .
Wait awhile: Ouraka.
Wait for me: Mantanekin.
We are staying there: Win-jidinura.
We are tired: Lal jirgugari.

E

We did not hear: Illa banandalie.

We don't understand: Gabo.

We killed the dog: Ngodli yelga bukana.

We shall come back: Wari wanjinju.

What do you want?: Nudbur wungawuduminji.

What is that?: Parepar.

What is the matter?:
Jamanda wule.
Titpeld ellin?

What is your name?:
Wangeganimba.
Yare matye mitye?

What shall I do?: Yarrura.

Where are you going?: Wungiana?

Which way?: Windana?

Why didn't you wait for me?: Wana ma nanudagbalaria.

Will you?: Yanima?

You are sulky: Konegranimba.

You bring it back: Yawoma gumdinda.

You go in front: Hungararacoola.

You liar: Orra-jerra.

You walk: Yentoo yanning.

THE LORD'S PRAYER

in the Darling River language, which was in use for 500 miles along its length:

Ninnana combea, innara inguna Karkania,
Munielie nakey, Emano pumum culpreathiea,
ona Kara canjelka yonagh patua, angella,
Nokinda ninnana kilpoo yanice, Thickundoo
Wantindo ninnana Illa ninnana puniner,
thullaga, Thilltill Chow norrie morrie
munda, lullara munie. Euelpie.

The superior figures shown in the following list refer to the following geographical areas:

1. Western Australia
2. South Australia
3. Northern Territory
4. Victoria
5. New South Wales
6. Queensland
7. Tasmania
8. Central Australia

WORD LIST
ABORIGINAL-ENGLISH

A

aalbawal[3]: head
abbulduppi[3]: cold
adaka-palai: let out
adjemot[4]: bad
adjo[1]: I
adjunepa[8]: goanna
adloo[2]: we
adnamira[8]: flowing, running water
adnummer[8]: yam stick
aiain: see aya
aijal[3]: sky
ainbu[3]: rain
aitye barkolo[6]: three
aka[6]: ground
akama[6]: whale
akamarei[8]: get up
al[2] (ald): with
alaijah: see kalajah
alait[3]: dog
alajah: see kalajah
alaok[3]: child
alba[8]: sandhill
albungec-nurra[8]: tall
albye[8]: go on
Alchera: place where the "Old People" lived
Alcheringa: Dreamland, or the Land of Baiame
algooma[8]: eating
alguna[2]: drink (verb)
alie: us
alinjarra[8]: north
aljerer[8]: dream
alkingar[8]: eye
alknarar-killja[8]: blind

alknarlba[8]: hip
alkoo: visitor
alkoomie: good
allabuckinee[8]: rain
allambee[4]: sit down, recline, remain (verb)
allambie: quiet place
allang-goola[8]: nostril
allar[8]: nose
alleari[8]: come here
alleena: we
alli[3]: dog; moon
alliebree[8]: shoulder
allinger: see allunga
allirra[8]: quartz
allue[8]: liver
allunga (allinger, arlunya): sun
allydung[3]: hear

ALOOTA

almeju³: fish
alondji³: sky
aloota⁸: kangaroo rat
aloripma⁸: flame
alpugi³ (elpugi): kangaroo
alquirta⁸: shield
alta⁸: hair
alteripa⁸: claypan
alye² (alyalle): here
alyenik²: near me
amayworra⁸: Orion's Belt
ambe²: for
ambo⁸: egg
amerjig: white man
amerjig-orok: white woman
ammaboolah³: fish
ammeara⁸: throwing stick
ammijeeler³: blood
ammonga⁸: see mongana
ammoula⁸: nose
ampan⁶: cut
amulla⁶: tree with edible fruit
an²: me
anaialye²: that there
anangkwarrin²: prepare
an anyril²: for them
anauwe: see nganauwe
anbirik³: hill
andek²: away (from the speaker)
andi⁵: who
andowach⁶: see
andri²: mother
angaikbirig³ (arnarigbirij): mouth
angbal³: hair
angk²: into, to
angorra⁸: box tree
angorra: see engorra
anjee-malla⁸: climb

anjigi³: hand; teeth
anka⁶: barramundi
ankana²: make
anowah⁶: give
antyan⁶: spear with four prongs
antye⁸: give
anyir²: from
apa: see appa
apanie: water
apari² (apirrie): father
apmurika⁸: boy
appa⁶ (apa): water
appointa⁸: cold
appunga⁸: cane grass
apurta⁸: stone
aquiaie: pink water-lily
aragoodgeawonga⁸: adolescent girl
aragudgeha⁸: married woman
arama⁶: bailer shell
arami² (urumi): for
aramut³: star
arangnulla: slaty gum
arcoona⁸: no good, stupid
arcoorie⁸: sweat
arcurrata⁸: plain
argadba³: star
argoonie⁸: catch (verb)
arika: blue water-lily
arilperill⁸: unpleasant
arinya: kangaroo
arkoola: hair
arlunya: see allunga
armoolya⁸: jew lizard
arnarigbirij: see angaikbirig
arndu²: come
arntuney⁸: lick (verb)
arnurna: blue water-lily
aroitj³: child

aroitja[3]: small
aroo: fan of emu tail feathers
aroo[4]: cygnet
arracoola[8]: front
arrah-cardie[8]: daylight
arrainya[8]: name
arrakata (aruckata): mouth
arrakutcha: snake woman
arrama[8]: louse
arrie-enpa[8]: lip
arrilla: aborigine
arrinyenin[8]: circle
arruleta[8]: neck
arrungwa[8]: do not have (no got)
arrunja[8]: devil
arrurrer[8]: kangaroo
artippa[8]: back
artoo[2]: I
aruaramba[3]: mouth
aruaroli[3]: foot
aruckata: see arrakata
arunta: white cockatoo
arutchie: native ferret, cat or tiger cat
atchina[8]: mine
atna[8]: womb
atnalure[8]: blood
atnaterta[8]: scorpion
atninebeemalla[8]: kick
atnitta[8]: belly
atta[6]: I
attong-giuilina[8]: cough
attower: skin water bag
atwa[8]: man
atye: see kitye
atyimba[6]: emu
au[2]: now
auminthina: remain (verb)
auwa[6]: hole, totem centre

awadabir[6] (rawadabir): goanna
awring-gamalla[8]: daylight
aya[3] (aiain, kaain): stone

B

ba[2]: he, it, she
baal[5] (bael, bail, bal): expression of disapproval; don't, no, not
baan[4]: dog
baanya[5] (baanga): camp
baapanannia: sunrise
baarlijan: platypus
babaneek: mother
babuk[4]: mother
bael: see baal
baelbael: gum tree
bagan[4]: sit
bagan[6]: sea
bagrook[4]: woman

ATNATERTA

bahal[5]: tree
bahlaka: salt bush
Bahloo[5]: moon, god of the moon, guardian of girls and women
bahn[5]: mistletoe
Baiame[5] (Byamee): culture hero or god, creator; literally, Great One
baiamul[5] (byahmul): black swan
baibaiye[2]: leaf
bail: see baal
bailaquar (bailiqua): bullock
bailpuli: see bilpuli
bailpulun[2]: foolish; forget
bakkano[2]: grandmother (maternal)
bakkare[2]: grandchild (maternal)

BAMI

bal: see baal
bal[1]: he, it, she
balemo: rough-leaved fig tree
balgon: see bulgoon
balgoungo: chop (verb)
balgul bullalel[1]: they
balgun[1]: they
balka[5]: hit, strike
ballamballam: see bullabulla
ballarat: camping place
ballat: cherry tree
balleroo: rain god
ballook: blue gum tree
balpewallin[2]: clean
balpi[2]: white
balumbah[3]: rain
balun: river
baluni[5]: die
balyarta[5]: stop, wait
bamarook (bamerook): oval shield
bambra: mushroom
bamburr: kangaroo
bamerook: see bamarook
bami[2]: girl
bananee[6]: dew
banarra: ear
banawara: limpet
bandera[6]: reed
band ngatoa[5]: I
bang[4]: hut
bangalay[5]: timber of the eucalypt
bangalow[5, 6]: feathery-leaved palm with edible leaves
bangnalla: golden perch
banjeeri: voice of ancestor spirit
banjora: native bear
banool: hill

banya: black-tailed possum
bara[5]**:** they
baragoola: flood tide
barakadan[6]**:** boomerang
baralgar: see brolga
barameda: fish trap made of logs
barega: wind
bareki: water
bargan[5] (barragan)**:** returning boomerang
bargi[5] (bargie)**:** grandmother (maternal)
barina: summit
baringa: light
baringup[1]**:** watering place
barkalonuke[5]**:** three
barkolobarkolo[5]**:** four
barkool (barkolo [5, 6])**:** two
barloona[2]**:** die
barn[4]**:** small
barno[2]**:** aunt
barook: teal
barperipna: morning
barragan: see bargan
barramundi: giant perch
barranduna: brush myrtle
baree: mountain
barreng: track
barribinda: sit (verb)
barrow: see parru
barru[1]**:** blood
barru[2]**:** meat
bartill[8]**:** parrot
bartoo[8]**:** man
bartoo-gilbee[8]**:** old man
bartungaran[8]**:** drop
bato kokoin[5]**:** water
battana[6]**:** hit
battur[6]**:** great

batturi[2]**:** bundle, heap
baylingyan[3]**:** die
baynilla[3]**:** girl
beal[4, 5] (bool, bull)**:** water sweetened with honey from the flowers of a Banksia
beal: see belah
beanga[5]**:** father
bedgery: see pitchery
beeargah: see biaga
beebeethung: red
beekbeek: ear
beela[5] (beeleer, beeler)**:** black cockatoo
beela: see belah
beelang: bag
beelarong: shining
beeleer: see beela
beenak (binnap)**:** basket
beenarra[3]**:** ear
beer[5]**:** long distance
beeree: lagoon
beereegan: quail
beereek: native cat
beereeun: small prickly lizard
beerwon: swift (bird)
beewee: goanna
beeyung: father
began[6]**:** beat
belah (beal, beela, belar, billah)**:** bull oak tree
belettah[3] (bellata)**:** throwing stick
bemkeah[5]**:** man whose brother is dead
benalla: musk duck
benang[4]**:** husband
benedba[3]**:** he, it, she
bengero[4]**:** two
bengeroganme[4]**:** three

bengeroobengeroo[4]: four
benjiman: husband
berallah: musk duck
berguna (biergoonera): wife
beri: claw
beria: sing
berigora[5]: orange-speckled duck
berley[5]: bait
berlkie[5]: see burlkie
bernarro[4]: gum tree
berontha: crow
berrimilla[5]: kingfisher
berringar[6]: sunset
Ber-rook-boorn: the first man
bertana[6]: day
Berwooland Babinger: god, son of Pundjel
betcheri: see budgeree
betcherrygah: budgerigar

BILLABONG

bettulun[2] (brattulun): disturbing from sleep
bi[1]: fish
biaga[5] (beeargah): hawk
biangri: night
biara: moon
bibba[6]: hill
bibbi[5] (bibbee): tree-runner
bibbil[5]: broad-leaved box tree; eucalypt
biergoonera[6]: see berguna
biggarroo: wombat snake
bigge[6]: sun
biggoon[5]: water rat
bigha[2]: moon
bilba[5] (bilber, bilbie, bilby): bandicoot, bandicoot rat
bilbungra: pelican
bilcom[5]: setting fire to a wurley
bilkurra: narrow-leaved box tree
billa[1, 5, 6] (bilo, pilly): river; water; fish. The common word billy, the tin can for holding and boiling water, came originally from billa
billabong[5, 6]: pool separated from a river
billah: see belah
billai[5] (billay): crimson-winged parrot
billambang: swamp oak
billeang: bat
billoo[5]: men with eagles' feet
billungah: creek
billy: see billa
bilo[1]: river (see also billa)
bilpuli[2] (bailpuli): fat, marrow

BIRRA-LI

bilyana (bilyara⁵): wedge-tailed eagle
bilyarra⁴: eagle
bimbil: poplar-leaved box wood tree
bimble: earth
biminya⁵: jealousy
binburra: white beech tree
binda: deep water
bindar⁵: kangaroo
bindaree: river
bindi⁶: see bingy
bindha⁵ (bindeah): prickle
bing⁶: father
bingami: mopoke
binganah: tree struck by lightning
bingarra: bark
bingelima: native orange tree
binga-wingul⁵ (bingahwingul): needle bush

bingee: see bingy
bingge-la⁵ (bingehlah): exclamation or ejaculation meaning, "You can have it!"
binghi: brother, later applied to all aborigines
bingui⁵ (binguie): wooden vessel, shaped like a canoe, for holding water
bingy⁵: (bindi, bingee, binji): belly, stomach
binking⁴: turtle
binnap: see beenak
binyana⁵ (binyanner³): chisel
biram⁶: heavens, sky
birra-ga⁵: stick for killing a man
Birrahgnooloo: see Birra-nulu
birra-li⁵ (birrahlee, birrah-li): baby, girl
birrana: throwing stick
Birra-nulu⁵ (Birrahgnooloo): Baiame's first wife. The name means "face like a tomahawk handle"
birrarl⁵: an exclamation
birrawa: go down
birri⁵: boy
birree gougou: see birri gu gu
birrie: danger
birri gu gu⁵ (birree gougou): a call to encourage someone to attack
Birubi⁶: Southern Cross
birwain⁵: bulrush
birwain⁶: boy
biteyee³: good
bittoorong⁵: red
blukkun²: afraid, alarmed, timid

blungbai[5]: father
boang[6]: die
bobbin[6]: father; moon
bodalla[5]: place where a child is tossed in the air
boelgi: willow
boge (bogey, bogie): bathe
bogong: see bugong
bohra[5] (bohrah, bowrah): kangaroo
bokara[5]: heat
bokka[4]: dog
boko[4]: head
boko: blind
boloke: lake
bolool: night
bombery: seaweed
bomboora: reef of rocks usually found at the foot of a cliff
bomburra: sleep
bonanyong: see buninyong
bonelya[5]: bat
bong[6] (bung): dead
bonganah[4]: boy
bonja[5]: hut
boobialla: see boobyalla
boobook: mopoke
booboo-tella[5]: feather from an emu's tail
boobyalla (boobialla): acacia, native willow
boodgeri: see budgeree
boodha[5] (budta, budtah, budtha): rosewood tree; salt
boodjerrie: see budgeree
boogarah[4]: keep away
boogoo[5]: long club
boogoo-doo-ga-da[5] (boogoo-doogahdah): rain bird

bookabooda: native gooseberry
bookang[4]: night
bookooi: rain
bool: see beal
boola (boolaboo, boolara, bolloween, bulli): two
boolaroo[6]: two
boolarra: twenty
boolea: cold
boolee[5]: whirlwind
boolgana: kangaroo
booloman[4]: two
booloman batha kootook[4]: three
booloman bathra boolung[4]: four
boolongena: emu
boolool: dark
boolooral: see bulooral
booloot[4]: above, heavens, sky
boolpooli[2]: chalk

BOOLTAROO

booltaroo: canoe
boolungal: pelican
Boomajarril: place of flowers where fairies congregate
Booma-ooma-nowi[5] (Booma-hoomahnowee): the son of Baiame
boomarrah: native plum tree
boomayamayamul and **boomayahmayahmul:** see bu-maya-mul
boomerang: weapon for throwing. The word is of doubtful origin. It is said that there is a close connection between the words for wind (boomori) and boomerang in some districts. Early forms of the word were boomering and bummering
boomori: wind
boonamin: sand hill god
boonari: "big boss"; anything supernatural
boondar: kangaroo
boonderoo: stony country
boondi[5] (boondee): club-headed weapon
boondoon: kingfisher
booner: beach
boongala: shade
boongurr: water beetle
boor[4]**:** one
boora and **boorah:** see bora
boorabi: see boor-bee
booral[5]**:** big, high
boorala: good
booragul: summer
booran: pelican
boorayo[4]**:** day

boor-bee: native bear
boorana: smoke
booreah[6]**:** fire
booreea: turpentine tree
boorlee[2]**:** see burley
boorook: warm
booroora (dooroogai): three
booroowal: day
boorrang: mist
bootoolga[5] (bootoolgah): blue-grey crane
booyanga (boyanga): egg
booyangan: female
bopup[4]**:** boy
bor (bur): girdle of manhood; circle
bora[5] (boora, boorah, borah): initiation ceremony. The word probably comes from bor, the girdle of manhood, worn in initiation ceremonies

BORA GROUNDS

borak[5]: banter, fun
boree: myall, weeping myall
boreen[5]: wooden shield
boringkoot: native raspberry
boroya: sing
borral[1]: spear head
borrinyer[5]: live (verb)
borun[4]: night
bougong: see bogong
bowrah: see bohra
boyanga: see booyanga
boyla: sorcerer
brael[4]: star
bra kini[4]: man
bralgah: see brolga
brate: see brauwarate
brattulun[2]: see bettulun
brauwarate[2] (brate): son, younger son
brenbun[4]: wife
bret[4]: hand
bri: see buri
brigge: messenger
brimbrim[4]: spring of water
brimhillah: go away
brinawa: place where water lilies grow
brolga[5] (baralga, bralgah): native companion
broon[4]: day
brumby: wild horse. It is doubtful whether it is an aboriginal word
brupe[2]: devil, evil spirit; spider
bruye[2]: forehead
buba[5]: father
buba-larmay[5] (bubahlarmay): game in which the players jump into the water with a splash

bubbera[5] (bubberah): boomerang that returns
bubbur[5] (bubburr): large brown and yellow snake
bucka[5] (puka): stink
buckali[8]: stand up
buckandee and **buckandeer**: see bukkandi
buckna[4]: rain
buddang[6]: mother
buddawong: see burrawang
budgel: sickness
budgeree[5] (boodgeri, budgeri): excellent, good
budgerigar: small bird also known by several aboriginal names, and by early settlers as warbling grass parrakeet, shell parrot, zebra grass parrakeet, etc.
budjor[1]: land
budta, budtah, and **budtha**: see boodha
buggoo[5]: flying squirrel
bugong (bogong, bougong): grey moth
bukkandi[5] (buckandee, buckandeer): native cat
bukkum[6]: land
bular[5] (bullae): two
bularbular[5]: four
bulga-nunnoo[5] (bulgahnunnoo): insects (literally bark-backed i.e. under bark and logs)
bulgoon[6] (balgon): stone tomahawk
bulkun[2] (bulgen): vomit
bull: see beal
bulla bulla[5] (ballam ballam,

bullah bullah): butterfly
bullae[6]: see bular
bullai bullai[5]: green parrot
bullarrto: place of plenty
bullen bullen: lonely place
bulli[2]: see bodla
Bullima[5] (Bullimah): Spirit
  Land, heaven, Sky Camp
bulli-medi-mundi[5] (bulli-
  medeemundi): south-east
bullito[4]: big
bulln bulln[5]: lyre bird
bullook: swamp
bullula[4]: kangaroo
bullyee[8]: navel
buln buln: green parrot
bulooral[5] (boolooral): night
  owl
bulpuli[2]: lime; pipeclay
bu-maya-mul[5] (boomayamayamul, boomayahmayah-

BUNYIP

mul): wood lizard, responsible for creating human
  babies
bumbel[5] (bumble): native
  orange tree
bunan[6]: make
bundah[6]: sing
bundara: clump of trees; edge
  of swamp
bunderra: black wallaby
bung: see bong
bungun bungun: see bun-
  yun bun-yun
buninyong (bonanyong): man
  lying on back
bungkee[8]: skin
bunmil[4]: hill
bunmilla[5] (bunmillah): fish
bunna[5]: cannibal
bunnener[5]: make
bunnyal: see bun-yal
bunnyyarl: see bun-yal
bunora[5]: long distance
bunto[8]: salt
buntor[8]: big
bunya-bunya: large tree with
  edible fruit, pine tree
bun-yal[5] (bunnyal, bunnyyarl): flies
bunyarra: sweet
bunyip: legendary monster,
  usually supposed to live in
  lakes. An early account of a
  native tradition describes it
  as "bigger than an elephant,
  like a bullock, with eyes like
  live coals, and with tusks
  like a walrus's"
bun-yun bun-yun[5] (bungun
  bungun): frog

bupper[6]: three
bur: see bor
burando[6]: windy
burgoin[5]: stone tomahawk
buri[5] (bri): acacia
buriagalah: species of acacia, literally place of the buria tree, sometimes corrupted to brigalow
burley[5] (boorlee, burle): star
burlkie[5] (berlkie): hair
burmpa: running water
burndo[5]: fish
burnta[2] (parnta): stone
burnu[1]: tree
burra: stop (verb), wait (verb); light (adj); large stone
burrabee: blood
burraburra: busy; quick; sheep
burrakay[3]: hill
burramaronga: wind
burramundi[6] (barramunda): Burnett salmon
burrandool: quail
burrawang (burwan): nut tree
burrawingie: diamond-leaved laurel
burremah: bring, come
burrendong: native bear
burrengeen: peewit
burrumbeet: muddy water
burudburang[3]: big
burwan: see burrawang
butterga[5] (buttergah): species of flying squirrel
buumbuul: manna
buyi[1]: stone
by-a-duk: stone tomahawk
byahmul: see baiamul

Byamee: see Baiame
byenie[8]: go on

C

caalang: sassafras
caberra: see cobbra
cabon: great, large
cadgee[8]: spear
caehngao[6]: snake
calca[4]: star
calimpa: bees' nest
callangun: blue fig
callemondah: many hills
caloola[5]: climb (verb)
canajong[7]: Tasmanian plant with edible fruit and leaves, known as pigface
cangella[6]: good
cappy[4]: water
carawatha: place of pine trees
carbethon: glad
carbora: native bear; water worm
cardeenie[8]: water vessel
cardo[4]: man
carina: bride, girl-wife
carlik[4]: four
carloo[8]: penis
carltooka[8]: bulldog ant
carndarah[6]: see kandara
carnka[8]: crow
carpoo[4]: three
carramar[6]: shade of trees
carrangall: athletic
carroo[8]: creek
carteta[8]: teeth
cartoo[8]: father
challing[4]: tongue
chenka: finish
cherrara[8]: shin
cheropin[8]: swim
chewenta[8]: thigh

CHURINGA

chicha[4]: small
chillberto[8]: rain
chilla[8]: poison fish
chillkalla[8]: prickle
chinkayackaby[4]: day
chinna[4, 8]: foot
chintillga[8]: grasshopper
chintoo[8] (chinto): sun
chintu-ruigin: daylight
chipala: whistling duck
chippia[8]: duck
chooka-chooka[8]: dream
chookola[8]: hole
choota[8]: gum tree
chucky-chucky: wax cluster
(an edible berry)
chucowra[8]: straight
Chucullba[8]: Southern Cross
chumbee: torpedo bug
churinga: bullroarer (see also tjurunga)

cobbie[8] (kabee, koppie): water
cobbra[5, 6, 7] (caberra, kabbera, kabura, kappara, kobbera, kobra, kobul): head, skull
cobbycoononyee[8]: rain (verb)
cobbyworrall[8]: rain (verb)
cocararra[8]: east
cockalella[8]: white cockatoo
cockanoorah[4]: hair
cocker[4] (cocki): head
colac and **colah**: see koala
colba[8]: go back
coleenie[8]: hear
collenbitchick: species of ant; double star in Capricornis
collin[4]: fire
collumbum: go back
colo: see koala
color[8] (warruc-color): flame
combo[1,3,6]: white man who lives with an aboriginal woman
comebee: see kumbi
comebo and **comeboo**: see kumbu
comebunyee[8]: hot
cooan-dunning[8]: suck
cooba: black stingless bee
coobah (koobah): species of acacia
coocoo-loora[8]: demon spirit
coo-ee (cooey): the call the aborigines gave to summon anyone, and quickly adopted by white settlers. One early explanation of the meaning was "Come to me"
coo-in-new: mahogany tree
coola: angry
coola: see koala

COOLAMON

coolabah[5]**:** eucalypt, flooded box tree

coolabun: native bear

coolah: tree

coolamon[6] (coolaman, kooliman)**:** wooden vessel for holding water or seeds, often made from a hollowed knot of a tree. Sometimes used as a term for the knot

coolbaroo: old

coolbyngga[8]**:** drawing, painting

cooler[5]**:** angry

coolie: sun

coolley[4]**:** tree

cooloongatta: fine view

cooma (combah, gaoma, kuma)**:** one

Coon undhurra: dragonfly woman

coondanie[8] (coontannie)**:** cut (verb)

coonmidjender[3]**:** sea

coorabin: barking lizard

cooragook: pause, wait

coorah[4]**:** woman

coorang: brown gravel

coordaitcha: see kurdaitcha

coorie[5]**:** husband, wife, spouse

coorigil[5] (corrigel, courigul)**:** sign of bees

cooroo[8]**:** eye

cooroonya: two women

cootrah[4]**:** two

cope cope: large lake fed by water from smaller lakes

coradgee: see koradji

coranderrk[4]**:** Victorian Christmas bush; wilga

cornu tribe[6]**:** hair

CORROBOREE

corowa[7]: rocky river
corrigel: see coorigil
corroboree[5] (corobboree and similar spellings): dance; meeting
courigul: see corrigel
cowirrie: rat
cudgel: tobacco
cudgewong: kangaroo skin
cue-on-buntor[8]: girl
cue-on-mema:[8] little girl
culgoa: river running through
cullebee[8]: hip
cullgenborn[8]: cough
cull-la (cull-lar): all right
culma: a spiny fish
cumbee: see kumbi
cundoonie[8]: kick (verb)
Cunmurra: carpet snake god
cunnenbeille and cunnunbeille: see kunnan-beili
curbarra: plenty
curla[6]: fire
currajong: see kurrajong
currawang: bell or black magpie, donkey bird, crow shrike
curreiquinquin: butcher bird
curringa: black duck
currong: silver wattle
curta[8]: head

D

dabber[6]: club
daen[5]: aborigine
daiyuwun[2]: keep, save
daku[2]: sand
dala[3]: eyes
dalo[6]: fire
dalthing[5]: end, finish
dalyo[5]: light (adj)

F

dandaloo[5]: beautiful
daraimin[2]: tear (verb)
dardur[5] (dardurr): shelter made of bark
darinana[5]: to put a water vessel near a fire
darri: track (of foot)
daya-minya[5] (dayah-minyah): small carpet snake
dayoorl[5]: flat stone used for grinding grass seed
dealk[4]: good
deentoo[2]: sun
deenyi[5]: ironbark tree
deereeree[5]: willy wagtail
degeen-boya[5] (degeen-boyah): soldier bird
dertoo[2]: hill
dhe[1,5]: hereditary totem
dheal[5]: sacred tree
dheran[6]: gully

DIDGERIDOO

dhilla: hair

diale[5]: food

didjeridoo (didjerido[3]): musical instrument, trumpet

dilkera: edge, shore

dilli[5,6] (dillee, dilly): bag for holding possessions, usually made of grass, cord, or fur. Although dilli means bag, the usual term is dillybag. Dilli was originally fine wood dust, and the dilli bag was used to carry sticks and tinder for fire-making, and the term extended to other bags

dindi[5] (dindee): pointed stick

dindin[4]: bad

dinewan[5]: emu

dinga[4]: stone

dinjerra[5]: (dinjerrah): west

dirdi[6]: day

dirrang: another term for dilli, q.v.

ditji toda[2]: day

ditter (ditta): mud, soft ground

ditye[2]: sun

dityiwakka[2]: star

djaat[1]: sun

djiimang[1]: see

djui[1]: bad

doleboin[8]: spit

dombart[1]: one

dombock: see jombock

dooliba[5] (dulibah): bald

dooloomai[5]: thunder

doonbur[5] (doonburr): grass seed

doongara[5] (doongairah): lightning

DILLY BAG

doonkami: rise (verb)

doonkuna: rising

dooran dooran[5]: see douran douran

dooroogai: three

doori[5]: grindstone

Doowi[5] (Doowee, Dowee): dream spirit

dora[4]: sleep

douran douran (dooran dooran, dourandowran): north wind

dowak[1] (dowak wirba): club

drekin[2]: chip (verb)

drekurmi[2]: hatchet, knife

drikdrik[4]: limestone

droonoodoo (droonooda): dream circle

dta[1]: mouth

dtallang[1]: tongue

dulibah: see dooliba

dullay-mullay-lunna[5] (dullaymullaylunnah): feud (literally vengeful hatred)

dulloora[5] (dulloorah): small grey bird

dumbog: see jombock

dumer[5] (dumerh, dummerh): brown pigeon

dummal[6]: small

dummerh: see dumer

dunburra-gee[3]: teeth

dundaldyn[6]: woman

dungel[5] (dungle): water hole

dunnum[6]: tongue

durabunun[6]: hut

durda[1] (durdd): fish

durdaak: pipeclay

durellie[5]: fight (verb)

durnin[6]: hand

durri[5] (durrie): cake made of flour ground from grass seed

durroon[5]: night heron

duwatyin[2]: yearning

dyintan[6]: nail fish

E

eake[3]: water

earmoonan and **ear-mou-nan**: see eer-moonan

echuca: meeting of the waters

echunga[2]: short distance

ecmurra[8]: big

edpeddo[3]: child

eebi: ghosts which inhabit the bodies of men

eehu[5]: rain

eeo eeo: alas!

eer-dher[5] (eer-dheer): mirage

eerilya: stone

eerin[5]: small grey owl

eer-moonan[5] (earmoonan, ear-mounan): monster (literally long sharp teeth)

egaie: mangrove

eggwarna[8]: see engwarnar

el[2]: is

elanora: home by the sea

el ap: I will

eleanba wunda[5] (eleanbah wundah): spirit monsters with two toes which live in the underworld

elilger: wire grass

elleenanaleah: beauty

ellhimalla[8]: day

ellimatta: our home

ellimeek: my home

ellin[2]: see ennin

ellin: move

elloi-jerra (eloi-jerra): large lizard

ellow[5]: yesterday

ellulger: ice

elod[3]: foot

eloin[3]: man

eloitj[3]: small

elouera: pleasant place

elpugi[3]: see alpugi

elunba: armpit

enamalla[8]: catch (verb)

enborra: heavy

enca[4]: one

endota[8]: beautiful

endracoon[8]: snake

engoordna: boil (noun)

engorra (angorra): bank

engwarnar (eggwarna): bone

engwura: initiation ceremony

enmaraleek[4]: give

enna[3]: nose

ennin[2] (ellin): have, wish

entoo[8]: feather
enunta[8]: bean tree
era cunalerme: play (verb)
erad[3]: one
erawar[8]: rock wallaby
erladgeer[8]: yam
erlicha[8]: raw, uncooked
erlinya: dry wood
ernar[8]: tree; stump of tree
ernar-injerika[8]: dry wood
errabunga: fish
erricha: arm
erringer[8]: neck
erringerrcoogum[3]: heat
err-reedy[8]: long time
errurraga: dry
ertargwar[8]: rat
etninja[8]: moon
etnurra: spear tree
etrakee[8]: lazy
euahl: see wahl
euloomarah: see yulu-mara
euloowirree: see yulu-wirree
eumina: repose
eurabbie: blue gum
eurah[5]: drooping shrub
eurobin: lagoon at foot of mountain

G

gaarn[4]: nose
gaat[4]: mouth
gabo: we don't know
gahrahgah: see ga-ra-ga
galah[5] (gilah): pink-breasted parrot or rose-breasted cockatoo
gallang[6]: good
gamboden[4]: one
Ganba: large mythical snake
gandjari[6]: bony bream

gaoma[2]: see cooma
ga-ra-ga[5] (gahrahgah, garargah): crane
garalin[2]: delay
garaweh[5]: white cockatoo
garbai[5]: forehead band made of string
garbarli[5] (garbarlee): shingle-back
garganj[6]: chicken hawk
gauware[2]: deep
gauwel[2]: midday
gaya-dari[5] (gayardaree): platypus
gayandi[5] (gayanday, gayandy): bullroarer, and therefore also a man's name for a bora spirit or bora devil. The woman was not allowed to use this name, but said gurraymi
gayardaree: see gaya-dari
gedala[1]: day
geebung[6] (geebong): Persoonia tree and also its fruit
geenong: footprint
geera[4]: see ghera
geewan: common fern
geewinnia[8]: see uwinnia
gelane[2]: elder brother
gelar[2]: brother
gena[4] (gerra): blood
geppmorra (gepmorra): fingernail
gerai[6]: sand
gerra[2]: see gena
gerringong: afraid; ambush
gheeger gheeger[5]: west wind
ghera (geera): gum leaf
ghilgai: see gilguy
Ghinda-inda-mui[5] (Ghinda-

hindahmoee): son of Baiame

gibber: rock, stone

gibber-gunyah: cave dwelling (gibber: rock; gunyah: shelter)

giddea: see gidya

giddie[8]**:** resin

gidgee (gidgeena): tickle

gidgee: see gidya

gidgerigar[5] (gidgereegar, gidgeereegah): small parrot (budgerigar), warbling grass parrot

gidji[1]**:** spear

gidju[6]**:** small

gidya[5,6] (giddea, gidgee): acacia tree; long spear made of this timber

gilah: see galah

gilanggur[6]**:** good

gilguy[5] (ghilgai, ghilghi): water hole

gimbi[5]**:** make

gin: aboriginal woman. Very occasionally used for female kangaroo

gira[6]**:** tree

girraween[5] (girrahween): place of flowers

giwar[5]**:** man

gnahwo: see na-wo

gnally geletcho[4]**:** we

gnamma: hole; rock

gnawela[5]**:** we

gnernpa[5]**:** my dear

gnertown[5]**:** a number of people

gnoka[5]**:** give, give me

gnolo[5]**:** wash; two people

gnoma[5]**:** yours

gnooloo-gail: see nulu-gail

GIBBER

gnoolooyoundoo: see nuluyoon-du

gnopowa[5]**:** two people

gnoyalanna[5]**:** afraid

goannar[6]**:** hut

goberta[8]**:** plum bush

goborro: dwarf box

goburra: see kookaburra

godarra[8] (kutthara): two

goditcha: see kurdaitcha

gogobera: see kookaburra

gondol[6]**:** canoe

goobita[8]**:** small

gooboothoo: done

goochagoora[8]**:** one

goodoo[5]**:** codfish

googarh[5]**:** goanna

googoorewon[6]**:** place of trees

goo-goor-gaga[5] (goug gour gahgah, gougourgahgah, gourgourgahgah): laughing jackass (literally take a stick)

go-oh[5]: come
goohnai: see goonai
goolabah: grey-leaved box tree
goola-gool[5] (goolahgool, goolahyool, goolayool): water-holing tree
goolara: moonlight
goolawa: yesterday
goola-willeel[5]: (goolah-willeel): topknot pigeon
goolay[5]: string bag
goolay-yali[5] (goolayyahlee): pelican
goolee: sand lizard
goolmarry[6]: shield
gooloo[5]: magpie
goomai[5]: water rat
goombeelga[5] (goombeelgah): canoe made of bark
goomble-gubbon[5]: bustard turkey
goomilla[5] (goomillah): woman's garment made of string; girl's garment with belt of possum sinews, with woven possum hair strands in front, about a foot square
goonagulla (goonagullah): sky
goonai[5] (goohnai): death wail
goonama: snow
goonaroo: whistling duck
goonarook: wood duck
goonawarra: swan
goonbar[3]: he, it, she
goonbean[5]: sweet excretions on the bibbil tree
goon-der-rah[6]: fight (verb)
goondie: see gunyah
goondnomda: water flowing over rocks

goondooi: see gundooi
goondool: stringybark tree
goongkoong[4]: nose
goongwar[3]: this
goonnear: carpet snake
goonur[5]: kangaroo rat
goorewon: tabooed woman
goori[5]: fat; tree
goornan: heat
goornung: see gunyang
gooroondoodilbaydilbay: south wind
goorung: fireplace
goorunna[2]: good
gootagoodo[8]: heart
gooweera[5]: pointing bone
gora: long
goroke[4]: magpie
goug gour gahgah, gougourgahgah, and **gourgourgahgah**: see goo-goor-gaga
Gowa-gay[5] (Gowargay): The Coalsack, which is the Emu in the Milky Way
gowdalie: hardwood fishing spear
goyarra[1,6]: sand
grantali[2]: big
grauwe: large
grauwe ru: larger
grauwun[2]: bury
gree[4]: canoe
grokumbalin[2]: stamp
grooee: see gruee
gruee[5] (grooee): tree with bitter fruit
guana[5]: me
gubba[5]: good
gubbera[5] (gubberah): crystals; clear stones used for magical purposes

GUNYAH

gudda[5] (guddah): red lizard
gudjal[1]: two
gudjal-gudjal[1]: four
gudjyt[1] (gudjyt barrab): heavens
gue[5]: blood
guie[5]: mine
guiebet: see gweebet
guineeboo: see gwai-nee-bu
guliba[5]: three
gulle: go up
gullee: see gulli
gulleemeah: see gulli-maya
gulli[5] (gullee): water
gulli-maya[5] (gulleemeah): water bag
gumalkoolin[4]: willy wagtail
gummy: spear
gunbower: tortuous, winding
gundai: see gunyah
gundar yuro[6]: cloud

gundoo[5] (goondooi, gundoo-ee): solitary emu
gunee: mother
gunmarl[5]: taboo; place where someone has died
gunni[5] (gunnai, gunnee): digging stick, yam stick
gununo[6]: black snake
gunyah[5] (goondie, gundai): hut, bark shelter
gun-ya-mu[5] (gunyahmoo, gunyahnoo): east wind
gunyang (goornung): kangaroo apple
gun-yanni[5]: tree
gurburra[5] (gurburrah): north
gurdar[1]: two
guridjadu[6]: carpet snake
gurkuk[4]: blood
gurra[2]: east; south-west
gurra malye[2]: south-west wind
gurraymi[5] (gurraymy): woman's name for gayandi, q.v.
gwabba[1]: good
gwai[5]: red
Gwai-billa[5] (Gwai-billah): Mars (the red star)
gwai-nee-bu[5] (guineboo, gwineeboo): robin redbreast
gwandalan: peace, quiet, rest
gweebet[5] (guiebet): thorny creeper with edible fruit
gweeon[6] (gwheh-un): stone tomahawk
gwineeboo: see gwai-nee-bu
gyn[1]: one

H

halcoppatunein[8]: sick
hanya[6]: stone
harnakar[2] (haranekar): these

Harrimiah: mythical black goanna
hatarear-amalla[8]**:** frightened
heeterra[8]**:** gum tree
hetarracadin[8]**:** pull
hetrala[8]**:** lazy
hii hii[2] (hiau hiau): any
hikkai[2] (hik): immediately, just now; this
hikkai nungge[2]**:** today
hillimung: shield
hill-lee[8]**:** fig
hillta[8]**:** hut
himbing: see humpy
hipmilta[8]**:** mirage
hokarra[8]**:** married woman
holanyee[8]**:** cry (verb)
holcoppa-tunein[8]**:** vein
holemunda (olemunda): dust
holtar[8]**:** stick
hong-gar[8]**:** reed
hontee: neck
hooray[8] (hooroo): hair
hotooworry[8]**:** cloud
humpy (himbing, oompi, yamba): bark shelter or hut
hundoeta[8]**:** see undooeata
hungappa[8]**:** crow
hungiaquar: hungry
hurramira[8]**:** goanna

I

ianuk[3]**:** I
ibi[2]**:** breast
icherramal[8]**:** shoot (verb)
idudar bungaru[1]**:** girl
igeelu[2]**:** father
igera[2]**:** mother
ignum: fall (verb)
ijawu[3]**:** fish

ikkati: sit
il[2] (ile): by
ilbanda[3]**:** earth
ilchar-atnitta[8]**:** hand
ildmurra[8]**:** dew
illa-illa[5]**:** no, not
illcarrie[8]**:** sky
illcha[8]**:** finger
illdo-malla[8]**:** cut (verb)
illginga: beefwood tree
illgulldenem: kick (verb)
ill-lamanoo[8]**:** long way
ill-loong[8] (ill-looka): dead
ill-lua[8]**:** salt
ill-luaquasha[8]**:** salt water
ill-lulta[8]**:** march fly
illpellpa: grass for thatching
illperippa[8]**:** leaf
illpilla: eyelash
illpun: along
illyer-manda[8]**:** ring
iluka: near the sea
ilumba: Moreton Bay ash
imba[2]**:** skin
imbunga[8]**:** cooked
imbye[8]**:** leave (verb)
imuran[3]**:** big
in anyril[2]**:** for him
inberra: shallow
incarnie[8]**:** laugh
indarnie[8]**:** frown
indenima: splinter
inger: foot, hoof
inger-godill[8]**:** horse
ingitja (ingitsa): new moon
ingualmulbil: foot
ingwa[8]**:** duck
injaracna: sneeze
injeer-mayjeer[8]**:** mist
injerima: breath

injerima unditta[8]: offensive breath

inkata: elder, wise man

inna[5]: this

innar-linger[8]: echidna

inntoo[8]: fur

interlina: shoe

intinne: necklace

intulka[8]: stubborn

inye[2]: also

inyeppa[8]: navel

inyerra-alcrim: shame

iona[3]: fire; tree

iperta: geranium; hole

ipminger[8]: altogether

ipoque[3]: cold

ippeeculca[8]: teat

ira[3] (jara): eyes

irinka[8]: dog

irita[8]: deaf

irriakura: edible tuber

irtaie[6]: giant nettle

irtalie: bean tree

ita[6]: scrub; swamp fish

iterika[8]: green

iterra[2]: be quick, run!

itickera[8]: root

itichika[8]: red

itichika: see ititika

ititika (itichika): blanket

ityan[2]: him

itye[2]: outside

itye[2]: see kitye

iwadi[3]: head

iwala[3]: man

iyebana[6]: peewit·

iyoura[8]: echo

iyouta[3]: spinifex

J

jaanga[4]: hut

JABIRU

jabiru: stork. It appears that this word has been imported into the aboriginal vocabulary from South America. The same word is used for the saddle-bill in Central Africa. In Australia it has also appeared in legend in the form djabiru

jackaroo (jackeroo): name for a young squatter, probably coming from the word tchaceroo, q.v., or from "Jacky Raw" a "new chum" on the analogy of the kangaroos

jalamari[3]: ears

jamida[3]: mouth

jane[4]: foot

janga[3]: foot

jara[3]: see ira

jarrah[1]: tree and timber

known variously as blue gum, mahogany gum, and swamp mahogany. It is a corruption of the native word jerryhl. It is known only as jarrah in Western Australia, where it is native, and throughout the rest of Australia, where "jarrah" is a familiar timber noted for its durability

jeeba: springtime corrobboree

Jeedara: large mythical water snake

jeetho: leave (verb)

jellan[4]**:** tongue

jeni[3]**:** nose

jenna[4]**:** foot

jenning-gherrie: willy wagtail

jenoong: foot

JUMBUCK

jerambitty yarka[4]**:** spear

jerilderie: place where reeds grow

jerron and **jerrund:** see jirrand

jerryhl: see jarrah

jewang[4]**:** star

jidi[1]**:** rain

jigi[3]**:** hand; teeth

jil-crow-a-berry: corruption of the aboriginal name for rat-tail grass

jilmil[3]**:** nose

jimara[3]**:** hair

jimari: stone knife

jimba: see jombock

Jimbun: spirit that controls love affairs

jimiramira[3]**:** big

jinang[4]**:** foot

jinchilla[6]**:** cypress pine

jindivik: destroy, lose

jinkana[2]**:** give

jinna: foot

jirra[4]**:** kangaroo

jirra: another term for dilli, q.v.

jirrand[5] (jerron, jerrund)**:** afraid; fear

jirriman[4]**:** knee

jitcha[8]**:** no

joatgba[4]**:** kangaroo

jombock (dombock, dumbog, jimba)**:** white clouds or mist which precede rain

jorrer[8]**:** shin

jumbuck: sheep. A corruption of jombock, q.v. When the aboriginals first saw sheep they compared them to white clouds

jumbunna: talk together
jumjum[4]: bellbird

K

kaain: see aya
kaandha: whale
kaar: white cockatoo
kabatang[4]: moon
kabbera: see cobbra
kabbin[4]: cold
kabbulin[2]: mock
kabee[2]: see cobbie
kabu[2]: three
kabura: see cobbra
kadaitcha: evil
kaddely[5] (kuddelee): dog
kadee[3]: mother
kaga[6]: water hole
kagailya[2]: hair
kagil[5]: bad
kahar[2]: root of tree
kaiaking[2]: tongue
kaidundun[2]: shout
kai hai: an expression of approval, equivalent to Encore! Hear! Hear!
kaiher[4]: spear
kaikai[2]: light (adj); plain (noun)
kaike: reed spear
kaikundun[2] (kaikulun): call (verb)
kaingani[2]: young man
kaintyamande[2]: bladder
kaiya[6]: spear with several stingray barbs
kakalan[6]: chicken hawk
kakee[5]: this
kaki[2]: bough
kakie[5]: that
kakke[6]: blood

kakowera: tree fern
kakuri: dry
kalajah[3] (alajah): ears
kalangbool[2]: swamp with many red gums
kalbe: pillow
kaldari[2]: tail
kalde[2]: language; throat; windpipe
kaldow[2] (kaldowinyeri, klauo, klauoanyeri): a long time ago, old
kaldowamp[2]: always, continually, ever
kalduke: bunch of feathers; umbilical cord
kalk[4]: tree
kalkerri[2]: liver
kalkkalk[4]: club
kalkree[5]: midday
kalkro[5]: jagged spear
kalla[1]: fire
kallakkure[2]: island
kallang[1]: heat
kallarak[1]: heat
kallarroo[1]: path leading to water
kalletulik[3]: two
kalparrin[2]: help carry a load
kalperri[2]: shoveller duck
kalpulun[2] (kalpundun): wink
kaltee[5]: emu
kalti[2]: spear
kaltin[2]: dig
kalun[6]: one
kalyan[2]: here; stop (verb)
kam[6]: head
kama[4]: spear
kamaroo[8]: uncle
kamballa[5]: young woman

kambara[6]: crocodile
kambera[5]: father
kambie[5]: garment
kambigo[4]: night
kameruka[5]: wait till I return
kami[5]: prickly lizard
kampa[6]: messmate tree
kan[2]: them
kana[6]: spear
kanake: fighting club, waddy
kanakie[5]: water vessel
kanamer[4]: heat
kanawinkie[5]: tomorrow
kanbigur mel[1]: eye
kandara[5] (carndarah, kandora): blood
kandari[2]: rope
kandauwe[2]: their
kandeer: branch
kandelka[5]: good
kandora[5]: see kandara
kaneky[5]: yellow-crested cockatoo
kangaroo: the famous animal which leaps on its hind legs, balances itself by its tail, and carries its young in a pouch. There has been much debate as to whether it is an aboriginal word, and many explanations have been given. There is no doubt that it was not used to any great extent by the blackfellows in the early days of settlement, for they regarded it as an English word. It was first recorded in 1770 when H.M.S. *Endeavour* was at Cooktown, but fifteen years later it was not known

KANAKE

to the aborigines of New South Wales. One explanation is that the word means "I don't know", but no similar sounding word or words with this meaning have been recorded.
kangernackie[5]: this side
kanggen[2]: laugh at
kangkin[2]: laugh
kangnarra: sweat (verb)
kan-guama[5]: sweat
kangulandah[2]: again, first, once more
kangulun[2]: another, other
kangulun nungge[2]: day before yesterday
kaning marrewan[4]: throwing stick
kanku[2]: boy

kanow[4]: he, it, she
kanpuka[4]: white water-lily
kantarli[2]: sweat (noun)
kaoga[5]: head
kaooroo: water-lily
kaoota[7]: dusk, evening
kapo[5]: silence
kappa[6]: moon
kappara: see cobbra
kappin[2]: mock
kar[2]: they
Kara: spider woman
karagata: umbrella bush
kara kara: gold
Karakarock (Kararock, Kur-ruk-ar-ook): goddess, daughter of Pund-jel
karangkarang[4]: hair
karawun: long leaf used for making baskets
karbeethong: laughter
karbolquar[3]: mouth
kardidi baldin[1]: small
kardingoola: midday, noon
kardo[1]: see kerdo
kare[5]: man
kargaruk[4] (kurruk): sand
kari[2]: smoke
karinga: today
karinye[2]: mother-in-law
karkalla: pigface
karkaro[5]: spear
karkarook: sand
karlo[2]: immediately, just now
karlowan[2]: behind, second
karlowan atye[2]: last, final
karlowun[2]: turn round
karlye[2]: crab
karndobara[4]: blood
karnick[4]: throwing stick

karobran: together
karoom: native currant
karraba: cut (verb)
karragain: stone tomahawk
karraka[5]: leg
karraninke[5]: day
karranga: up
karri (kari): eucalypt
karrit[4]: rain
karte[2]: island
karthro[5]: there
karu: spear with stone head
karumba: soul or spirit of an old man
karwin: grass tree
kaso[5]: another
kata[6]: mother
katan[6]: cut (verb)
katata[4]: cold
katee-wailwo[5]: small
kathowart[4]: you
katoa[5]: short
katta[1]: head; hill
kattamangara[1]: hair
kattidj[1]: hear
kaṭṭik[1]: night
katya[6]: far away
katye[4]: heat
katyil[2]: yes
katyin[4]: water
kauerti[2]: swan
kaukau[2]: bless, thank
kauwul[5]: big
kaya: uncle
kayannie[4]: water
ke[2] (keh): eh!
kearka[8]: bowerbird
keda[2]: boomerang
kehla nyauwe[4]: day
keilambete: brackish lake

kein[6]: moon
kekuyan[6]: spiny ant-eater
kelgalli[2]: infant
kelgelli[2]: caterpillar
keli[4]: dog
kelunji: galah bird
kembla: abundant
kena[6]: fresh water crocodile
kendi: lizard; mythical frilled lizard
kene[2]: firestick
kenggun[2] (kengk): they two
keni[2] (kene): cinders, ember
kenkank[2]: grey-haired
kenkulun[2] (kenk): grey
kerau kiath[2]: above
kerdo[1] (kardo): husband, wife, spouse
kerlpa[5]: knot
kerlpra[5]: finger
kertum[4]: boomerang
kertun[2]: bend (intrans. verb)
ketchum[4]: hut
keyakki[2]: five
keyap[4]: one
kia[2]: spear
kiambram: dense forest
kiar[4]: bad
kiata: heat; summer
kibulyo: whistling duck
kiewa: sweet water
kielpa[5]: short distance
kikinummi[2]: black snake
kiley[1] (kyli, kylie): type of boomerang
kilkie: water hen
kilkilyalin[2]: destroy, scatter; rub (verb)
kilkulun[2]: smooth
killara: permanent

kilpa[2]: cool, cold
kilpalie: cold
kilpanie: winter
kilto[5]: grassy
kimba[5]: bush fire
kimmuli (kimmule): teatree
kin[2]: him
kinankurnunk[2]: day after
kinauwe[2] (kinauwurle): his
kindyerra: grass
kindilan[6]: joyful
kine[4]: fish
kinedana[5]: laugh (verb)
kineman[2] (kinemin): black
kineyah: rice
kinga[4]: he, it, she
kinie-ger: native cat
kinka: laugh
kinkindele[2]: tortoise, turtle
kinkuna: laugh (verb)
kinma[4]: this
kinma[6]: awake
kinner[5]: they
kinpin[2]: sweet
kinyet[4]: they
kirkuwe[2]: itch (verb)
kirli[2]: coot
kirra[6]: leaf
kirrang: wattle
kirrkie: whistling hawk
kirrpiyirrka: seagull
kitye[2] (atye, itye): he, it, she
klallin[2]: fiery hot, scald, thirsty
klallin ruwe[2]: parched ground
klare[2]: short-tailed goanna
klartin[2]: shine
klauo: see kaldow
kldeimindin[2]: fetch
koa[2]: crow

koala (colac, colah, colo, coo-la, kool-la): native bear
koala³: man
kobbera: see cobbra
kobi: medicine man
kobra: see cobbra
kobul: see cobbra
koiranah: eagle
kodala⁶: reed
koiyung⁵: fire
koka²: see kukaa
kokate²: see kukathe
kokereka⁵: black
kokeri⁵: hut
kokipijira⁶: rain, storm
koko⁵: see kokora
kokora⁴: rain
kokora⁵ (koko): head
kolet⁶: dove
kolge² (kilgi): she-oak
kolkon⁴: boy
kollah⁵: tree
kolle: water
kolora: fresh water lagoon
kolya⁵: winter
kombona⁵: old woman
komlia⁵: big
konak³: earth
konamba⁴: woman
konda: cabbage tree
kondarle²: whale
kondu⁴: club
konegerana⁵: sulky
kong⁶: water
kongaroo⁸: sister
kongoola²: fresh water fish
kongwak: catch(verb)
koninderie⁵: rainbow
konk²: away
konkaer⁶: head

konkea: aunt
konkinyeri²: alone, apart
konkon⁶: white fish hawk
konkonbah²: hunt (noun)
konkuwarrin²: send
konnung: man-killing stick
konol³: sky
koobah: see coobah
koob-bor: native bear
Koobooboodgery: night spirit
kooberry: bidyan ruffe (fresh water fish), also called silver perch or bream
kooding³: mother
koodnapina: brown duck
Koodyoorinadyal⁶: Southern Cross
koo-ee-lung: porpoise
kooim⁴: kangaroo

KOOKABURRA

kooka: animal food, flesh, game

kookaburra (goburra, gogobera): laughing jackass

koola² (koolar⁶): kangaroo

koolein: man

koolena: sandy plain

kooliman: see coolamon

koolin⁴: man

koolkuna: protect

kool-la: see koala

koolyangarra: children

koolyer⁵: cold

koolyn: black swan

koolootaroo: magpie lark

koombar⁶: bark

koomeela: fly (verb)

koonappoo: mouse

koondi⁵: hut

koongarra: noise of the flight of birds when rising from the ground

koongarra⁸ (koongarroo): kangaroo

koongawa⁴: good

koongoora: elder sister

koongun: scorpion

koon-ja-gilbee⁸: old woman

koonje⁵: camp

koonkie: doctor

koonthooi: kelp

koonwarra⁴: oyster

koora²: day

kooraba⁴: blood

koorala: walk (verb)

kooraltha: spotted ferret

koorang: snake

kooranya: other daughters

koorngoo: food bag

koornkoo²: camp

koorong⁴: canoe

kooronya: myself

kooroorook: stick

koorowar³: water

koorowera: black diver

koorpa: flood

koorrnong: creek which dries up in summer

koort-boork boork: grove of she-oak trees

koortgang: speckled teal

kooruck: soil

koorunga: four

kootopan⁴: one

kooya² (kuya): fish

koppie²: see cobbie

kopulun²: avoid a weapon thrust

kor⁴: sea

kora⁶: native companion

koradji⁵ (coradgee): clever man, medicine man, sorcerer

korana³: see orana

kore²: woman

korne²: man

korneok: whistling duck

korobra: dance (verb)

korowalkin²: lie on the back

korpi⁶: mangrove

korra²: grass

korraco⁸: red ochre

korrorook: stork

korrumburra: blowfly

koruldambi²: white owl

kotbityerowe²: bull ant

kotla²: tail

kotyap⁴: stone

kow⁴: nose

kowa⁵: plenty

kowallong-cowling: outside place

kowandi[2]: smoke signal

kowan worang[4]: head

kowia[5]: come here

kowinka: red mangrove

kowundun[2]: step (verb)

koyuga: plain surrounded by forest

koynaratingana[7]: sandy beach

kraiyelin[2]: jealous

kralin[2]: bury

krambruk: landing place

kramburk[4]: sandy place

kranalang: crab

krangnark[4]: hill

krepauwe[2]: bread

kringgun[2]: grow

kringyang: sand mullet

kroman[6]: kangaroo

krowalle[2]: blue crane

krugarupe[2]: oven

krunkun[2]: name (verb)

kruwalde[2]: bloody

kruwe[2] (krui): blood

kua[6]: dingo

kuarun[2] (kuun): distant

kuboin[4]: scrub pigeon

kuddelee[2]: see kaddely

kudgee: castor oil plant

kudla[2] (kurla): fire

kuging-cudgen: red pigment

kukaa[2] (koka): head

kukabuka[2]: die

kukai[6]: mother's older brother

kukathe[2] (kokate): orphan

kuke[2]: elbow

kukki[6]: blood

kuk kuk ki[2]: five

kula: bloodwood tree

kulagook[3]: one

kulai: echidna

kulan[6]: possum

kulde[2]: farm; froth; saliva

kuldi[2]: mate

kuldoo: edible seed

kulduke[2]: doctor

kuldun[2]: see kulkun

kulgarnie[2]: hot wind

kulgulankin[2]: see kulyulaikin

kulgutye[2]: motherless

kulka[2]: star

kulkawura: afternoon

kulk turring[4]: tree

kulkuldi[2]: crooked

kulkulook: fishing net

kulkun[2] (kuldun): burn (scorch), scorch

kulla (kullah): native bear

kullack[4]: club

kulletulik-kulagook[3]: three

kullin[4]: throwing stick

kullun[2]: pliable

kulmul[4]: blood

kuloomba: native clover

kulpana[5] (kulpanah): speak

kultha[5]: another

kultown[5]: duck

kulu: seed

kulyulaikin[2] (kulgulankin): ashamed

kuma[2]: see cooma

kumala[6]: mud shell

kumalie[5]: small duck

kumaloro: sign language

kumarie[6]: blood

kumbargang myardack[1]: night

kumbelin[2]: sweetnesss

G

kumbi[5] (comebee, cumbee):
kangaroo skin bag
kumbokumbo: death dance
of warriors
kumbooran[5]: east
kumbu[5] (comeboo, comebo):
stone tomahawk
kumbumbana[5]: a number of
women
kummaiyem[2]: distant
kummun[2]: deep
kumpa[2]: urine
kumpun[2]: blow (verb), blow
the fire
kuna[5]: grey hair
kunabinjelu[2]: mosquito
kunakuna[5]: box tree
kunakunakasno[5]: bark (verb)
kunar[2]: excrement
kunara[6]: tiger shark
kunarle[2]: emu feathers
kunda[6]: dog
kunda: decorated digging stick
kundart: cloud
kundemer[4]: mouth
kunden[2]: kiss; rest
kundgulde: butterfish
kundolo[4]: eye
kundy[5]: mosquito
kunewallin mewe[2]: cross (ill-
tempered)
kung[6]: water
kunga[4]: make
kunga-gnarra[5]: throat
kungenyeriwallin[2]: epileptic
fit
kungkungullun[2] (kungkung-
under): love (verb)
kungkungundun[2]: loved
kung our[2]: listen!

kungullin[2]: think
kungun[2]: hear, understand
kungyuttulun[2]: eat greedily
kuniekoondie: crayfish
kunkulde[2]: Murray mouth
sprat
kunkun[2]: swallow (verb)
kunnai[6]: spear
kunnan-beili[5] (cunnembeille,
cunnunbeille): Baiame's second wife; pigweed root
kunpie: jew lizard
kunnogwurra[3]: canoe
kuntnama-cuerana[5]: smile
(verb)
kunthold[2]: gladness, joy
kunthun[2]: glad
kuntun[2]: blaze (verb)
kuntyan[6]: pandanus
kuntyari: plant with edible
roots
kunye[2]: enough
kupa: white man
kupala[6]: white
kuppa: water
kur[2]: calf (of leg); river
kuracca: white-crested cockatoo
kuranye[2]: closely woven
kur-bo-roo: native bear
kurda[2]: man
kurdaitcha (coordaitcha, goditcha): shoes made of emu
feathers, pointed at both
ends so that trackers cannot
tell which way the wearer
has gone. The term is ap-
plied to the shoes by the
white man, but by the aborigine to the wearer, who is

usually being hunted by a vengeful enemy

kure²: neck

kurla²: see kudla

kurla²: wood

kurle²: head

kurmoonah⁶: honey

kurnkuni²: relative

kurra: fierce storm, gale

kurragong: shade tree

kurrajong⁵ (currajong): tree *Sterlucia* (also called noonga); also used of fibrous plants

kurrara: place frequented by possums

kurramilla: small pink shell

kurrawa: rough sea

kurrawan: reed

kurreah: see kurria

kurrengk²: see tarrukengk

kurria⁵ (kurreah): crocodile; also the name of the crocodile who lives in the Milky Way

kurrin²: ask

kurrin⁵: sand

kurrinyerengk²: trousers

kurrnung: small creek

kur-rook-ar-rook: koala with young

kurrowera: shag

kurruk⁴: see kargaruk

Kur-ruk-ar-ook: see Karaka-rock

kurrung⁴: big

kurta²: excrement

kurtli: she-oak

kurtoo²: wife

kurunkun²: blow (of wind)

kurunto⁵: belly

kur-ur-rook: native companion

kutha²: club

kuti²: cockle

kutjara²: ear

kutkuti²: crooked

kutsha²: another, more

kutta yang⁴: head

kutthara²: see godarra

kutyeri²: thin

kutyo²: small

kuun²: see kuarun

ku-utyun²: far

kuwullun²: stick (verb)

kuya²: see kooya

kuyan⁶: honey bee

kuyulpi²: parrot

kwa⁵: dance of the crows

kwaky⁴: day

kwimpy⁶: kangaroo

Kwoolcudee: lizard god

kyeema⁴: kangaroo

kyeema: dawn

kyena: barracoota

kyli and **kylie:** see kiley

kynkar¹: father

L

laane-coore (lanacoora): home of the kangaroo

laane-pyramul: home of the emu

laap: see lerp

lakebi²: few, small number

lakkari²: honeysuckle tree

lakkin²: throw a spear

laldilald²: round about

lalirra³: sun

lal-lal: small quantity of water

lamaldar[2] (maldamaldar):
curl (noun)

lamaliala[3]: mouth

lamangurk[4]: girl

lamgalio[3]: small

lamilla[3]: stone

lammin[2]: carry on the back

lanacoora: see laane-coore

lane[4]: good

langi: dwelling place

langi-dorn: bellbird nest

langi-gherim: home of the
yellow-tailed black kangaroo

langi-giran: nest of the black
cockatoo

langmong[4]: stone

lanyalin[2]: fester

lapoinya[7]: tree fern

lar[4]: hut

larayelarra[3]: hair

larelar[2]: circular, round

lare muntunt[2]: on the other
side; upside down

lark[4]: cloud

larolk[3]: fire; tree

lawitbari[3]: two

lawitbarimot[3]: three

lea (leang, leanyook): tooth

leawill[4] (langeel, leangeel,
leanguel, leeangle, leawil,
le-ow-el): wooden club bent
at the head. The name leeangle is probably half aboriginal and half European, the
"angle" referring to the bent
head, but bearing a resemb-
lance to the aboriginal word

leeang[4]: teeth

leemurra[3]: eye

leena[7]: possum

leetunger[3]: fire

leewin[2]: bend (intrans verb)

leita[3]: small

leongatha[4]: tooth

leripma: flame

lermalner[3]: hair

lerp[4] (laap, leurp): sweet;
manna secreted by an insect

lerra[8]: river

lerunna: flounder

lewurmi[2]: buttocks

lianwill[4]: club

licka[8]: prickle

lidjet: fish

lielu: husband

likoo[2]: canoe

likoorler[3]: spear

lilla[8]: gravel

lilliri[2]: shade, shadow

lillkar[8]: wind

lilyerwer[3]: hill

LEAWILL

limga[3]: stone
lintyeri[2]: young root of weeds
lirok[4]: woman
lirralirra: wren
lirt[4]: hair
liyer[3]: fish
loa (lowa): woman
loaranneleah: blue sky
loilyer[3]: moon
lokkin kaye[2]: make a basket
lokulun[2]: howl (dog)
lokure[2]: mussel
loldu[2]: down in; go; go down
lom[2]: you two
lomar[3]: ears
longerenong: dividing of the waters
longootpar[5]: kangaroo
loombark: water grass
loongana[7]: swift
looranah: brushwood
loorapa: caught
loorea[3]: moon
loorl[3]: sit down
loru[2] (moru): ascend, go up
lottheggi[2]: bat
lowalde[2]: summer
lowan[2,4]: scrub turkey, native pheasant or mallee fowl
lowana[7]: girl
lowanna[7]: beauty
lowralarree[3]: we
lubra[7]: woman
luderick (ludrick): black-fish
luk[2] (lun): as, like
lukun[2]: sour
lulur[2]: broken
lurki[2]: lizard
luwun[2] (lulun-intrans. form): break

luwun-turtangk[2]: kneel
lyaleetea[7]: sea
lyeltya: breakers

M

ma[3]: eye, see
maa[4]: eye
Maamu: leader of evil spirits
mabingi mulko[1]: cloud
mackunya[5]: turn over
macooloma[7]: draw, paint
madba[3]: kangaroo
madbarra[3]: tree
madhi[5] (mahthi): dog
madlanchi[2]: bad
mado[5]: trumpeter-perch, bleak
magra: pouch or sling in which women carry their children
mague[5]: eyebrow
magul[6]: head
mah[5]: totem; brand; hand
mahmak[4]: father
mahn: long
mahrung[4]: see
mahthi: see madhi
mai: fruit and vegetables, food
maiatta[6]: sugar-bag
maigamaigwa: thumb
maimah: see mayama
mai-ra[5]: paddymelon
mairn[4]: heavens
maitlia[2]: clay
maiya[6]: vegetable food
maiyanowe[2]: grand-mother (paternal)
maiyarare[2]: grand-child (father's side)
maiyingar[2] (maiyinggar): cloak, garment, possessions
maka: small fire

make²: cheek
makga⁵: doctor
maki: hunting boomerang
makkin²: pick up
mako: edible wood grub
makoo: cloud
makoro⁵: fish
mal⁵: one
malangenna⁷: infant
malbooma⁶: wind
maldamaldar²: see lamaldar
malde²: foreign, strange, different
maleye⁵: husband
mali⁴: he, it, she
mali: non-material form of both human beings and inanimate objects
malie⁵: man
malkin²: creep
mallana⁷: canoe
mallanbool⁴: pool with reeds
mallee⁴: scrub of dwarf eucalypts
maller⁴: throwing stick
malloomar³: head
mallowe: Murray mouth salmon
malpuri²: guilty of murder
maltaiar² (malde, malte): few, some
maltthi²: night
malunna⁷: nest
malyar²: flock
mam²: animal food, meat
mama⁶: hold, pick up
mamalla³: star
Mamaragan: the lightning man
mamarap¹: man

mambamya pumo⁵: widow
mambo⁵: sister-in-law
mame²: fish
mamiliri³: hand
mamma² (mamman): father
mammal¹: boy
mamman¹: see mamma
mammart¹: sea
mammerool³: dog
mamook⁴: father
mamun³: tree
mana⁶: neck, run
manai²: see mani
manamana⁴: hand
manar²: fin
manba⁵ (wanga): flesh
mandigara¹: girl
mandurama⁵: water hole
manenee³: hand
maneroo: plain
mangaroo: phalanger, flying squirrel

MALLEE

manga tandra[2]: head
mangka[6]: behind
mangnoo[2]: rain
mani[2] (manai): equal
manillirra[3]: hut
manity[3]: sun
mankara[2] (munkara): girl
mankuri[2]: belly, stomach
manna[7]: wattle tree
manninkki[2]: leech
mant[2]: gently, slowly
mantaba[6]: bustard
manya[6]: small
manyeekerrik[3]: spear
mao-warang: native pepper tree
mapa[6]: flap (verb)
mar[3]: cloud
maragajang[4]: small
marandoo[4]: plenty
marangane[2]: crowd (verb)
marangani[2]: autumn
maranowe[2]: elder sister
maratulde[2]: empty
marauwe[2]: sister
maray[5]: pilchard
marbangye[2]: black diver
marbeangrook: evening star
maremuntunt[2]: beneath, inside
marhra[1]: hand
mari: wallaby
marila[6]: man
markrah[5]: dark
markulde[2] (markulli): shoulder, shoulder blade
marloo: pipeclay; kangaroo
marloorie[8]: claypan
marloorie-buntor[8]: lake
marma[8]: sore
marman[4]: father

marmingatha: prayer
Marmoo[8]: demon spirit
marnditye[2]: because
marngowi[2]: sugar
marnmin[2]: beat (verb)
maroo[4]: pine tree
maroong (mahrung, maron): pine tree
marpanye[2]: club
marra[2]: see murra
marram: kangaroo
marro: instruction of initiates
marrongie: spear shaft
marroo[8]: black
marte[2]: stone
marti[2]: limestone, rock
matari[2]: man
matong: great, strong
mattini: double-pointed club
matyimuk[4]: wife
maunanyuk[4]: hand
mawiliri[3]: teeth
may[5] (mayr): wind
mayama[5] (maimah): stone
Maya-mayi[5] (Meamei): the Pleiades (the seven sisters)
mayra[5] (mayrah): spring wind
mbal[3]: hair
mea[6]: eye; open mesh
mealler[4]: husband
Meamei: see Maya-mayi
meangener[3]: man
mearann[8]: call (verb)
meauke[2]: crayfish
meekyluka: Sturt's desert pea
meelitshel[3]: small
meelugger[3]: woman
meetawarri: old woman
mega[1]: moon
melape[2]: devil, evil spirit
meli[2]: company of people

melinya[5]: fingernail
melkin[2]: shade (verb)
mell[1]: eye
memerangi: cough
mempin[2]: beat, kill, strike
menaikulun[2]: turn inside out
menaikundun[2]: bend (trans. verb)
menamenakarin[2]: roll (verb)
menane[2]: penis
menarte[2]: blunt
menbi[2]: fat
mendemullar[6]: nose
mendic: sick
mendin[2]: fight (verb)
mendolo[5]: nose
menengi[2]: mud
mengye[2]: how; whose
meningkundun[2]: bow
menmenengkuri[2]: martin, swallow
menperre[2]: frog
menurte[2]: short
mera[5]: string bag
meralde[2]: spear with quartz head
meraldi[2]: dried, withered
meralke[2]: tree root
meralte[2]: boat
merammin[2]: see nammin
merate[2]: bare, naked
merbuck[4]: cold
merendamin[2]: drink (verb)
merippin[2]: cut (verb)
merkani[2]: strange, wild
merkawatyeri[2]: riddled with holes
merke[2] (merki): hole, small hole
merlaga[5]: the other side

mermawer mokiter[3]: die
Merpulla: rain woman
merrenetta: see murranudda
merri[4]: stone
merrican-kein[6]: moon
merrina: deceit, pretence
merringannee[5]: south wind
meta[2]: land
metpadinger[3]: club
mewe[2]: bowels
mewultun[2]: want (verb)
meya[6]: lift
mi[6]: eye
mia[2]: sleep
mia[5]: cold
miah[1]: moon
miailler[4]: eye
miala[2]: sleep (verb)
miam[4]: hut
mia-mia: hut, shelter
mian[4]: wife
mianameena[7]: pool
Mickibri: messenger of the bird goddess Nulgin
mickie[5]: quick
middip[3]: live (verb)
midgee[8]: blood
midjee[5]: species of acacia tree
midjeer[5]: barbed stick for prising grubs out of crevices
midna[2] (mina): eye; see
mie[5]: girl
miga[6]: dog
miintinta[6]: sea turtle
mije: little
miki[1]: moon
mikurri[2]: spotted bandicoot
mil[5]: eye
milbung: blind (literally eye-dead)

milki[2]: eye
milkurli[2]: orange (colour)
millair and **millear**: see millia
milla milla[6]: baby
millemurro: pelican
millia[5] (millair, millear): kangaroo rat
millin[2]: bewitch, charm (verb), sorcery
millin-dulu-nubba[5] (millin-dooloonubbah): bird
milling-kalla[6]: four
milloo: river
milo[6]: eye
milpara (milpera): company
miltee[8]: nail
milterree[5]: stiffness
milyali: infant
milyali tinyeri[2]: offspring
milyarm[1]: star
milyaroo: dusk
mimbo[8]: water vessel
mina[2]: see midna
minamberang: clematis
minar: mark
minarto[5]: what name
mincarlie[8]: rain
mind[2] (mindenanyir): why
minderin[4]: hair
mindi[6]: teeth
mindi (myndie): bunyip-snake
mindyah[6]: cloud
minga[2]: ill, illness, pain, sick, sickness
minga[5]: hole in the ground, well
minga[8]: small black ant
minga: bad
Mingara: good spirit which

controls the clouds
ming-ari (min-jin, minnnarie): mountain devil
mingga[5] (minggah): spirit-haunted tree
miningkar[2]: worm
minkie[5]: daylight
minna: beach; what; wrist
minnear: see myrna
minninger[3]: night
minn-narie[8]: mountain devil
minnta[8]: shadow
minntin: pinch (verb)
mintambi[2]: string
mintchie[6]: foot
minti[2]: small portion
minya[2]: small
minyai[2] (munyarai): how many?
minyaka: tomorrow
minyandai[2]: how often?
minyun[4]: kangaroo
miowera[4]: emu
mirambeek: mine
mirimp[2]: half
miriyan[6]: star
mirla[2]: throwing stick
mirnyong[4,7] (mirrnyong): midden containing shells
miro[1]: throwing stick
mirpin[2]: sink (verb)
mirr[4]: eye
mirramirildin[2] (mirramerildin): decayed, rotten, withered
mirreen: south
mirria[5] (mirrieh): polygonum shrub
mirrin[5]: cloud
mirror[8]: country

mirru[6]: wife
mirrung[6]: girl
mirta[2]: white ant
mitamit: speed
mittagong: small mountain
mityak[4]: rain
mityan[4]: moon
mitye[2]: name
miyer[6]: send
moa[6]: run
moabu[2]: dark
moatah[7]: pigeon
mockra[5]: rain
modda: stone
modla[2] (mooller): nose
moerlina: friendly spirit
moerpun[2]: take care of, watch
moerty[3]: canoe
mogo[5]: axe; stone
moilong: advancing tide
moilwer[3]: stars
moinpunden[2]: kiss
moiya[6]: bullroarer
mokari[2]: new
moki[2]: cloudy
molbangen[2]: warm (verb)
molbangimindin[2]: warm oneself
moldar[2]: breath
moliagulk: wooded hill
mollineux[3]: man
molta (molltee[8]): wrist
moltu[4]: night
moma: ghost
momar[4]: father
monatandra[2] (munathandra): teeth
mongan: a mammal
mongana (ammonga): fly, insect

monkeit[4]: make
monmondik[4]: girl
monomeeth: agreement, benevolence, enjoyment
monoro[6]: eye
monti[6]: stork
mooaloonyah[7]: pigeon
moochambilla: kangaroo
moocoo[8]: heel
moodai[5]: possum
moodla: corroboree
moodunna: finish (verb)
moogaray[5]: hailstone
moogana: white-breasted shag
moogra-ba (moograbah): bell-magpie, black-backed magpie, crow-shrike, or donkey-bird
moola: shady place
moolgewanke: bunyip
mooller[4]: see modla
moolyera[8]: curlew
moomowroong[4]: pebble
moona[2]: plenty
moondah: beyond
moondak: squeeze (verb)
moondara: periwinkle
moondani: embrace (verb)
moonga[8]: dark
moongan[4]: father
moonoon: see mooroon
moonoroo[6]: eye
moonthalie: ourselves
Moora: spider which brings girl babies to earth
mooro-moora: good spirit
moorang[4]: cloud
moorapoo: back
mooregoo[5]: mopoke
moorelli: thirsty

moorillah: see morilla

mooroo: bitch

mooroocoochin[4]**:** black swan

mooroola[5] (mooroolah)**:** waddy (weapon)

mooroolbark: red bark

mooroomin[5] (murroomin)**:** bark of kurrajong tree

mooroon[5] (moonoon, moornin)**:** emu spear; fat

mooroop: spirit

mooroopna: deep hole

mootcha: native cotton bush

mootta: wood

mooyi[5] (mouyi)**:** white cockatoo with yellow crest; also the pointers of the Southern Cross

mopa[5]**:** no

morala: see morgalal

morallie[2]**:** low (of cattle)

morang[4]**:** sky

moranjee[8]**:** steady

morannie[8]**:** relative

morequirta[8]**:** see morquita

morgalal[3] (morala)**:** sea

morilla[5] (moorillah, morillah)**:** stony ridge

mornee[3]**:** rain

morokkun[2]**:** bring, get, hold, obtain; sieve

moroko[5]**:** sky

moron[5] (morrun)**:** live (verb)

morquita (murequirta)**:** hat

moru[2]**:** below, down, go down, go

moruga[2]**:** sweet

moruldun[2]**:** adultery

morwong[5]**:** carp, jackass fish

motepa[5]**:** child, girl

motthari[2]**:** seal

motu[3]**:** one

mouyi: see mooyi

mowan[3]**:** sun

mowantyi[2]**:** pine tree

moye[3]**:** sun

mrangalli[2]**:** stony ground, place full of stones

mree[4]**:** eye

mubbo (mubboo)**:** beefwood tree

mubboon: small tributary

mubbu[5] (mubbo, mubboo)**:** beefwood tree

mudla[2] (mutla)**:** nose

mudlo[3]**:** head

mugana: willy wagtail ("teller of tales")

muggil[5]**:** stone knife

mukka[2]**:** no

mulali[2]**:** bone

muldarpe: devil-devil, evil spirit

muldi[2]**:** bough, foliage, leaves; smoke

muldurie[2]**:** magpie

mulga: acacia

mulgamurra[8]**:** blowfly

mulgar naggaman[1]**:** cold

mulla-munale[6]**:** throwing stick

mulla-murrale[6]**:** boomerang

mullara[5]**:** cloud

mullauna: together

mullaya[5] (mullayerh)**:** companion, friend, mate

mullee mullee[5]**:** dream spirit (of wirinun)

mullian[5] (mullyan)**:** wedge-tailed eagle

mullian-ga[5] (mullyangah):
morning star
mullo[6]: stone
mulloka[5]: water devil
mulloona: each other
mullyan: see mullian
mullyangah: see mullian-ga
multara: covering of emu
feathers used for warmth in
cold weather
multuwallin[2]: many
multuwarrin[2]: too much
mulundar: swallow (bird)
mulwala: possum grass
mulya: nose
mumalwar[3]: blood
mumberleya[2]: live (verb)
mummjeeli[8]: take, take it
mummu[2]: good
mumnunah[6]: mouth
munainpulun[2]: languid
munangpallan[2]: soft
munathandra[2]: see monatandra
munda[8]: earth
mundamunda: string ornament
mundara[4]: thunder
mundarra[8]: garment, shirt
mundawora: native blackberry
munde-wudda[5] (mundehwuddah): north-west wind
mundho[4]: mouth
mundi[2] (munde): man's breast
mundil[6]: night
mundill[6]: big
mundoe: big toe
mundooie[5]: foot, leg
Mundook: goddess or spirit of
fertility

mundroola: two only
mundurra: hunter
munengk[2]: lip
mungaiyin[2] (mungaiyulun):
write
mungaiyuwun[2]: tattoo
munganye[2]: again
mungara[2]: thirst, thirsty
mungedma[3]: wife
mungeenie[8]: pick up
munggai[2] (mungow): close
(to the person spoken to),
near
munggaiyuwun[2]: cut the body
munggan[2]: in that
munggar: tattoo marks
munggi[5] (mungghee): mussel
munggi-wurray-mul[5] (mungghe-wurraywurraymul):
seagull
munggow[2]: in there, there
mungi[2]: eat; message stick
mungi[3]: child
mungkule[2]: lake
mungoon-gali[5] (mungoongarlee, mungoongarlie): goanna
mungow[2]: see munggai
mungrie[2]: see munkuripa
mungunni: evil
munguwun[2]: feed (verb)
muninyeri[2]: moustache
munja[4]: fish
munjong: new chum
munker[2]: small hawk
munkora: dilly bag
munkumbole: clever, expert,
superior person
munkuripa[8] (mungrie): three
munmunde[2]: barter
munnari[2]: short-tailed goanna
munniger[4]: he, it, she

munnura[6]: mouth
munta[8]: sand
munte[2]: thumb
munthu[2]: kangaroo
muntye[2]: lame
munung[4]: hand
munyarai[2]: see minyai
munyertoo[2]: cold
munyeru: small, black edible seeds
muralappi[2]: little, young
murang[6]: fish
muranpun[2]: seize
murde-ejit[3]: hill
murdu: totem
mure[2]: dust
muremelin[2]: quick
murga muggai[5] (murgah muggui): trapdoor spider
muri[3]: sun
muritpun[2] (muriltpun): close shut, shut in (verbs)
murna[2] (murnna): big, great, many, much
murndiella: wave
murra[2,5,6,8] (marra, murrah, murramamlunya): finger, hand
murrai[5]: good
murrakeen[5]: girl
murramai: talisman made of quartz crystal
murramaner[4]: we
murranudda (merrenetta): bustard
murrara[2]: duck
murra-wunda[5] (murra-wondah, murrawundah): climbing rat
murree[5]: fish
murri[5] (murry): many, very

murri[6]: kangaroo
murri: hand, root, or cavity which holds water
murri-cooler: fiercely
murr-nong[2]: plant with edible root; yam
murromin: see mooroomin
murrumbidga: big water
murrumbinner[4]: you
murrumbooee: waterfall
murrumbung: pleasant
murrumnuller[4]: they
murrun[4]: see moron
murrunmil[2]: hurry
murry: see murri
murta[5]: husband
murtama[5]: your husband
murtee[8]: knee
murti[5]: my husband
muruke[6]: day
murule[2]: mosquito
murungar[2]: steady
murunkun[2]: cool
mutla[2]: see mudla
muttun[2]: drink (verb)
mutto[6]: boy
muttun[2]: smoke tobacco
muttura[5]: land
muwe[2]: sleep
muwe watyeri[2]: sleepy
muwityiwallin[2]: wakeful
mya[1]: hut
myall: wild, wild man, untamed, stranger. In a modern sense it has come to mean amateur or new chum
myee: native, native-born
myhee[8]: bread
myimbarr: black wattle
mying myrongatha[4]: eye
myndee: sycamore

myndie: see mindi
myneam⁴: moon
myorli: small red kangaroo
myrna (minnear): food
myrniong: cooking place

N

nacooma: see!
nagga¹: cold
naggi³: dog
nagooroo²: see
nai-ari: mountain devil
nainkulun²: depart
naityi²: alone
naiya⁶: hold on to
naiyuwe²: that there
naiyuwun²: curse, scold, swear
najan⁴: mother
najina²: see
naka⁶: water
nakame⁵: name
nakelang⁴: see

naki⁶: eyes
nakilli⁶: see
nakkare²: black duck
nakkin⁴: see
nak our²: look out
nalgarmyeri²: bull ant
nalgo¹: teeth
nalin² (nalurmi): lightning
nallak: come on
naltra⁵: how many
nalurmi²: see nalin
nam²: us, we two
nama⁶: teatree
namaga⁶: pearl shell
namagan⁴: see
namana⁵: see namarra
namarra⁴ (namana): mother
nambucca: winding river
nameropinah⁵: hole in the side
namma: breast. A namma-
   hole is a well or water hole
nammana²: sit
nammin² (merammin): cook
   (verb)
nammuldi²: hidden, unknown
nampulun² (nanampundun,
   nampundelin): conceal, hide
namtuk⁴: husband
nanampundun²: deny, per-
   suade
nanampundun: see nampulun
nananook: behind
nanarinyeri²: sandfly
nanarlin²: flat
nanauwun²: look round
nanbean⁸: eyelash
nanbimba⁸: eyebrow
nanbundelin²: caught
nanbundun² (nanbundun):
   catch (verb)

NAMMA

nandalie[5] (nandale): fire
nandroya: man and wife
nangalla[5]: fall, sit
nangana: see
nangare[2]: shelter
nangarikelerad[3]: three
nangkero[5]: pelican
nangoran[4]: husband
nangurwallin[2]: exult
nanni[2]: I
nannygai: snapper
nanowande[2]: hooked stick for pulling banksia flowers
nanowie: corner
nantoo[8]: thirsty
nantuma[5]: bend (verb)
nanwai[5]: canoe
nanyee[8]: womb
nanyima[4]: play (verb)
napa[5]: I
napa[6](nopa): water
napalle[2] (nape): husband
napanopa[6]: water
napowatyeri[2]: married man
nappa[5]: I
napwallin[2]: marry
nara[5]: companion. (yato nara: his companion)
narahdarn[5]: bat
narana[2]: hear
narang: little
narbeethong: cheerful, lively
narcoolba[8]: ashes
narcoonah[4]: see
nardu (nardoo): clover fern, a plant with edible seeds
nare[2]: tame
naretha[4]: salt bush
nargarawarat[3] (nargilwarat): three

nargarik[3]: two
nargariknargarik[3]: four
nargoneit[4]: hear
nargoon: native bear
nari: my companion
naripal[4]: spear
narkindie[8]: cave
narkale[2]: thumb
narkowalle[2]: his mother
narluk[2]: see ngalluk
narluke[2]: half full
narmar[8]: grass
narmare[2]: spring of water
naroa-mine[6]: man
narr[2] (ngarr): distinct, intelligible
narrah[4]: sea
narrawa: spring water
narrinyee[8]: breathe
narrinyeri[2]: people
nartee[8]: spring of water
narteol[2]: small piece
natan[6]: fig tree
natoah[5]: me
natto[6]: I
naweenda: fine day
na-wo[5] (gnahwo): yes
nauwe[2] (nauwurle): whose
ndruila[6]: native companion
neanga[4]: sit
neanwert[4]: sit
neanya: fly (insect)
neecoo[8]: elbow
neeghinee[3]: sit
neelong: bone
neena[7]: you
neenjeweny[8]: kiss (verb)
neenca[8]: sparrow
neerim[4]: hut
neetee[8]: fat

neeyangarra: eagle
neilyeri: pointing bone or stick
nemmin[2]: leave, leave off, stop
nemmuran[2]: remain
nenartin[2]: spread
nenengkin[2]: fall backwards
nenggatauwe[2]: pliable
nent oura[2]: out of the way
Nepelle: ruler of the heavens
neppaldar[2]: three
nerambo: against
nerbungeron: grand-father
nerndaik[4]: teeth
nerndoa: teeth
nerntoma[5]: more
nerntulya[5]: well, hole in the ground
nerreman: river bend
netangee[3]: yours
newchin[8]: sneeze
ngadhungi[2]: bewitch, charm (verb)
Ngaetelli: evil spirit which inhabits the black cockatoo
ngai[1,6] (ngaia): I
ngaiambin[2]: return
ngai-i[2]: I
ngaikung[5]: eye
ngaitshi[2]: mine
ngaityapalle[2]: grand-mother
ngaitye[2]: friend
ngaiyeri[2]: father
ngaiyuwun[2]: abuse (verb)
ngak[2]: almost
ngake[2]: close (adj)
ngalata ngillel[1]: we
ngalluk[2] (narluk, narluke): half, half-full

NEILYERI

ngama: bottle-shaped pits in rock for holding water
ngammaura[5]: mother
ngan[2]: me
ngan[5]: who
nganauwe[2] (anauwe): my
nganden[2]: cause to fly, frighten, scare
ngangan[1]: mother
ngangaranden[2]: cry out
ngangga[1]: sun
ngangge: see ngongi
ngangor[1]: star
nganmil[1]: me
nganna[6]: they
nganni[1] (ngan indi): who
ngarakkani[2]: shark
ngaralin: linger, wait
ngarari[2]: log
ngarbinya[2]: lie down

ngarlengarl[2]: small branch
ngarma[5]: they
ngarneit[5]: see
ngarningi[2]: fig
ngarntin[2] (ngartin): fly (verb)
ngarpin[2]: sorry
ngarr[2]: see narr
ngarra[2]: daughter (form of address by mother to daughter)
ngarraraipari[2]: ship
ngarrin[2]: build, make
ngarring[6]: boy
ngartang[6]: mother
ngarte[2]: river bend, corner
ngartin[2]: see ngarntin
ngathungi: instrument used in witchcraft
ngauandi[2]: nest
ngauka[6]: see
ngauwire[2]: son
ngauwun[2]: pass (verb)
ngeane[5] (ngeen): we
ngele[2]: heart
ngembelin[2]: spin
ngempin[2]: twist
ngende[2]: darkness
ngenempin[2]: grind
ngenna[5]: he, it, she
ngenyarin[2]: stare
ngeragge[2]: scrub
ngerake[2]: teal
ngerakowun[2]: overturn, turn inside out
ngeri[2]: fishing net
ngerin[2] (ngirin): catch fish with a net
ngerla[2]: fine
ngernka[2]: beard
ngerwein[4]: sun
ngiakkai[2]: armpit

ngiampi[2]: backbone
ngia ngiampe: bond between families or tribes
ngibalin[2]: paddle a canoe
ngikunde[2]: tadpole
ngilde[2]: cobweb
nginbundim[2]: flee
ngindai[5,6]: you
ngingeranggi: cough
nginno[1]: sit
ngipi[2]: shell
ngio[4]: I
ngiralin[2]: open (intrans verb)
ngirin[2]: see ngerin
nglaiye[2]: grass tree
nglalin[2]: as, like, resemble
nglelin[2]: grope with the feet, know
nglelurumi[2]: faith
nglulun[2]: top
ngodli[2]: we
ngoinkun[2]: shiver, tremble
ngoiyir[2]: promise (verb)
ngoiyun[2]: farewell
ngokkun[2]: disappear
ngolika: wattle flower
ngolkun[2]: bite (verb)
ngolun[2] (ngolamindin): wear (verb)
ngomerna[2]: go
ngommi[2]: convicted, guilty
ngomon[1]: big
ngongi[2] (ngangge): what, who
ngontha[2]: bad
ngoppano[2]: uncle on mother's side
ngoppun: move, step (verb)
ngopuld[2]: walk (verb)
ngorkulle[2] (ngokulli): bright, flame

H

ngottha[2]: me
ngowalle[2]: go
ngowalour[2]: go!
ngoweyin[2]: destroy
ngrakkuwallin[2]: angry, growl (verb), passion
ngraldi[2]: rage
ngrallin[2]: cure
ngramal[2]: open!
ngrammin[2]: open (intrans verb)
ngranyeri[2]: wonderful
ngraye[2] (ngragge, ngraldi): anger
ngrekkaldo[2]: tomorrow
ngrelggi[2]: contrary
ngrelggimaiyi[2]: contrary wind
ngrengkulun[2]: cough (verb)
ngrilkulun[2]: dance (verb)
ng'rui moch: native cat
ngruinyerar[2]: much more
ngudela[5]: see nguobela
ngunkurawallin[2]: go before
ngruwar[2]: abundance, abundant, all, many, much, whole
ngthummulun[2]: green
nguba[1]: blood
ngubbo-numma[5]: this
nguldamul-mindin: tire
nguldammulun[2]: tired
ngulde[2]: animal food, flesh, muscle
nguldin[2]: finish (verb)
nguldun[2]: cure, healthy
nguldunguldelin[2]: fist fight
ngulli[2]: long ago
ngullun[2]: remember
ngultun[2]: bruise, hit with fist, kick

ngumba[5]: mother
ngumperi[2]: milk, nipple
ngumpura[2]: woman's breast
ngumundi[2]: black snake
ngune[2]: vegetable food; you
ngungango[4]: he, it, she
nguni[2]: tea
ngunggurank[2]: before (in front of)
ngungyen[2]: kindle, light
nguobela[5] (ngudela): sit
ngupe[2]: down (of bird)
ngura[2]: hut, house, or shelter of any kind
ngurangpar[2]: brain
ngureng[5]: ear
ngurintand[2]: many times
ngurle[2]: mountain
ngurle[2] (ngurleuwar): you two
ngurnauwe: our
nguroo[2]: hair
nguruguldun[2]: knock
ngurukwar[2]: outside
ngurukuwarrin[2]: last (final)
nguta[6]: black
ngutam[6]: banana bird
nguwa[5]: give
nguyanowi[2]: cousin
nhamba[6]: we
nia: here, this
nidja[1]: this
nielongan[6]: mother-in-law
nierrina[7]: hawk
nihooloo[8]: me
nilee: bush rat
niley[5]: shell
nillam[4]: bad
nimi[2]: mouth
nimmitabel: source of many streams

ninder[5]: heavens
nindethana: ours
nindoah[5]: you
nina[2]: see ningana
ningana[5] (nina): fall, sit
ninkaiengk[2]: pair
ninnai[6] (ninna): sit
ninnann[8]: sit down
ninndwer[5]: we
ninwoa[5]: he, it, she
niu[2]: I
njugur: see wunjugur
noa[2]: husband
noinpalin[2]: soft
noiyulun[2]: I grope with the feet
nokarugge[2] (nolkaruggi): locust
noko[6]: water
nokuna[2]: look
noma uwe[2]: yours
nompie[6]: wedge-tailed eagle
nompulun[2]: plant (verb)
nonedia[5]: cousin
nonga[6]: kurrajong tree
nongo[5] (nonjo): woman
noojee: content
nooko[6]: give
noonameena: sleeping place in the bush
noondha: at
noonga[5] (noongah): kurrajong tree; him
noora-gogo[5] (noorahgogo): orange and blue beetle
nooroo: quick
nooroobunda: morning
nooroonooroobin: see nuru-nuru-bin
noorumba: hunting ground
noorwanang[4]: nose

nootoo[8]: chin
nopa: see napa
norabeetya[7]: green
norachanda[4]: make
normananyee[8]: snore
noro[5]: three
note[4]: cloud
nowaiy[2] (nowaiy ellin): none, not, nothing
nowantareena[7]: sister
nowego[4]: sun
nowieya: there
noyang: eel
nruwi[2]: a cold
nuba[6]: you
nucka[5]: eat
nucko[5] (nukou): water
nukee[5]: one
nukung[5]: woman
nulgerong: moonlight

NULLANULLA

Nulgine: bird goddess

nullanulla[5] (nullahnullah): club with heavy head

nullar[8]: forehead

nullegai: we two

nullgoonie[8]: bite, eat

nulu-gail[5] (gnooloo-gail): white painted headband

Nulu-yoon-du[5] (Gnoolooyoundoo): monster of legend

numald[2]: secretly

num-ba-di[5] (numbardee): mother, maternal aunt

numbe[2]: chin

nummunin[4]: heat

nunbalo[5]: to be drowned

nunden[2] (nunten): suspect

nunga[6] (nungge): day

nungana: cause

nunggaiyi[5]: wife

nungge[2]: see nunga

nunggi[2]: fishing line, rope

nungheenah[7]: elf, fairy

nunghungee[8]: look out

nungkutu[1]: give

Nuninjeeri: old man of the black frost

nunkalowe[2]: light (noun), sunlight

nunkardeol[2]: short club or waddy

nunkeri[2]: beautiful, excellent, good, handsome, pretty, right, tasty

nunkeri-mari[2]: right hand

nunkowallin[2]: being good

nunkuluthen[2]: running water

nunkumbil[6]: morning star

nunnoo[5] (nyunnoo): grass shelter

nunta[4]: bad

nunten: see nunden

nunthy[4]: he, she, it

nunungki[2] (nunukke): flour, fruit

nunyin[5]: see

nura[5]: you

nurawordubununa: carpet snake

nurong: bread

nurriga[6]: moon

nurroobooan and **nuroolooan:** see nuru-buan

nurrumbeek[4]: I

Nurrumbunguttia: old spirits who were responsible for darkness, storms, and evil spirits

nurrumpi[4]: native bear

nurrungar: listen

nuru-buan[5] (nurroobooan, nuroolooan): south

nurula pundi[5]: club

Nurunderi: teacher sent by the Great Spirit

nuru-nuru-bin[5] (nooroonooroobin): south wind

nuta[6]: night

nutam[6]: banana bird

nuttoo: grub

nyampulun[2] (nyampundun): walk softly

nyang[4]: sit

nyangow[1]: see

nyauwe[4]: sun

nyenkulun[2]: dissatisfied

nyenkundun[2] (nyiukundun): cross (ill-tempered), offended

nyerin[2]: cry (verb); depend on; expect

nyerpulun[2]: pant
nyiddin[1]: cold
nyinna[6]: sit
nym[3]: child
nyrangkin[2]: burn (verb)
nyringgen[2]: singe
nyrippin[2]: clean (verb), wash
nyumap bottyu[1]: small
nyungie: moon
nyungu[6]: Torres strait pigeon
nyurang[1]: you

O

oba[3] (obait, obaitj): water
obernilimer: whistle (verb)
odenpa[8]: ironbark tree
odern[1]: sea
odneler: midnight
odunepa[8]; white ant
ohi[3]: woman
oiyangopan[6]: carpet snake
ojalli[3]: fire; tree
ojena[3]: fire; tree
okolyer[8]: cloud
olba[8]: red ochre
old-burra[8]: dust
ol-dorry-e-way: kiss
oleara[8]: string
olebrya[8]: south
olemunda[8]: dust
ollo: brown bee
olltoo[8]: nostril
olono[3]: hill
oloorinann[8]: shame
oltarkim: broke
olumbera: swear
omalwin[3]: kangaroo
omenderry[8]: chest
omil-dadgee[8]: bamboo, large reed

onak[3]: earth
onbellera[8]: whirlwind
onengarkwa[8]: starve
onya[6]: ghost
Oobi Ooobi[5]: sacred mountain in Bullima where Baiame lives
ooboon[5]: blue-tongued lizard
oodoolay[5]: rain-making stone
ooeena[7]: fuel
oogee: head-dress
oola[5] (oolah): red prickly lizard
Oola-pikka: imaginary tribe which lives at the back of the south wind
ooliekirra: bright, clean, new
oolyarra: young man
oomborra[8]: maggot
oomoomurla: superior
oompi: see humpy
oompi bong: deserted camp
oongarra: asleep
ooraa[8]: see oura
ooranye[2]: rainbow
oorgker[3]: heat
oorla[2]: camp, hut, nest
ooroowinannee: grey owl; also daughter of Merpulla the rain woman
ooya[5] (ouyah, ouyarh): quarrian parrot
ooyan[5] (ouyen): curlew
ooyella: compassionate
ooyu-bu-lui[5] (ouyouboolooey): black snake
opera-yenpa[8]: bark (noun)
orad[3]: earth
orialk[3]: two
orialkeraroka[3]: three

orana³ (korana, orani): moon
oridji³: sea
orinjetta⁸: spark
orodina: chin
orojiimul³: nose
orowa medinda³: sea
orra curra: desert oak; large owl
orrapoora⁸: magpie
orucknurra: large fire
orumbera: large spear
otama⁶: porpoise
otayba⁸: bird
oticha: half
otorkweta⁸: heart
ottinna⁸: hot
oura⁸ (ooraa): wood
ouraka: wait awhile
ourapilla⁸: black
ouratita: black beetle
ouyah and ouyarh: see ooya
ouyen: see ooyan
owadema⁸: more
owingee: he, hers, his, it, its, she

P

pademelon: scrub wallaby
padewer⁸: go
    padewappa: I go
    padewaimba: you go
    padewaley: we go
    yato padewa: he goes
padilpa⁸: parrot
padmur²: point (noun)
padmuri²: sharp
padmurwallin²: pointed
padmurwarrin²: sharpen
paiala²: cold
paialla⁵: tell
paieri perna²: big

paipan⁶: black ibis
paipe² (paiapowallin, paiapu-lun): stiff
paitcha: breast, anything that develops with maturity
paiyin²: hate
pakapaka⁶: bullroarer
palberry: corruption of word for native currant
paldharar²: hail
paldi² (palli): by and by, future
pallai²: while
pallarang⁴: bow down
palli²: see paldi
palpera⁸ (palperipa): leaf
palthawangalana⁵: ashamed, naked
    palthawangalnappa: I was ashamed
    palthawangalnimba: you are ashamed
pama⁶: man
pan⁶: liquid
panamuna: ocean
panda⁵: heart
pandana⁵: spear (verb)
pandappure²: gun
pandelanen⁵: tired
    pandelnappa: I am tired
    pandelnimba: you are tired
pandin² (panden, plunden): carry in the arms, embrace, lift, nurse on the knee, seize, embrace
panelgorana: be noisy, speak
    panelgorappa: I speak
    panelgorimba: you speak
pangalarke²: eldest daughter
pangali² (panggalli): eldest son

pangari²: shade, shadow, soul

pangarinda²: evening, twilight

panggalli: see pangali

panichie⁴: wife

panimillie: small river

panitya⁴: area of land

panje: black-eared cuckoo

panketye: boomerang

panpande²: cherry tree

pantin²: two people sleeping together; squeeze

papa⁶: teat

pappa: seed food

pappora⁵: appear

parattah⁷: frost

Parawanga: spirit of madness which appears in the form of a mirage

parehana: all

pargi²: wallaby

pariwilpa²: heavens

parlcoon⁸: tattoo

parn⁴: water

parnggi²: deep water

parnta²: see burnta

parpin²: cry (verb), sorry

parpinga⁶: father

parpin mewe²: anxious, desire (verb), yearn

parpun⁴: mother

parra²: hair

parragilga: narrow-leaved ironbark tree

parru (barrow): fish

parrumbal: mushroom

partambelin²: wrestle

partin²: rub

partumbe²: infant

partyi (partch): shoal

parumin⁴: rain

pateenah⁷: egg

patter²: eat

patya⁶: flower

patyuwarrin²: cure

pecarf⁴: hand

pedgery: see pitchery

peer⁸: mouth

peggeralin²: dream (verb)

peggerambe²: breakfast

pehah⁵: bone

pek: empty; very

pekeri²: dream

pekin²: empty (verb); finish

pelberri²: tea

pelberrimunt²: lungs

pelde²: musk duck

pele²: greedy

pelepe²: land

pellati²: edible grub found in banksia

pempin²: give

pendin²: smell

pengana⁷: hawk

penghanah⁷: ford

pentin²: decayed, stinking, withered

peppee³ (pipee): father

pera⁵: club

peranbim²: divide amongst, share

Perindi: mythical yellow-brown striped goanna

perke² (perki): hole, large hole; steep

perlka⁵: fishing line

pernmin²: flick

pertill-lerra⁸: cheeks

pertorrue⁸: string

peta[2]: tree
petachall-lily[8]: scorpio
petamalde[2]: thief
petcheual[4]: two
petcheualenea[4]: three
petcheual-petcheual[4]: four
peti[2]: frost
petin[2]: refuse (verb)
pettin[2]: abduct, steal
petye[2]: face
pewingi[2]: swamp hawk
piallano[4]: die
picca[8]: sore
pichi-malla[8]: come on
pidne[6]: hear
piealah[4]: girl
pierah[4]: see pirra
piggi-billa[5] (piggie-billah):
    ant-eater; echidna
pikuwa[6]: salt-water crocodile
pilar[5]: spear
pilbe[2]: dirty
pilbiwallin[2]: dirty
pildin[2]: drive
pilepi[2]: dew
pilgeruwallin[2]: see pulkeri
pilkundun[2]: frown; stare at
pillambe[2]: black cockatoo
pillara: spear with two barbs
pilli: see billa
Pilliethillcha: aurora austra-
    lis
pillcoo[8]: vein
pill-ler: spit
pilpati[2]: hip
piltengi[2]: hard, strong
pilyaulun[2]: man
pilyan-undun[2]: shake the head
pimble: country, district
pimpa[5]: tree

pimpala[5]: pinetree
pinah[5]: hole
pinaroo (pinarroo): old man
pinbittulun[2]: push (verb)
pindan[1]: desert
pindattulun[2]: lay an egg
pindyin[2]: pick out
pinera[5]: climb
    pinerappa: I climb
    pinerimbo: you climb
pinggen: throw down
pinggi[2]: seaweed
pingkin[2] (pinggen): cause to
    fall, fall, overthrow
pingyin[2] (pindyin): find
piningi[2]: buttock
pinjaroo[2]: make
pink-hi: holiday
pinna[8]: ear
pino[6]: female ghost
pinpan[8]: lightning
pinpi[6]: parrot
pinpin[2]: push; put
pinpuna: share (verb)
pinta: bamboo spear
pintamin[2]: carry off, take
    away
pintannie[8]: open
pintapinta[8]: moth
pinterry[8]: star
pinyali: emu
pintyin[2]: pick up
pinyatowe[2]: sugar
pinyin[2]: see pingyin
pinytowe[2]: honey
pipa[6]: father
pipa: bent
pipee[3]: see peppee
pipi[2]: egg
pipipa[6]: sandpiper

piralko: native companion
pirilah[4]: cold
pipirbin[6]: small
pirra[2,6] (pierah): moon
pirramurra: shield
pirri: small leaf-shaped spear point of chipped stone
pirria[2]: clay
pirriwee: possum skin rug
pirron-yallock: little water
piruwallin[2]: breathless, dead, fainted, insensible
pita[6]: bamboo spear with four points
pitchery[5,6] (bedgery, pedgery, pitchiri, pituri): shrub, the leaves being used as a narcotic
pitchie: wooden vessel used for holding water
pitchingga: gum of pine or gum tree
pitereka[6]: white
pitja[4]: fire
pitoa[5] (pito): moon
pitti[2]: line
pityi[2]: cape, headland
pitura[5]: light
piyaller: speak
plaityinggin[2]: proud, vain
plangge[2]: drum made of skins tightly rolled and beaten by the hand
pleppin[2]: feel
plewalauwun[2]: grope in the dark
plomare[2]: ice
plombatye[2]: deaf
plombatye[2] (plomb atye wallin): disobedient

plombewallin[2]: stupid
plongge: club, knobbed weapon for inflicting punishment
plorte[2]: egg yolk
plotye[2]: childless woman
plowallin[2]: cramp; lament (verb)
plunden[2]: see pandin
plurampe[2]: valley
poenghana[7]: ringlets
pogal[3]: head
poi: dust
poka mala[5]: lie
pokkoremin[2]: heap up
pola[6]: paternal grand-father
polgumpi[2]: backbone
poli[3]: man
pollit[4]: two
pollit kepap[4]: three
pollit pollit[4]: four
poltha[2]: see pultha
pombulun[2]: flow; leaf
pomeri: mudfish
pombindho[5]: earth
pompo: egg
pomponderoo[5]: land
ponda[4]: stone
ponde: Murray cod
pongo: flying squirrel
pooet: treefern
pookanah[7]: albatross
pookerah[4]: heat
poolkrinna: mischievous spirit
poolooloomee: firework made of gumtree bark
poomong: tin
pooney[8]: blow (verb)
poonganyee[8] (poonganie): hit, kill, strike
poonja[8]: sing

poonta buckanee[8]: heavy
poontee[8]: grub
poora: tail
poork[4]: head
poorlie[2]: stars
poorp[4]: kill
poorparta[2]: sparrow-hawk
poortge[6]: heat
pootikkatikka: wattle-tree
poottoo[4]: land
popa[4]: blow, shoot (verb)
popogina[5]: gun
pordenpar: calf of leg
porle[2]: child
porlta[2]: possum
porn il[2]: died
pornumindin[2]: kill
pornun[2] (pornunil): dying; like (verb); love
pornurumi[2]: death, death-causing
poroany[8]: press (verb)
potoroo: kangaroo rat
potyanambe[2]: food for a journey
pouraller: mist
powdingella[6]: cold
powenyenna[7]: magpie
poymalangta[7]: kill
poyyou[8] (puya): smoke
prakkin[2] (prakour): rise (verb)
prandyi[6]: butter-fish
pranggiwattyeri[2]: tiger snake
prangpin[2]: diarrhoea
prantin[2]: start (jump with fright; wonder
premin[2]: tie (verb)
prempun[2]: cook (verb)
preppin[2]: lift, raise

pretella[6]: moon
prewarrar[2]: rib
prewirri[2]: side
prilde[2]: ant
prildin[2]: pursue
prilpulun[2]: spring of water
pringgarimmin[2]: tie (verb)
pritye[2] (prityin): firm
prityururmi[2]: strength
proi: big
prolggi[2]: brolga; Magellan Clouds
prolin[2]: red
prumpun[2]: drive flies away with smoke; prepare an oven
pruwuttar[2]: pieces
Puckowe: the grandmother spirit
pudding-ball: corruption of name for a fish
puka: see bucka
puka[6]: baby
pukara[2]: heat
pulca[8]: toe
puldan: see pultin
pulhiner[6]: dying
pulkeri[2] (pilgeruwallin): greedy
pullatye[2]: two
pulley[8]: stone
pulliner[6]: die
pullun[2]: bathe, swim
pullybuntor[8]: mountain range
pulpilla[4]: heavens
pultera[5]: canoe
pultha[5] (poltha): bark, covering, skin, skin garment
pultin[2] (puldun): receive, take
pultue[2]: weak

pultuwarrin[2]: rot (verb)
pulwaiya[6]: totemic ancestor
pulyara: long-nosed rat
pulyugge: ball, ball game
pumdo[5]: smoke
punauwe: kangaroo skin bag
punde[2]: bag
Pundel: another name for Baiame
punden[2]: childbirth
pundeol[2]: mouse
pundi: dog
pundira[6]: conch shell
punga[6]: hut
punjil: finger
punka[8]: large lizard
punkerri[2]: brown duck
punkulde[2]: fish spear
punkunduleol[2]: bandicoot
punkunduli[2]: bandicoot rat
punnamoonta[7]: emu
puntaman: fishing net
punthari[2]: scrub
puntin[2]: arrive
puntyaiya[6]: swamp turtle
puppa[8]: dog
pupperimbul: diamond fire-tail or spotted-sided finch
puratte[2]: black and white shag
pure[2]: waddy
purinyeriol[2]: wild man
purkabidni[2]: ghost, spirit
purni[2]: oven
purni ngomerna[2]: come here
purnung: dingo
purpuck[4]: cold
purpuk[4]: head
purragia[6]: lie (falsehood)
    purragiappa: I tell a lie
    purragimba: you tell a lie

purreung[5]: day
purri[2]: hill; kidney
purrinunggi[2]: right hand
purroin[4]: night
purtia[2]: kangaroo rat
purtin[2]: hurt
puthawing[2]: lower arm
putta[8]: grass; lazy
puttheri[2] (putte): end
puttun: pinch (verb)
puya[2]: see poyyou
puyulle[2]: emu wren
pyabea[4]: woman
pyala[4]: tree
pyingerra[6]: pine tree

Q

quabara: sacred song
qualpar: large rat
quandong: native peach tree
quarail[4]: big
quarallia[8]: star
quarragwan[4]: heat
quasha[8]: water
quasha-booga[8]: small water
quasha-iperta-quorna[8]: deep water hole
quasha-unjewma[8]: drink
quasha-ul-kurry: rainy sky
quasha-undema[8]: rain (verb)
quasha-yerra-pichica[8]: swim (verb)
queeabraabra[3]: who
queeal[3]: foot
queenguarr[3]: nose
quear[8]: crooked, no good useless
queearr[3]: hand
queeneeda[3]: fire
quei: little girl

quei-marla: big girl
quei-marla[8]: adolescent girl
quei-marla-goobita: adolescent girl
quemilla[3]: tongue
quillagee[3]: big
quinja: ash
quorna[8]: deep
quunder[3]: club

R

ragaralti[2]: egret
raiaralin[2]: flow, overflow
raiaramin[2]: pour
rammin[2]: inform, tell
rampaullun[2]: persuade someone to go with the speaker
randi[2]: widower
randli[2]: childless father, father who has lost a child
ranwul[2] (rande): ancient, old
raraityungun[2]: beg
rarkee: bush food
rata: plant, vegetable
rattulengk[2]: mother and child
rawadabir: see awadabir
rawan[3]: rain
rawlinna: wind
rekaldi[2]: water rat
relbulun[2]: suffer
rengbari[2]: stop
retulengk[2]: father and child
retyinne[2]: heel
rewuri[2]: spring (season)
reyin[2]: show
reytyunggun[2]: ask
reytyuwundun[2]: forbid to accompany
riawena[7]: games
riawunna[7]: circle

rikkara[2]: south
ringbalin[2]: chant, sing, song
ringmail[2]: hunger
rogoona[7]: forehead
roka[3]: one
ronggi[2]: brother-in-law
rongummun[2]: bark (verb)
ronumdo[5]: boy
roragarin[2]: shake
rorari[2]: rotten
rumalduwallin[2]: joke (verb)
rumaiy[2]: west
runde[2]: cousin, friend
rupulle[2]: chief, land-holder
ruwe[2]: land

S

saleng[4]: tongue
shoo-ho: death word
su[2]: curse, expletive, or imprecation

T

ta[6]: land
taa[6]: foot
tackan[4]: see
tagera: cockle
taikundun[2]: cry out
tainbarilin[2]: arrive
tainke[2]: swamp
tainki[2]: salt
tainpulun[2]: forget
taipan[6]: brown snake, rainbow snake
taitpullun[2]: jump (verb)
taiyi[6]: maternal grand-father
taiyin[2] (tarraiyin): command, go away!, send
takkin[2]: eat
takkure[2]: plucked
taldauwin[2]: squeeze out disease or sickness

taldree[5]: young man
taldumande[2]: house, substantial house
taldumbarrin[2]: hold (verb)
talga: sow-thistle
talkinyeri[2]: bustard turkey
talkiwallin[2]: cross (ill-tempered), miserable
tallaim[6] (talla): tongue
tallangge[2]: tongue
tallara[2]: rain
tallarook: wattle bird
tallawong: bell or black magpie, donkey bird, or crow-shrike
tallbee[8]: wet
tallerk: thistle
tallon[4]: see tully
tally[8]: sandhill
talpa[2]: ear
tamba: ibis
tambelin[2]: choose
tambur[6]: mouth
tampin[2]: walk
tana[6]: stand up
tandan: catfish
tang[2]: where
tangari[2]: edible gum
tangulun[2]: stand
tanpundun[2]: put together
tantan[6]: cold
tantin[2]: lie down
tapang[4]: father
tapangk[2]: near, near you
tappak: bronze-wing pigeon
tappan[6]: stake
tappenitin[2]: yawn
tappin[2]: fierce
tar[8]: mouth
taralye: throwing stick

tarangk[2]: between
taranna[7]: wallaby
taree: tomahawk; wild fig
tareena[7]: basket
tari[2]: opening
tarkee: evil spirit in the form of a woman who drinks blood
tarki: perch (fish)
tarkoori[2]: bittern
tarlarang[4]: red-billed plover
tarlina[5]: see therlinya
tarlina[6] (tarlina aitye): one
tarlina barko[6]: three
tarlit[4]: small
tarlo bra womba lettie[4]: boy
tarloorin[8]: yawn
tarl worcat[4]: girl
tarmaroo[6]: possum
tarnalo[2]: never
tarno[2]: not
tarntunnerrin[8]: tired
tarra[4]: white
tarraiyin: see taiyin
tarralangi[6]: see therlinya
tarrangower: rough; high hill
tarrgoorn: reed necklace
tarrinyeri[2]: middle one
tarrukengk[2] (kurrengk): leg
tartar burlke: hair
tarte[2]: younger brother
tartengk[2]: stick for beating time in singing
tarti[2]: younger sister
tata[6]: frog
tatea[6]: whistling duck
tatya[6]: goanna
tauel[2]: neighbour, neighbouring tribe

tauo²: don't, no!, not
tauwa⁶: talk
tauwangi²: firestick
tauwin²: lean on
tchaceroo⁶: magpie
tchaik: an expression of contempt; unreliable person
tealedyan⁶: shark
tean⁶: take
teangi: earth
teepookana⁷: kingfisher
teeta: ant, insect
Teetya: swallow which brings boy babies to earth
teeya²: teeth
teeyar-tarlina⁶ (teeyir-tarlina): see therlinya
tekin²: escape
tellingiter³: one
tempi: swamp duck
tenan⁴: foot
tendi² (thandi): decision of the elders in council
tendu²: climbing frog
tenjumar: drink (verb)
tepi²: live (verb)
tergoonee²: sit
teriltin²: pluck feathers
terninyeri²: boot
terpulun²: appear, come in sight, come out of, emerge
terrara: place of shrubs
tete: kingfisher
tewart: see tooart
thacka⁵: bank
thackory⁵: heavy
thadelee²: sea
thalaak: sow-thistle
thalan⁴: tongue
thalera: manhood, strength

thalinya²: see therlinya
thalme²: bay
thambaroo: spirit; also in some parts the name for a white man because he is believed to be the reincarnation of a spirit or someone who is dead
thame²: shallow
thammi²: seashore
thandi²: see tendi
thandwalla: gumtree on the edge of a river
thanga²: down
thankomalara⁵: island
thanpathanpa: snipe
thappin²: open (to make a hole in)
tharalkoo: duck
tharamba⁴: make
tharook: convolvulus
theen-who-ween: an ancient, legendary name for the platypus
therlinya (tarlina, teeyar-tarlina, teeyir-tarlina, thalinya): tongue
therna-perty⁵: kidney
therto⁵: head
thettherre²: dray (a word which comes from its movement)
thiar⁴: land
thickathickana⁵: pour water into a vessel
thidna²: see thina
thidnamura: toad
thiewie: flowers
thilhya⁵: strong
thina⁶: ear

thina[5] (thidna, tshina): foot, footprint, track

thinana: beside

thindu[4]: this

thingairipari: spear belonging to a medicine man

thirti[2]: mean, selfish

thirlta[6]: kangaroo

thirtawalla[2]: head

thita thata lana: itch

thockyar[6]: land

thoma talko[4]: good

thonku mundil[5]: night

thooma: sandhill creatures which belong to the Dream Circle

thoomie: peace, silence

thoopara: native pear tree

thoorka[4]: big

thopramolla[5]: get inside, get on, sit on

thorom[5]: smoke going up a hollow tree

thowla: spoonbill duck

threttin[2] (threllin, trattin): divide, part, split

thriggi[2]: message stick

thrintin[2] (thrinden): pluck

thrippin[2]: sprinkle

throkkun[2]: throw away, toss

throttun[2]: attack one man, place, put down

thrumari[2]: cape (point of land)

thrunkkun[2]: go away!

thrunkun[2]: frighten

thuckara[5]: river bend

thuiye[2]: stump

thulanja[5]: bad

thuldi[2]: pus

thuldun[2]: meet

thulga[5]: bad

thulloo-munal[6]: camp

thulloo-nurral[6]: hut

thulti[2]: floating mass of reeds

thultie[2]: ear

thumelin[2]: green

thummyerloo[6]: sun

thumpun[2]: hunt (verb)

thunbira[2]: mouth

thundarta[5]: nothing

thungana[5]: fill up a hole

thungge[2]: see tunge

thungy[4]: land

thuppun[2]: carry

thur[2]: truth

thurakami: swim

thurkuna: swimming

thurar[2] (thure): straight

thurre[6]: sit down

thurto[5]: head

Tickalara: spirit world, hereafter, happy hunting grounds

tiddalick: frog

tidnah[6]: foot

tiendi[1]: star

tier[4]: live (verb)

tiewiwar: see tyiwewar

tikki[6]: live (verb)

tilpulun (tilpuldun): cracking of lice, crackling of flames, sparkling

tiltili[2]: pied crow shrike

timbelin[2]: smoke tobacco

timpin[2] (timbelin): lick (verb), tasty

tinabulka: boot

tinar[5]: woman

tingin[2] (tinkin): stoop

tingowun[2]: inform, tell

tinka[2]: day
tinkelin[2] (tinkin): swell (verb)
tinna-punni: bone carried in dilly bag to repel evil
tintauwa[6]: black snake
tin-tookie: gnomes who inhabit the bush and hear the last words of those who are dying
tin-tuppa: imaginary plant people
tinuwarre: bream
tipi[6]: guts; root
tipuldun[2] (tipundun): break in pieces, crush
tikeri[2]: knot
tirkundun[2]: dive
tirra[4]: teeth
Tirtelak: sacred frog who guards underground rivers
tirtygan[4]: die
titna[2]: foot
tittadi[2]: flea, vermin
tittimballin[2] (tittimbarrin): tickle
tityarokan[6]: willy wagtail
tityowe[2]: death-adder
tiwiwarrin[2]: fast, speedy
tjukaro[2]: kangaroo
tjurunga (often corrupted to churinga): sacred object of wood, stone, or shell
tloppere[2]: ibis
tlopulun[2]: grope in the mud for crayfish
tluiye[2]: short
tluyeol[2]: shortest
tokai[5]: night
tokiejonburnba[8]: bulldog ant
tokkun[2]: crowd, pinch (verb)

tokorauwe[2]: narrow
tolai[2]: beardless
tolkun[2]: poke, stamp
tolkundun[2]: stab
tolloiyer[3]: two
tomin[2]: swallow hastily
tonaleah[7]: sun
tonde[2]: blind
toney[8]: thunder
tonga jija[1]: ear
tong kongka[5]: early morning; evening
tooart (tewart): tuart gum-tree
toogaadya[2]: small
toolangatta: many kurrajong trees
toolain: brown wattle
toolka: Cape Barren goose
toora[4]: woman
toorange: jealous
toorlie: poison stick
toorutbambam[4]: die
toota[4]: star
topyrun[2]: star
torarin[2] (tȯrauwun): assemble, collect
tore[2] (torengk): mouth
tortuwallin[2]: delay, quiet, silent
totolar[5]: hill
tottumbarrin[2]: eat meat and vegetables
tottung[2]: disappeared, out of sight
Totyargeril: the star Aquila
tour-ur-rong: good grass
towa: bladder
towarnie[8]: dig
towera[4]: fire

---

towulun[2]: blaze (verb)

towun[2]: tread

trandararin[2]: divide amongst

trangkin[2]: drive away

trata[6]: night-fish

trattin[2]: see threllin

trawalla: much rain, wild water

trelin[2] (tremin): tear, torn

trelin ngreye[2]: dawn

trippin[2]: drip, drop (verb)

tshina[2]: see thina

tshinta[2]: sun

tshuppana[2]: kiss

tuan: flying squirrel

tuat[4]: fish

tuckatuck[8]: tickle

tuckie: see tukkie

tuckonie: little man of the forest

tudhuki[2]: bed

tuki[2]: bullfrog

tukkeri: flat, silvery fish forbidden to women

tukkie[2] (tuckie): bream

tuldar[2]: star

tuldi: forequarter

tuldin[2]: net (verb), surround

tulgeen[2]: put together

tullangapperi[2]: mat

tullun[2]: howl (wind); scrape

tully[5] (tallon, tullon): tongue

tulpi: "talk stick", used for tapping out messages

tultun[2]: chip (verb)

tuma[6]: fire

tumakowaller[2]: swan

tumaquoi[2]: look

tumbe[2] (tumbelin, tumbewallin): alive, live (verb)

tumbe an ngulde[2]: raw meat

tumbeelluwa: evergreen

tumbetin[2]: heal, save

tumbi[2]: raw

Tumbutilamaldi: Saviour

tummun[2]: choke, hiccough

tumpinyeri[2] (tump): life (belong to life)

tumpun[2]: count

tundi[2]: spark

tunge[2] (thunggi): ankle

tunggar[2]: joint

tunggerar[2]: language

tunggare[2]: word

tungge[2]: wrist

tuni[2]: ground

tunka[6]: day, month

tunkeri[2]: louse

tunkun[2]: fondle, nurse

tunkuwallin[2]: play (verb)

tunta[6]: spear

tunte[2]: middle

tunthun[2]: rejoice

tupong: marble fish or freshwater flathead

tupun[2]: guard

tura[5]: spear

turelin[2]: cover up

turika[8]: bone

turi kalkir[2]: covered

turlemindin[2]: frightening

turlin[2]: frightened

turnar[2]: toe; track

turni[2]: hand

turninyeri[2]: shoe

turnit[1]: boy

turokkul[2]: lame

turrammelin[2] (turramulun): make a noise

turro[2]: fire

I

turrumturrum[6]: rain
turt[4]: star
turtangi[2]: knee
turuwun[2]: guard
tuta[6]: parrot; palm leaf
tuu[6]: spear with three prongs for spearing bony bream
tuyalie[6] (tuyalie-dusali): teeth
tuyulawarrin[2]: look for, seek
Tya: Earth; flowering time
tyalli[4]: tongue
tyarbuk[4]: mouth
tyarmorak[4]: you
tyelde[2]: clay
tyele[2] (tyerle): upper arm, wing
tyeli[6]: swamp fish
tyelokuri[2]: mussel
tyelyerar[2]: ray of light, sunbeam
tyepi[2]: quail
tyerle: see tyele
tyetyin[2]: anoint
tyilye: fly, maggot, worm
tyilyi[2]: rice
tyinkulun[2]: screech
tyintin[2]: remain in one place
tyinyeri[2]: child
tyirpin[2]: deny
tyit[6]: fish hawk
tyiwallin[2]: become dry
tyiwar[2]: loud
tyiwewar[2] (tiewiwar): hurry
tyiwi[2]: dry
tyiwiwallin[2]: withered
tynrmeargorak[4]: we
tyrilly[4]: heavens
tyrintyin[2]: sneeze
tyurmik[4]: I

U

ua[4]: give
uaburika (umburika): centipede
ubeeterra[8]: fog
uc-aliebra (ucaleebra): reed
uckillya[8]: brother
uc-neer[8]: father
uc-nulla-mull: swing
ucnullya[8]: dog
uc-nun-alemem: shake
ugundyi[6]: crab
uka[6]: white sand snake
ularit[3]: star
ulbra-cullima[8]: claw
ule[2]: wave (noun)
ulla: well
ulluricna[8]: dirty water
ulpirra: flute; love-horn made of hollow sticks
ulwai[6]: paternal grand-father
umanbang[5]: make
umbacoora[8]: baby, child
umbee-leedin-gorra[8]: kneel
umbeeramalla[8]: tired
umbellditta[8]: orange tree
umboa: urine
Umborn-ditchalicka[8]: a fabulous female being who lives in mountain ranges and cures people of their ills. It is also the name for a red stone which is powdered and put on wounds to heal them
umburika[8]: see uaburika
ummal[3]: foot
ummee[3]: sun
umorra[8]: rat
umpara[6]: stingray
umpiya[6]: water-lily

unchurunqua: painted finch
uncoo[8]: sleep
unda[6]: see ungda
undarnga: bush food
undeanya[8]: see undeneya
undee-lablab[8]: butterfly
undeneya (undeanya): wasp
undia: gap, gorge
undie[5]: teeth
unditter (unditta): stink
undooeata (hundoeta): string
undoolya[3]: shadow
undunga: wet
undurra[3]: silver wattle
unengoo[2]: they
ung[2]: after
unga[2]: see ungooroo
ungai[2]: to, with
ungamala[3]: sea
Unganti Barachi[4]: "the land beyond the sky"
ungarunya: rush
ungawilla: black magpie
ungda (unda): he, she, it
ungee-gungee (ungee-gun-jee): grasshopper
unggoingee[3]: I, we, us
ungiverta: crooked
ungjeeburra[8]: crane
ungolar: native currant
ungooroo[2] (unga): give
ungroo[2]: hear
ungun[2]: if
ungunai[2] (ungul, ungunel): before (of time)
ungunuk[2]: when
ungunyer-pollipa: shoulder
ungurgal[3]: sea
ungwarlyer: medicine
ungwyndei[8]: sleep

ungwyner[8]: yours
unja: mating fever
unkee[2]: woman
unkeegeega[2]: girl
unmaturra[8]: hungry
unmerta[8]: buckbush
unnee[2]: who
unoyie: broad-leaved tea tree
unti[8]: run
untita: down feathers
untoo[8]: windpipe
unya[8]: louse
upmoa[8]: snake
upmurra[8]: camp
uralla: big hill; by-and-bye; camp; running water
uran[6]: heat
urdera[6]: sand ridge
ure[6]: ear
urnin[3]: woman
Uroo: mythical water snake
urpalk[3]: sky
urra-quarra: grey goose
urrie urrie[5]: soul
urtathurta: shoe
urumi[2]: see arami
urungari: bees' nest, sugar bag
utam[6]: corpse
utyana[2]: initiated youth
uuna[4]: sun
uwa[6]: leech
uwan[6]: meet
uwinnia (geewinnia): mosquito
uwoppa (youwoppa): spider
uworra[8]: road
uwurta[8]: bush wallaby

W

wa[6]: give

wa-ah[5]: shell

waaljerrumbuddy kewat[4]: spear

wacka[5]: chin

Waddahgudjaelwon: see Walla-gudjail-wan

waddy: war club, also used for any stick for striking. There is a theory that it is the aborigines' pronunciation of the English word "wood"; another that it is the Tasmanian word "wi" (wood, or fire), with a modifying particle

wadelang[2]: tree

wadleena[2]: bad

wadna[2]: boomerang

wah: an exclamation

wahgoo[5] (whagoo): game of hide-and-seek

wahgunyah: place where crows are found

wahl[5] (euahl, youal): no

wahler[5] (wahlerh): manna which runs down the trunks of trees

wahn[5]: crow (the most mischievous of all birds)

wahrang[1] (warhrang): three

wahroonga: see warooga

wahroonga: our home

wai-i[2]: afraid, fear

waiirri: heavens sky

waikerdumai[6]: hill

waimba: you

wainbaru[2]: rain

wainkan[6]: curlew

waiye[2]: light brown snake

waiyin[2]: drive

wakaje: emu

wakbok[3]: head

wakerdi: crow

wakka elji[2]: small

wakkalde: shield

wakkin[2]: spear (verb), wound (verb)

wakkin-turtangk[2]: kneel

wakoola: girdle of human hair or kangaroo skin worn by men who have been initiated

wakulun[2]: caw (verb)

wal[2]: place (noun)

wal[3]: ear, hear

wala[6]: blue-tongued lizard

walbeeatta[8]: see wolbitta

walkandi[2]: north

walla: jump (verb)

walla-boondie[5] (wallahbdee): topknot

WAHN

wallaby (wallabee, wallobi, wolloby): small kangaroo

Walla-gudjail-wan[5] (Waddahgudjaewon, Wallahgudjailwon): female spirit, guardian of unborn spirit children

wallahboondee: see wallaboondie

Wallahgudjailwan: see Walla-gudjail-wan

Walla-guroon-bu-an[5]: the messenger of Baiame, guardian of male spirit children awaiting birth

wallangar: burnt stump

wallaroo[5,6]: large species of kangaroo

walla-walla: jump quickly

wallin[2]: accompany, hang, pendant

walloobahl: see wallu-barl

wallong: pounding stone

wallowa: broom wattle

wallu-barl[5] (walloobahl): barking lizard

wallung[4]: stone

walmat[3]: rain

walpa[5]: lift

waltra[4]: fire

waltye[2]: childless father, father who has lost a child

wamba[1,3,6]: white man who lives with aboriginal woman

waminda: companion, friend

wanappe[2]: mushroom

wanbanalong: place where kangaroos are found

wanbanna: lack of understanding, stupid

wanbin[2]: pity (verb)

wanda: sandhill

wandelana[5]: chin

wandoo[1]: wandoo gum

wane[4]: moon

wanga[5]: see manba

wangarang: tortoise

wangin[4]: boomerang

wangkin[2]: ascend

wangoora[6]: baby

wanji: bird dance

wanka[6]: dilly bag

wankin[2]: ask, beg

wankin mewe[2]: pant

wanna: digging stick

wanni[1]: die

wanowe[2]: paternal uncle

wanta[6]: discard

wantan[6]: leave tracks

wantyandyindan[6]: spear with three prongs for spearing bony bream

wantya pian[6]: young married woman

wanya[4]: boomerang

wanye[2] (wunye): then

wanye[2]: mountain duck

wappilka[5]: hot

war: up

wara[6]: oyster

warama: dugong

waranyukbeal: large gum tree

wararuwnaji[3]: child

warat[3]: one

waratah: tree with red flowers

warbang[4]: canoe

warde yallock: big water

warea[5]: small

warhrang[1]: see wahrang

WARATAH

wari[3]: head
wariat[3]: stone
wariatanbirik[3]: hill
wari-comomo[3]: woman
wariga[4]: hear
waring[4]: sea
wariya: string of wombat or wallaby hair
warka[6]: tortoise
warkolala[4]: two
warkolala boor[4]: three
warkolata-warkolata[4]: four
warma: stop a while
warna[2]: sea
warooga[5] (wahroogah): child
warra[1]: bad
warra[2]: over there
warraba: see wayamba
warrah: honeysuckle
warrain: belonging to the sea

warralewar[2]: see warre
warramba: see wayamba
warrambool[5]: flood water on polygonum flats; Milky Way
warrame[2]: left hand
warrannie[8]: sing
warrang[6]: bad
warra-nunna[5] (warranunnah, wurranunnah, wurrunnunnah): bee
warraroong: hillside
warratinnah[7]: sky
warrawee: come here
warre[2] (warralewar): high, high up
warreeah: mountain ash
warreen[4]: sea
warreen: wombat
warregal[4]: dog
warrew[8]: wallaby

WARREEN

warreyin[2]: follow
warridanga: midday
warrie[6]: dog
warrigal: dog, i.e. dingo; later used as a word meaning wild, and then applied to wild horses, wild men, etc.
warri-kundall[6]: dog
warrina[6]: give
warring: the Galaxy
warringa[4]: sea
warritsha[2]: emu
warriuka[2]: boat, ship (from warr ngukatha, lit. wind go)
warriwillah: twisting water
warroo[4]: kangaroo
warroo[6]: boomerang, day
warroo[8]: fire
warroo-culla[8]: moth
warroong[4]: dew
warr-ringa[8] (warringo-beeny): cold
warruc-color: see color
warta[2]: wallaby
Warte[2]: Venus (planet)
wartin[2]: track (verb)
waru[2]: see woora
warwanbool[4]: growing tree
wata[6]: crow
watangrow[2]: yesterday
watnah[6]: boomerang
wato[5]: take hold
wattangger[2] (wattangerind): evening
wattar[2] (wattangri): twilight
wattora[8]: long
watye[2]: polygonum shrub
watye[4]: man
watyin[2]: have
waukatte[2]: small hawk

wauwakkeri[2]: grey hawk
wauk-wauk-wa: pigeon
waukyn warra[1]: bad
wauwauwi[2]: fear
wayamba[5] (warraba, warramba, wayambah, wayambeh, wayembeh): turtle, tortoise
waybung: chough (bird)
waycoot: much
wayembeh: see wayamba
waylehmina[7]: swallow (bird)
waywa[5] (waywah): belt worn by man, made of possum sinews with pendant strips of paddymelon skins
wayway[5]: devil's bread fungus
weagolalameit[4]: die
weagoon murmbool[5]: live (verb)
wee-ar[8]: none
weedah[5]: bower bird
weehi: boy
weekin[4]: die
weelar[8]: stomach
weeloo[8]: curlew
weelya[7]: parakeet
weema[8]: small
weenduga[8]: goanna
weeombeen: see wi-oombeen
weerap: blackfish
weeriga: fire-walking
weeronga (werona): quiet, rest, sleep
weeroona: resting place
weeyehr[3]: nose
weeyer[3]: tongue
wee-y-tena[7]: rainbow
weing[4]: fire

weire[4]: mother
wela[6]: barter shell
welappe[2]: mullet
weloorarra[8]: west
welya[4]: summer
wenbener[3]: throwing stick
wenjoitj[3]: kangaroo
wenkana[2]: speak
wenkin[2]: refuse (verb)
wenyerang[4]: child
wepe: quiet
werderh: west wind
werendun[2]: lead, pull
werentun[2]: answer (verb)
werguttulun[2]: fish (verb)
weringerong: lyre bird
werite[4]: banksia
werkin[2]: fish (verb)
wernma[8] (wonma): long way
werona[4]: see weronga
werrilah[4]: cloud
werring[4]: ear
werrook: root
werrup: red ochre
wertun[2]: skin (verb)
wertuwallin[2] (wurtuwallin): sweat (verb)
werunnunn[4]: dog
wettinnie[8]: hold (verb)
weumpa[8]: no
weya[3]: hair
whagoo: see wahgoo
wherto[5]: old man
whilpra: aborigine's pronunciation of wheelbarrow, applied also to carts and wagons
whinya[4]: where?
whippoo[8]: tail
whitkitha[6]: girl

whytalla[8]: tell
wi[5]: clever; fire; a small fish; wood
wia[2]: mother
wi-bulloo[5]: fire; women who lived in a country where there was no fire
widawok[3]: big
widdidna: truffle
wiena[7]: firewood
wietatenana[7]: nautilus
wiinki[6]: arrowroot
wiitii[2]: sting (verb)
wika[6]: speech
wikky: bread
wilari[3]: star
wildin[2]: stare at
wilga: dogwood, willow, (always known as wilga)
wilgee: yellow clay
wilgu-wilgu[5] (wilgoo-wilgoo, willgoo-willgoo): painted stick with feathers at the end
wili[2]: pelican
willa[2]: wife, woman
willang[4]: rain
willanjo[5]: boy
willarra[6]: tomahawk
willawallin[2]: stubborn
willawatta-thuyin[6]: woman
willkilla[4]: look round
willum[4]: hut
willy-willy: storm, whirlwind
wilpa[2]: cloud
wilpy[5]: camp (verb)
wiltcha[2]: night
wiltja: hut, shelter
wiltun[2]: spread
wilyango[5]: boy
wima[2]: four

WIRINUN

wimmera: uncle
wimmin[2]: work
wimouyan: clever-stick
winamin[2]: beat time
winani: hollow tree
winberongen[8]: whistle
windarra: where?
windawityeri[2]: bullock
windtha: grey owl
wingamin[2]: sow
wingaro[5]: see
winin[2]: deceive, lie
wininaru[2]: deceit
wining: live (verb)
winkulun[2]: whistle
winkundun[2]: breathe, blow a fire
winmin[2]: make
winni[2]: be off
winnea[4]: they

winninger[3]: day
winnungi[5]: hear
winta[2]: spear
winthunga: somewhere
winyangun[6]: man
winyar[6] (winwar): big
winyer[4]: who
wi-oombeen[5] (weeombeen): small bird like a robin redbreast
wipa[6]: wash up against
wirake[2] (wiraki): friend, mate
wirakulun[2]: bleat
wirildar[2]: an acacia
wirin[2]: ache, hurt (verb), ill
wirinun[5] (wirreeneen, wirreenun, wirrinun): "clever man", medicine man, sorcerer
wirlpa[2]: hare
wirngill: koala
wirpa[2]: ant
wirrah[1]: fish
wirralee: gin fish
wirrangi[2]: wrong
wirrannie[8]: scratch (verb)
wirrap[4]: fish
wirratye[2]: childless mother, mother who has lost a child
wirree[5]: vessel for holding water, made of bark and shaped like a canoe
wirreebeeun[5]: adolescent girl, young woman
wirreecoo: tea-tree
wirreeneen: see wirinun
wirrelyerna: level ground
wirre-oobra: "dust shadow" which indicates that no water is present

wirrie: stick inserted in dead body

wirrinun: see wirinun

wirritin[2]**:** rough

wirrullummi[2]**:** itch (noun)

wirruna: sunset

wirtoo[6]**:** big

wirwy[4]**:** I

witchetty: edible grub

withinka[2]**:** green frog

wititurar[2]**:** small snake

witjuti: acacia

wittha: leg

witwit: throwing stick

wityeri[2]**:** fig leaf

wityungyin[2]**:** overcome, press heavily

wiwieringgere[2] (wiwirring-ille)**:** native pheasant

wiwirremalde[2]**:** doctor

wiwirimalde[2]**:** sorcerer

wiwirri[2]**:** pain, sickness

wobbegong[5]**:** carpet shark; snapper

wobma[2]**:** snake

woga[4]**:** give

woggara[5] (woggarah)**:** wooden axe used in fighting

wogghee and **woggigai:** see woggi

woggheeguy: legends (stories from the plains.

woggi[5] (wogghee, woggigai)**:** plains

woggoon[5]**:** mallee fowl

woggul: sacred water snake

wohn[6]**:** night

woka[6]**:** swim

wolbah[4]**:** hill

wolbitta (walbeeatta)**:** billy

WITCHETTY
GRUB

woldra[2]**:** heat

wolka[6]**:** spear with stingray barb

wolka[8]**:** drawing, painting; ice

wolkolan[6]**:** bony bream

wollomai: snapper

wollombi: meeting of the waters

wollowra[8]**:** eagle

wollumbin: high mountain

wolpa[8]**:** wind

wolter (wolta)**:** rib

woltsha[2]**:** eagle

womah[6]**:** boomerang

womba[5] (wombah)**:** deaf; mad; the star Canopus

womba[8]**:** knife

wombalano: beautiful; love

wombat (womback)**:** a marsupial

wombul[5]: sea
womma: fat, colour of fat
wommee[8]: snake
wommera: see woomera
wommurrur[5]: throwing stick
wompa[2]: hill
wompinie: sheltered from the sun
wondah: see wunda
wonenie[8]: fall (verb)
wonga[5]: bulrush; pigeon
wongalyer[3]: what, which, who
wonga-wonga: pigeon
wongguri[2]: ring-tailed possum
wongoonoo[8]: grass
wonka[8]: spider
wonkana: sing
wonma: see wernma
wonna[8]: stick
wonnewarra[8]: hold on
wonninny[8]: throw
wono[3]: sky
wonthaggi: pull
woodgera: daylight
woolladge-ilkna[8]: milk
woollung[5]: hard
woolta[2]: heart
woomelang[4]: poor
woomera (wommera): throwing stick
woonah[6]: lie down
woonda[1]: shield
woongarra: sleeping place
woora[6] (waru): kangaroo
woorail[4]: lyre bird
woorak[6]: honeysuckle
woorak: plain
woorarra: mountainous place
woorawa[6]: wedge-tailed eagle

wooremolleen[4]: day
woorin[4]: sun
woorinyan[4]: affection, love (verb)
woorkarrim: blue
woornack: sunshine
woorookool: fine weather
wooroonga: sea
woorree: sea
woorun[4]: day
woorwoorr[4]: sky
woowookarung: plentiful
worippa[6]: storm bird
workat[4]: woman
worlba[2]: boy
wornkara[2]: crow
worooa: green
worpa[6]: nest
worraworra: fighting stick
worru[4]: mouth

WOOMERA

worrue[8]: wood
wotiya[6]: yam
wrack[4]: land
wring[4]: ear
wruwallin[2]: hope (verb)
wu[6]: fire
wuka[6]: flying fox
wulde[2]: wedge-tailed eagle
wulgaru: devil-devil, made from a wooden figure
wullaki[2]: black cockatoo
wullanti[2]: string bag
wullun[2]: blue sky
wullundigong: goblin, little man of the bush
wunba: fin
wunbi[2]: puppy
wunda[5] (wondah, wundah): ghost, evil spirit, white person, white devil

WURLEY

wunde: long heavy black spear
wundurra: warrior, young man
wune[5]: give
wungghee: owl
wunggi: seashore
wunjugur[6] (njugur): well
wunmullun[2] (wunmun): stretch out the hands
wunmun[2]: throw
wunta[8]: fish
wun-u-wa-tirring[4]: sunrise
wunye: see wanye
wur[6]: fire
wuralparin[2]: stir
wurang[6]: bad
wurchiewurchie: white owl
wurdawurda (wurtawurta): band made of emu feathers
wurgulin[6]: short-legged kangaroo
wuri[2]: red gum tree
wurley[5] (wurlie): hut, shelter
wurranunnah: see warranunna
wurrawilberoo[5]: whirlwind, whirlwind devil; Magellan clouds
wurrook: flat
wurrunnunnah: see warranunna
wurruntun[2]: crush
wurruwallin[2] (wurruwarrin): believe
wurtawurta: see wurdwurda
wurte[2] (wurtuwallin): wet
wurtun[2]: warm (verb); feel (verb)
wurtuwallin: see wertuwallin
wutherama: hurry (verb)

wutta[6]: dog
wyah[5]: an exclamation
wyang[2]: second
wyebo[4]: small
wyebokooroon[4]: canoe
wyeera: dig (verb)
wyehoota[8]: possum
wyelangta[7]: large timber
wyena[7]: small timber
wyeriguru: spirit of fire
wyerow[1]: make
wyirre[2]: white of egg
wyralla: black and red cockatoo
wyterrica[8]: wattle
wyuna: clear water

Y

ya[2]: yes
ya[3]: teeth
yabber: talk
yabbie: small crayfish
yabm-irriti: quarrel (verb)
yackan[4]: mother
yackatoon: happy
yacker: see yakka
yackhoo[8]: mother
yacki: celebration, big noise
yago[1]: woman
yaitcha: yes
yakake: bathe
yakalya[5]: break
yake[5]: cold
yakea[5]: widow
yakka (yacker): work
yakkai[2]: ah! oh!
yakkoeela[6]: father
yakoolabarri: place where water lilies grow
yalabidji[3]: hand

yalakki[2]: carpet snake
yaldeenie[8]: come back
yalgin[2]: soak
Yalkara: spirit of drought
yalkin[2]: full; wet
yalkuldun[2]: melt
yallaban[4]: native raspberry
yallambee: live at, stay
yallane[2]: mat
yallara: long-eared bandicoot
yallart[2]: flock of emus
yalta[8]: charcoal
yam[2] (yammin): other
yaman: speak
yamba: see humpy
yambalin[2]: play at cat's cradle
Yammacoona: female ruler of sky spirits who made rivers on earth
yammalaitye[2]: one
yammamel[2]: one more
yamma murru[6]: hand
yammiam[2]: each
yammin[2]: see yam
yamminuwar[2]: another one
yammin uwar korn[2]: foreigner
yamminye[2]: another
yan[5]: go
yandala[6]: spear with a long point
Yananamaka[6]: "Trample the hair", the first man child to be created
yandarlana[5]: cry
yande[2]: old, useless
yanedana[5]: unfasten
yanga[6] (yanganna, yangena): mother
yangalla[6]: sit down

yanganna and **yangena**: see yanga

yangatin[6]: native cat

yangennanock[4]: all of us, we

yangoora[4]: stringybark tree

yangor[1]: kangaroo

yanima: will you?

yanka[6]: tail

yankulun[2]: loose

yanmulun[2]: drip, drop (verb)

yannathan: walk (verb)

yanning[8]: walk (verb)

yant[2]: peace

yan yean[4]: unmarried man

yap[3]: fish

yapar[2]: stick

yape[2]: tree

yapinga[3]: big

yappera[5]: camp

yappulun[2]: enter

yappundun[2]: bring in

yara[6]: seagull

yaraan[5]: white gumtree

Yaraandoo[5]: Southern Cross (place of the white gumtree)

yarakai[5]: bad

yaral[2]: when?

yaramin[2]: pour, spill

yaran[5,6] (yarra): beard, hair

yari[2]: what?

yarild[2]: how

yarluke[2]: path, track

yarn[4]: water

yarnde[2]: spear

yarngge[2]: vein

yarnimindin[2]: talk

yarnin[2]: saying, speak

yarnirumi[2]: conference, discussion

Yarra: spirit woman of the sand storm

yarra[4]: hair

yarra: speak (verb); tree

yarra: see yaran and yarrah

yarraga[5]: see yarrageh

yarrageh[5]: south-east wind; gentle spirit of spring

yarragerh mayrah: spring wind

yarrah: river red gum (but also applied to many trees)

yarrak: fight (verb)

yarraman: horse (from yeera —teeth; mahn—long)

yarramba[4]: throwing stick

yarran: an acacia

yarrara[5]: wood

yarraringy[5]: possum

yarrawah: storm of wind, gale

yarrawonga: nesting place of cormorants

yarra yarra: ever-flowing

yarri: native bear

yarrum[5]: throwing stick

yarrumba[5]: boomerang

yartamin[2] (yartin): stretch out the hand to receive anything

yartin[2]: stretch a skin out to dry

yarto[5]: wind

yartuwe[2]: big girl, young woman

yarumpah: honey ant

yarunmundule[2]: bat

yataotbidji[3]: teeth

yato[5]: he, his

yatta[4]: good

yattoo[4]: live (verb)

yatye[4]: bad
yauoanggi[2]: porpoise
yawoma[5]: come back
yayin[2]: chew, eat
yea[6]: mussel
yeatoura[5]: who
yeera[5] (yiera): teeth
yeildo[2]: blood
yelga[2]: dog
yelka[4]: dog
yelka: mouth; yam
yellawa[4]: day
yelpia[5]: count (verb)
yelpulun[2]: deceive, lie
yenamalde[2]: enemy
yenara[5]: that way
yenben guala[4]: man
yenembelin[2]: wrestle
yenempin[2]: entangle, twist
yenpar[8] (yenpa): skin
yentoo[8]: you
yeppa[2]: hole
yepperta: deep
yera[4]: teeth
yeramba: sugar ant
yeranda[5]: black cockatoo
yerang: thicket
yerdlee[2]: man
yergutta[8]: bag
yerhillgar[8]: liver
yerilla: ground
yerlata[2]: oyster
yerlieyeega[2]: boy
yernd[5]: stone
yerra: ant
yerracharta[8]: spear
yerracolya[8]: water vessel, also used for carrying babies; made from a hollowed out piece of bean tree

yerra-coppa: desert oak
yerrakincha: disease
yerrawar[8]: boomerang
yerrear[8]: salt bush
yerricknar[8]: blood
yerta[2]: land
yertauwullar[2]: remain
yetni[2]: he, she, it
yetto[2]: good
yeyauwe[2]: hungry
yeyeko[3]: small
yeyen[3]: hand; teeth
ygo[1]: I
Yhi[5]: sun goddess
yhuko[5]: sun
yhuko hippy[5]: sunset
yhuko pappora[5]: sunrise
yiallinah[4]: sit
yiarculrer[4]: teeth
yiarrih[4]: mouth
yiera[2]: see yeera
yikkowun[2]: enough
yikowalle[2]: his father
yilgi[2]: salt water
yilin[2]: broken
yiltoo[4]: blood
yinai[5]: boy
yinbaikulun[2]: go away
yindi: sun
yingge[2]: wool
yingoorna: today
yirtuggi[2]: bucket
yirum[6]: woman
yityumbarrin[2]: carry on the shoulder
yluppun[2]: to bring fire
yoldi[2]: black shag
yolla[7]: mutton bird
yondun[2]: wade
yonga[1]: give

yongga[4] (yonggadyr): sun
yonguldye[2]: darkness
yooralanni: will love
yooralla: love
yoorami: love (verb)
yoorana: loving
yoothapina: good luck
yorlin[2]: go into deep water
yorlun[2]: descend, come down
yorte[2]: winter
youa[4]: throwing stick
youal: see wahl
youamalla[8]: throw
youayah: see yuaia
youhi[8] (youi): give
youko: see yuroka
younger[4]: give
youngoloy[5]: swan
youracudda[4]: hear
youria[4]: ear
yourula (youroul): bullock's
   horn
youwoppa[8]: see uwoppa
yowi[5] (yowee): soul, spirit,
   warning spirit of death
yowi[5]: yes
yoyangamalde[2]: champion
yoyangi[2]: bed; fight (verb)
yrottulun[2] (yuruttulun): thin
yuaia[5] (youayah): frog
yuka[2]: stand
yuka[6]: tree
yuke[2]: boat
yukkay[5] (yuckay): an exclamation
yukunder[3]: kangaroo
yul-arai: satisfied
yulde[2] (yullukke): tall

yulthi[2]: bark of tree
yultun[2]: draw towards, drag,
   lead; save life
yultuwarrin[2]: mix
yulu-mara[5] (euloomarah):
   grub
yulu-wirree[5] (euloowirree):
   rainbow
yumbera[2]: fly
yummun[2]: stand
yun[2]: by and by
yunbeai[5]: familiar spirit, individual totem
yunde[2]: down (feathers)
yune[4]: man
yungana[2]: cockatoo
yungara[2]: wife
yunka[6]: make
yunkara: stranger
yunkimp[4]: canoe
yunkundun[2]: extract
yunt[2]: crowd, together
yuntheyunthe[5]: kidney fat
yuntuwarrin[2] (yuntuwallin):
   assemble, crowd (verb); useless
yuppun[2]: arrange, lie down,
   place
yuppundelin[2]: dress (verb)
yuri[2]: ear, hear
yurlunggur: rainbow snake
yurnga: extensive view
yuroka[6] (youko): sun
yurru[6]: cloud
yurruttulun: see yrottulun
yurung[6]: rain
yutthero[5]: road
yuwam[6]: black snake

...the story of the world's longest continuing art tradition

JOURNEY IN TIME
George Chaloupka

By the foremost authority on the subject, *Journey in Time* documents the 50 000 year story of the Australian Aboriginal rock art of Arnhem Land, easily the longest continuing art tradition in the world. Apart from its aesthetic value, the art provides a pictorial record of the longest-surviving culture on earth, taking its viewers on a compelling journey in time.

This stunning book was published with the permission of the members of the Gagudju Association Inc., the traditional owners of the Kakadu National Park and other areas of western Arnhem Land. It features 276 colour photographs, as well as maps and diagrams—a comprehensive documentation of the art treasures of Kakadu.

George Chaloupka was awarded the Order of Australia Medal for his services to Aboriginal art and culture in 1990. *Journey in Time* represents his lifetime work.

330 x 230
256 pp., 276 colour photographs, and maps and diagrams, hardcover
ISBN 0 7301 0310 2

OTHER BOOKS BY A.W. REED

Aboriginal Stories of Australia, A.W. Reed. This is a collection of authentic Aboriginal myths and legends that retain, as much as can be possible, the full impacts and strengths of their original traditional tellings.
180 mm x 112 mm, 120 pages, paperback.

More Aboriginal Stories of Australia, A. W. Reed. This companion volume to *Aboriginal Stories of Australia* presents a further twenty-two stories that are a rich reflection of Aboriginal thought and culture.
180 mm x 112 mm, 120 pages, paperback.

Aboriginal Words of Australia, A.W. Reed. Words used by Aboriginal tribes with their meanings, as well as an English Aboriginal section which is useful for those who wish to choose names for houses, boats, etc.
180 mm x 112 mm, 144 pages, illustrated, paperback.

Aboriginal Myths, A.W. Reed. This book is divided into three parts, dealing first with acts of creation by the Great Spirit or All Father, second with totemic ancestors and third with the origin of natural phenomena and specific features of animal life.
180 mm x 112 mm, 144 pages, paperback.

Aboriginal Legends, A.W. Reed. A large selection of Aboriginal legends dealing mainly with the origin of different forms of animal life. The legends come from a variety of tribes from all parts of the continent.
180 mm x 112 mm, 144 pages, paperback.

Aboriginal Fables, A.W. Reed. The wisdom of the Australian Aboriginals in this varied collection of short fables, with illustrations by Roger Hart.
180 mm x 112 mm, 144 pages, illustrated, paperback.

Aboriginal Place Names compiled by A.W. Reed. A comprehensive collection of names and their derivations from all parts of Australia. The book includes a section giving English words and their Aboriginal translations, as well as an appendix of present day names with earlier Aboriginal names.
180 mm x 112 mm, 144 pages, paperback

Reed for Books